BRITAIN, EUROPE AND THE WORLD 1850–1986:
DELUSIONS OF GRANDEUR

Britain, Europe and the World 1850–1986: Delusions of Grandeur

Bernard Porter

London
GEORGE ALLEN & UNWIN
Boston   Sydney   Wellington

Allen & Unwin (Publishers) Ltd,
40 Museum Street, London, WC1A 1LU, UK

Allen & Unwin (Publishers) Ltd,
Park Lane, Hemel Hempstead, Herts, HP2 4TE, UK

Allen & Unwin, Inc.,
8 Winchester Place, Winchester, Mass. 01890, USA

Allen & Unwin (Australia) Ltd,
8 Napier Street, North Sydney, NSW 2060, Australia

Allen & Unwin NZ Ltd,
Private Bag, Wellington, NZ

First published in 1983
Second edition 1987

British Library Cataloguing in Publication Data

Porter, Bernard
 Britain, Europe and the world 1850–1986 :
delusions of grandeur.—2nd ed.
1. Great Britain—Foreign relations—19th
century 2. Great Britain—Foreign relations
—20th century
I. Title
327.41   DA560
ISBN 0-04-09040-2

Library of Congress Cataloging-in-Publication Data

Porter, Bernard.
 Britain, Europe and the world, 1850–1986.
Includes index.
1. Great Britain—Foreign relations—1837–1901.
2. Great Britain—Foreign relations—20th century.
3. Great Britain—Foreign relations—Europe.
4. Europe—Foreign relations—Great Britain.
5. Great Britain—Politics and government—1837–1901.
6. Great Britain—Politics and government—20th century.
I. Title.
DA550.P59   1987   327.41   86-28719
ISBN 0-04-909040-2   (pbk. : alk. paper)

**Printed in Great Britain by Billing and Sons Ltd,
London and Worcester**

Contents

In memory of
Alan Lee

Preface

The subject of this book is the change that has come over Britain in her relations with the rest of the world during the last century or so. The most obvious feature of that change is her decline, in material terms, relative to certain other countries, with the implications this has had for her power to influence events abroad. One of the aims of this book is to offer an explanation for that decline; not, I think, a highly original one, though the degree of fatalism involved in it may be new — and uncongenial — to some readers. Very broadly, I believe that Britain's decline as a power in world affairs was inevitable because it was implicit in the reasons for her rise; that, like the Marxists' version of capitalism, Britain's dominance in the mid-nineteenth century carried within it the seeds of its own destruction. It could not therefore have been prevented: not by wiser statesmanship, nor by more favourable world conditions, nor by any measures to restore (for example) Britain's economic health, which measures themselves would (and did) only serve in other ways to make her position worse. Britain's decline derived from fundamental, ineradicable and eventually fatal contradictions in her situation, so that the more she struggled at the end of the rope, the tighter the knot became.

This view of Britain's recent history begs, of course, many questions, and in the pages that follow it will not be put so baldly and simply as that. In the first place the word 'decline' itself is not an altogether ideal one to describe the process that has gone on: not, for example, if it is taken to imply that Britain's downward path has been a steady and continuous one, or that her material weakening as a 'power' is the only or the most significant change that has taken place. So far as the material symptoms of her decline are concerned it certainly has not been steady and continuous; by most criteria the graph took its sharpest dip after 1945, before which date Britain could still claim, with justice, to be one of the great powers. My argument is not that her strength and influence were significantly weakening before 1945, but that her ability to sustain them was limited all along: that Britain from the middle of the nineteenth century onwards was always weak in certain directions, and always bound to suffer as a result of that weakness in the end. The weakness was not primarily a material one: it was not that she lacked the material resources needed to finance a position of national strength. That came to be a factor later, but the initial flaw, the decisive one, was to do with the nature of her economy and society, the kind of nation she was. That qualitative factor influenced her policy towards and relations with the rest of the world far more than the quantitative one, and it also makes the history of those relations far more interesting than a mere story of national decline.

The second difficulty about this argument is that it spares little room for individual initiative or volition, for the contributions of statesmen, who were — by this way of looking at it — essentially ineffective, the prisoners of events rather than the authors of them. This is certainly my impression of the last 150 years of British history, though I should not like to say whether it is true more generally: that politicians had far less freedom of action than they thought. In the long run (and even in the shortish run) it did not matter who was at the head of Britain's affairs: Derby or Russell, Disraeli or Gladstone, Baldwin or MacDonald, Churchill or Attlee, Heath or Wilson, even Thatcher or Healey or Benn. In this sense Britain has been 'ungovernable' for years. Prime ministers and Cabinets swam with the tide or they were out; if Gladstone did not pass a Reform Bill Disraeli would have to; if Disraeli did not take Egypt Gladstone would have to; it signified very little who held the reins of power — or rather, who appeared to. Political parties to a great extent were frauds, deceiving their supporters that alternative policies were available when, on the fundamental issues, they were not; even Parliament itself was a kind of fraud, encouraging what was really only an illusion of popular determination and choice. This of course is not a new idea. That British political parties often converge to the 'centre' when they attain power is a well-known phenomenon; it was called MacBaldwinism in the 1930s and Butskellism in the 1960s (though it is interesting that no one has yet dared to coin the expression 'Gladraeli-ism' for the period before). So too is the idea that democratic processes are a sham, that the real determinants of events lie outside: which has been a common view on the Left of British politics for years. The Left, I believe, sometimes puts the blame in the wrong places — currently with conspiring capitalists, the civil service and the press, none of whom may be responsible at bottom for what goes on. Nevertheless the notion of parliamentary and even governmental impotence is a familiar one; most familiar of all, of course, to Marxists, to whom the primacy of 'base' over 'superstructure' is a fundamental article of belief. Whether or not the argument of this book is 'Marxist' I do not know. I suspect not, but I shall be interested to find out – if they can agree together – from the Marxists themselves.

What it certainly is, however, is deterministic. I realise that this will cause all kinds of problems. For a start it will go against a lot of people's grains, as it goes against mine too. (I am not a *general* determinist; I do not believe that all history is predetermined, only this particular piece of it, for reasons peculiar to itself.) People do not like to think that their political environment is determined for them by factors outside their control: though in this case it is possible that a few might draw some comfort from the obvious corollary that Britain is not after all responsible for her own 'decline'. A more serious problem is that it may seem to run against the evidence, much of which, especially in the field of Anglo-European diplomatic history, inclines towards more voluntaristic kinds of interpretations of events. Diplomatic history is particularly rich in documentary sources, the recorded testimony of the diplomats, which testimony, for reasons I shall go into later, is supposed to be peculiarly pertinent in this field. By many diplomatic historians it is assumed that the way to find out why a thing was done is to explore the reasons the people who did it gave for doing it: this way the truth can be established, and errors rectified, quite objectively, with chapter and verse. If we abandon this assumption we are left with nothing, no evidence anything like so voluminous as the voluntarists', no empirical criteria, therefore, to test our findings by. This is the chief difficulty with any kind of deterministic argument: that it is, by its very nature, impossible to prove.

This is the main reason why the argument of this book is necessarily a tentative one: hardly more, really, than a hypothesis. What I have tried to do – the best, I think, that *can* be done – is to demonstrate that it is consistent with the facts: consistent that is with what happened, rather than what was sometimes thought to be happening. All the way through I have tried to distinguish rhetoric from reality: Palmerston's apparent provocation of war from his actual avoidance of it, for example; the idealism of Gladstone's words from the very practical realism of his actions; the 'internationalism' of the Common Market-eers' arguments from the harsher truth underneath. This I believe will give a far better idea of Britain's true relations with the world over the past 150 years, and a firmer basis from which to deduce the fundamental factors affecting them.

It may be that more can be deduced from it than that. Because this book goes up to the present day, and seeks to explain the position Britain finds herself in now, it may be found 'useful' by those with an interest in present politics as well as those with an interest in the past. Nevertheless it is not intended to carry any kind of constructive 'lesson' for the present. If it does have a contemporary purpose, it is merely to undermine certain other lessons that are commonly drawn from the past. It is done all the time: messages and morals read into ill-digested and distorted versions of history, to back up one view or another of the present. Sometimes it is done by drawing direct parallels: especially, for example, with Munich, which is constantly being cited as a salutary lesson in situations which appear to be – but are not – the same. Another way, increasingly common nowadays, is to pick over the past like a piece of knitting, to find out when and why we started to go wrong. When did our decline set in? Was it in 1945, when Attlee started diverting resources into welfare, or in 1939, when Britain mortgaged herself to America, or in 1900, when she began to lose her Faith, or maybe in 1870, when Britain's long entrepreneurial decline is now supposed to have begun? Unravel the garment until the dropped stitch comes to light, and perhaps it can be knitted up soundly again. This is not the approach of this book; which will take notice along the way of one or two suggestive little historical 'parallels' (such as the obvious one between the Liberal Unionists of the 1880s and the present-day SDP), but will not presume to draw lessons from any of them. Its main lesson, if there be one at all, is that these are the wrong kinds of lesson to expect from history, and the wrong kinds of props, therefore, to shore up a contemporary political position by.

One more thing that needs to be made clear at the beginning is that this is not a textbook, but an extended interpretative essay, and so is not intended to replace, but rather to supplement, the admirable narrative accounts of Britain's external relations that already exist.[1] If I had tried to write a book that would serve as a textbook too it would have come out too long, obscured the main themes, and maybe not been as stimulating as I hope this book will be found. If, even with its faults and its hostages to fortune, it does stimulate some thought about Britain's place in the world, today and in the past, it will have done its job. With this aim it is directed both to the historian and to the general interested reader, who will disagree with much of it, but who I hope may find a little sense in it somewhere.

It has been a difficult book to write, and has gone through two or three different drafts before the present one. Several people have read it at various stages. Some of them have disliked the version they read, but I trust will approve more of this one, which takes grateful account of many of the criticisms they have made. Others will no doubt still dislike it, and for good reasons as well as bad. Among more sympathetic – but still critical – readers I should like to single out Paul Kennedy and Andrew Porter for special thanks. Their aid and encouragement have been invaluable, as have the patience of my publisher and, most of all, the cheerful tolerance, and help with medical metaphors, of my wife Deirdre.

BERNARD PORTER

Cottingham,
East Yorkshire
June 1982

Preface to the Second Edition

I have taken advantage of the appearance of this book in a paperback edition to make some changes. The most significant are in Chapter 5 and the Conclusion, which have been substantially rewritten in order to expunge some extraneous matter, modify the argument slightly, and bring it up to the present day. Chapter 5 now incorporates, therefore, a general analysis of the foreign policy of the first one-and-a-half Thatcher governments. I have left the original Preface as it was, though some details in it have obviously been overtaken by events. If I had made any substantial alteration there, it would have been to the third paragraph, which I would have modified in order to hedge my bets a little over the question of the 'freedom of action' of governments since 1979. This is one of the matters discussed in the new Chapter 5.

BERNARD PORTER

Cottingham
August 1986

1
Mid-Victorian Heyday
1848–70

In the middle of the nineteenth century Britons felt more distinct from foreigners than at any time in their history. One of them wrote in 1850 that they were 'in reality now . . . more the *toto divisi orbe Britanni*' than ever before, especially, he thought, in the 'spirit and principle of our social institutions'.[1] He was not the only one to notice the difference. It was part of the accepted wisdom of the time. Generally it was seen in terms of 'progress' or 'maturity'. Britain was different from other countries because she was ahead of them. She was particularly ahead of them at that moment, because of a kind of revolution she had passed through recently, which had taken her on to a new and higher stage of human development. This 'revolution' had been a slow, undramatic and comparatively bloodless one – none of your French histrionics and excesses; but it was no less efficacious for that. Its twin signs, in the Victorians' eyes, were the bounding prosperity of their economy, and an enormous accession of a quality they called 'freedom'. It was these that set Britain apart from the rest of the world then, and for some years afterwards.

Later generations might hesitate a little over the word 'freedom', and prefer to see the 'revolution' in rather less abstract terms than contemporaries: as a straight transfer of power from one class of society to another. But the difference is one of emphasis rather than substance. Contemporaries sometimes described it in terms of class too. What had happened, in their view as well as that of most modern historians,[2] was that the aristocracy had been replaced by the middle classes as the dominant force in British society. The transformation had taken many decades, and was not quite complete yet: but it was very nearly so. The Reform Bill of 1832 and the repeal of the Corn Laws between 1822 and 1846 had been its most recent stages. By 1850 the ideals and interests of the British middle classes had become

1

supreme. Each of the other main classes of society, the aristocracy and the working class, had either been coerced or persuaded (usually the latter) into accepting the new state of affairs. From now onwards it would be plain sailing. The bourgeois age of gold had arrived.

In very many ways it was indeed a golden age. Materially, for example, it was a wonder. Industrial Britain, the new creature of this 'revolution', was like nothing that had ever been seen before. Such productive vigour as the north of Britain especially displayed was unparalleled. In 1850 Britain had more factories, consumed more coal and iron and raw cotton, and employed more men and women in manufacturing industry than the rest of Europe put together. And the creature was not yet full-grown. Coal output, pig-iron production, railway mileage and the manufacture of textiles were all to double in the next twenty years. Trade with foreign countries was to triple. This was a dynamic economy, still expanding, *ever* expanding, perhaps, and with everyone standing to gain. Many were gaining already: capitalists of course, and also workers, whose real wages rose by nearly a fifth in these years. Things were not merely good – they were getting better. Scarcely anyone denied it. Scarcely anyone could.

Maybe this was why so many of them acquiesced in the new order. For this was the other remarkable thing about it: that during most of these twenty-odd years of prosperity there seemed to be no threat to it from anywhere at all. Chartism, which had threatened it in the 1830s and 1840s, was effectively dead. Socialism – indigenous socialism – was in a kind of hibernation until well into the 1880s. What remnants there were of working-class revolutionism in these years were not considered by the authorities to be significant enough even to set a watch on. Foreign revolutionaries were tolerated in Britain because they were believed to offer no danger to their hosts. On the other flank the danger was even less – reactionaries as impotent as revolutionaries. The new order appeared to be absolutely secure, impervious to subversion from any direction: and yet with no visible protection against it, none of that apparatus of surveillance and repression, for example, without which most continental states (and Britain too not so long before) had felt naked in the face of it. Britain did not need such things. Her order was intrinsically, naturally, safe.

Of this the Victorians were, if anything, prouder than of their prosperity. They had cause to be, especially in 1848, which saw the most dramatic demonstration of the resilience of their system. On the continent 1848 was the 'year of revolutions', with thrones toppling nearly everywhere and anarchy rife. But in Britain it passed almost without a shudder. This experience strengthened the confidence of the British in their new style of life immensely, not least because not all of them had been entirely confident when it began. When the Chartists had started amassing for their climactic demonstration on Kennington common in the spring, and rumours began flying that socialists and foreigners were planning to light the British revolution from it, many people had become nervous, and the government took precautions. When in the event it did not happen – the demonstration passed over, and the propertied classes blinked and found they still had their heads – the chorus of self-congratulation was deafening. Even in the most perfectly constituted societies, reflected the *Annual Register*, there would be found some violent and subversive men who in times of general turbulence would seek to use the occasion to undermine society's fabric. In those circumstances 'A system which has been supported only by the strong hand of power' was terribly at risk.

> On the other hand, a loyalty, based on reason and conviction, and an enlightened appreciation of the benefits derived from well-tried institutions, proves a sure bulwark in the hour of trial against the machinations of conspirators and anarchists. Such was the lesson exhibited by England in the revolutionary era of 1848.

Order in Britain stood firm while all around her it was breaking down; and the reason for that was the excellence of her governance, which in the end, as the *Annual Register* claimed again, 'was materially strengthened by the futile efforts made to undermine it'.[3] What better test could be devised? What more positive proof of the vessel's seaworthiness, than to have sailed unscathed through the hurricanes of 1848? A few years later the Great Exhibition pointed the same lesson even more clearly. Continental powers could never have contemplated staging such an event so soon after 1848. Some of them sent warnings of the perils she was courting: in such uncertain times positively to encourage the congregation of such crowds of revolution-fodder was foolhardy beyond belief. But again, she survived. 'I walked about the park,' wrote a diarist after the opening, 'and never saw a more good-humoured multitude, and there was nowhere the slightest disorder or confusion.'[4] It was a tribute, again, to the excellence of Britain's political and social institutions, by contrast with everywhere else.

The Victorians might have attributed all this to their innate racial or cultural superiority, but by and large they did not. Instead they explained it in terms of a general theory. That theory stated that both prosperity and security rested on what was called 'freedom': by which was meant the kind of freedom that was left to men when the hand of the state – even for protection – was taken away. It was a kind of economic and political naturism: polities, like people, were healthiest without bureaucratic clothing. Leave men free from state interference and regulation to follow their own selfish interests as they liked and it would redound to the good of all. Industry would flourish, the nation's wealth would accumulate, and everyone would prosper. Interfere with the plant and you would only stunt it. So taxation to help the poor, for example, only depleted the stock out of which the poor could be paid. Tariffs designed to safeguard British industries against foreign competition had just the opposite effect — raising prices, holding back growth, blunting competitiveness. The best defence was no defence at all. The same principle applied to politics. The best way to disarm dissidents was to tolerate them. This was what 1848 had proved. Britain then had been the European society most permissive of political dissent, with the freest press and the least obtrusive police and the fewest restrictions on the personal liberties even of known subversives, and yet Britain was the society which in the event proved to have least to fear from dissent. This was not mere coincidence: it was not just that Britain had been strong enough to withstand the storm despite the fact that she had no defences against it. She was strong enough *because* she had no defences against it. It worked this way. People on the whole — so the Victorians believed — were rational beings. They turned to extreme measures only when reasonable courses were denied them. Subversion could appear anywhere, but it could only succeed where the people were repressed. To resort to repression in order to contain subversion, therefore, was counter-productive. To tolerate extremists was to ensure that they remained impotent. It was also cheaper — repression after all cost money, which meant taxation, which again was a kind of incubus on industry and prosperity; so that the two kinds of freedom, political and economic, were complementary. Freedom was the fount of everything: of prosperity, of stability, of happiness. It was a simple idea, and not original with the Victorians; but in the European context of the time it was revolutionary. It stood on its head the customary continental way of looking at these things. Not surprisingly, it left the continentals sceptical.

Perhaps their scepticism was justified. Britain after all could be said to have been prosperous and dynamic and stable before she was 'free'. Maybe she was only 'free' now because she could afford to be: politically free, for example, because she was stable, and not the other way around. Many socialists of the time believed so, and believed also (as do some Marxist historians today) that what really kept the proletariat down in the 1850s and 1860s was not consent, but the recollection of repression in the recent past, and the knowledge that it could be used

4

again. The horse had been tamed – now the reins could be loosened. In much the same way it could be argued that free enterprise capitalism was merely right for its time: that its success in the mid-nineteenth century had much to do with the favourable circumstances it encountered then. After all, when the vessel had been launched it was into very sheltered waters indeed. Its early stages had been protected closely: even Adam Smith knew that 'infant' industries needed nursing. Only when it was strong enough was it given the full range of its freedoms. When that was done the conditions were perfect for it. With a docile labour force, plentiful capital, limitless markets and virtually no foreign competition, it could scarcely fail. So it prospered: and the myth grew up that the source of its prosperity was its freedom. Which it was – in those circumstances: but would it have been so in others? And would it have been so even then, if the rules had not been bent for it just a little? For in fact the Victorians never did adhere rigidly to those rules: which was one of the reasons for their success. Men were never allowed, for example, to pursue their economic self-interest entirely unfettered. If they had been the system might have collapsed in a week, destroyed either by the mass rebellion its suffering would have provoked, or by the drain on productive industry which the measures necessary to contain the rebellion, or the threat of it, would have involved. Its dynamism and prosperity may have depended on the freedom allowed to it; its survival, however, depended on (for example) the Factory Acts, which clearly contravened the pure canons of free marketism, and on charity, which could be regarded in one sense as a considerable waste of investment capital, but was not a bad price to pay for domestic peace, and for social acquiescence, therefore, in the system. This is not to imply that the Victorian middle classes necessarily saw it like this – that their charity was consciously intended as a cynical bribe. Hypocrisy is a charge historians should be very sparing with. The Victorians learnt their charity from their religion; maybe the particular leaning of their religion can be said to have grown, *au fond*, from a kind of economic necessity, but if so it was not their (or even their priests') doing. Nevertheless charity, whatever its motives, performed the function of oiling capitalism's most abrasive edges, and had the effect therefore – together with Reform Bills and habeas corpus and the rest, all buttressing the Englishman's sense of freedom – of neutralising dangerous dissent for a time at least, until capitalism's more general benefits could percolate through: or until impatience grew that they had not.

However this may be, the Victorians clung to the idea that it was their 'freedom' that lay at the root of their good fortune, and of the essential difference which they believed existed between Britain and her national interests on the one hand, and most other countries of the world and their national interests – or their conception of their national interests – on the other. That difference was not just one of degree, but of kind. Britain was not merely more prosperous or more stable than foreign nations: she was in a different category from them. Maybe Britons exaggerated the contrast – continentals tended to think so. When Britain proclaimed herself invulnerable to political subversion, for example, continentals were sceptical: England in fact was 'sleeping on a volcano', warned a French propagandist in 1858, and would be consumed before France was.[5] Others saw the difference, but would not admit that it indicated any advance on their own condition. What about Ireland? And the sufferings of England's industrial proletariat? And what price Britain's much vaunted political freedoms, when set against the slavery of her social conventions: for as foreigners were constantly pointing out, though there might be 'liberty in the laws of England', there was 'tyranny in many of its customs'.[6] This much was admitted too by very many British commentators on affairs abroad (few of whom were as thoughtlessly chauvinistic as they are generally painted); but it did not alter the fact that Britain was different in some quite fundamental ways from even her closest allies. The difference arose, not from her religion, or her culture, or from something inherent in the Anglo-Saxon 'race', but from her political economy, and her 'freedom' – or her particular brand of it.

Most Englishmen were struck by it, at one level or another. On a very superficial level it was noticed the moment any British tourist set foot in France, when he was immediately beset by a French officialdom which was the more resented for the fact that such a plethora of state bureaucrats was entirely unknown in England. This itself – the *douaniers* and the *gensd'armes* – was seen as a sign of tyranny ('tyranny' being defined in this context as an imposition you are not used to). For those travellers with a more serious purpose, who delved deeper, it was a symptom of a prevailing disease on the continent called 'functionarism'. Of course continentals had other failings too, like their Sundays and their 'superstitions', and their breakfasts, and French immorality, and the German habit of spitting, and so on; and they had their virtues, which marked them off from Britain almost as much: French sobriety, for example, and German domesticity, and their superiority in all the arts except the 'useful' ones, which was the virtue most commonly remarked on. But none of these was as significant as the fundamental structural difference which was thought to exist between 'free' Britain and 'functionary' Europe: between a country in which people were left to do broadly as they liked, and a whole continent where even the smallest detail of life was regulated by an enormous class of state employees. The effect could be seen in productive industry abroad, which functionarism stifled in three ways: by over-regulating it, by drawing human talent away from it, and by crippling it with taxes to pay for these parasites. Everywhere on the continent the free play of natural forces was restricted and repressed: enterprise held back, opinion curbed, political activities spied on, freedom of movement and trade (even sometimes within a country) restrained and suppressed. This vast public sector of officials, together with police forces and standing armies far larger and more intrusive than Britain's, were sapping all the vital juices of continental states. This was the real difference, which others were incidental to or maybe in a way merely symptoms of: Roman Catholicism, for example, just another manifestation of the continental preference for authority; continental universities breeding-grounds for more functionaries; even art a mere distraction from the real and proper business of life. (For how really useful was a statue or a sonata? How many mouths could it feed, how many comforts did it minister too, how many people did it *employ*?) All these things were signs of the gap between them: evidence, to many Victorians, that the continent had not yet grown out of a stage of society that Britain had passed entirely beyond.[7]

What is called xenophobia in Victorian Britain, therefore, may really have been just an expression of this difference between her and her nearest neighbours, which all classes were aware of, but which the liberal middle classes tended to use more to berate the continent: not because they were more bigoted or ignorant or even 'patriotic' than Tories or aristocrats, who tended to side more with the continentals, but because they were more in tune with the new spirit of their age. If the continent had gone bourgeois (or more bourgeois) in 1848 it would have been the other way around. Tories and aristocrats favoured the continent because they saw the old values honoured there still; Liberals and the middle classes disapproved, for the same reason. Both sides saw it as a dichotomy between an old order and the new. Britain was a novel and unique political and social phenomenon: the first and for the time being the only tadpole in the pool to have become a fully fledged frog.

The implications of this for Britain's foreign relations were profound. The fact that Britain regarded herself as having grown out of one particular stage of national development and into another meant that she had grown out of a particular stage of international development too. She had grown out of 'power politics', for example; of

7

territorial ambitions; of the ethos of military rivalries and 'prestige': all of which were, as we shall see, widely believed to be inappropriate to her new situation. Other countries, however, had not yet made this transition: which meant that in international affairs they and Britain were somehow out of kilter, had divergent values and priorities and interests. Sometimes they were so divergent that they did not even conflict with one another, like planets turning around different suns. At other times they did conflict or, more often, gave rise to mis-understandings, which was natural. (It must after all be difficult to understand a frog's point of view if you have not been one yet.) In any event it was this which mainly lay behind the relations between Britain and the rest of the world in the mid-nineteenth century: this imbalance between them arising from Britain's new status then, as the first liberal and mature capitalist polity in the world.

Some of the men who actually implemented Britain's foreign policy in these years, however, might have disputed this. Many of their middle-class critics certainly did. Richard Cobden for example, one of the bitterest of their critics, believed that the Foreign Office could not reflect the true interests of the middle classes (and therefore the country) while so few of its personnel came from that class, and while they remained so little accountable to the House of Commons, which by and large did come from that class. In a new bright bourgeois Britain the foreign service remained a solitary survival from older times, a branch which had yet to be lopped. It followed – did it not? – that foreign policy was exceptional, outside the range of middle-class control, and unlikely therefore to reflect the structural changes in British society associated with that class.

There was a lot in what Cobden said. The Foreign Office and the diplomatic service were both predominantly aristocratic throughout the nineteenth century – intentionally so. Every foreign secretary between Canning and Grey was a peer. Most of their underlings too came from the aristocracy or from its fringes, as they were bound to, in view of the fact that they had to be personally known to the foreign secretary before they could be appointed. In the foreign service there was none of this new nonsense about selection by 'merit'. Every other department of state capitulated at some point in the nineteenth century to the middle-class shibboleth of entry by competitive examination: but not this one. In 1855 it did institute a qualifying test in handwriting, spelling and arithmetic: but with the reassuring proviso that it would contain 'nothing of a puzzling character', and with the final choice still made by the chief.[8] This of course did not satisfy the critics, whose basic complaint against the Foreign Office's personnel had never been that they were illiterate or even incompetent, but only that they were unrepresentative, which they were, and largely immune from parliamentary control. This seemed to be true also. The reason lay partly in the nature of foreign policy, which did not generally lend itself to legislation – did not involve budgets or bills. Foreign policy decisions were basically executive decisions. Ultimately of course all governments were accountable to parliament for their executive decisions too: but in this area the accountability was really *very* ultimate. Debates on foreign policy could be initiated on the address from the throne, or the estimates, or an emergency motion, which theoretically could put a ministry out. The fact however that this so very rarely happened on a foreign policy issue[9] suggests that the sanction was not a particularly effective one. The decisive factor was that governments had no statutory duty to consult Parliament.[10] From this it followed that they had no duty to *reveal* anything either. The excuse for this was that revealing your hand to your constituents would reveal it to your enemies too. But who in any particular instance was to know that this was not merely a cover, to hide from the public gaze measures which might be unpopular at home? 'Blue Books' printed for the perusal of Parliament quite often omitted key passages from documents with no indication even that the excisions had been made, and of course no way of checking. Sometimes documents were contrived purely for public consumption and mystification.[11] Over large areas of policy no documents were revealed at all: sometimes because the Foreign Office refused to publish, as it was entitled to, but more often because their existence was unknown to anyone who might wish to have them revealed. The cards therefore were stacked in the Foreign Office's favour. Foreign policy in the nineteenth century was not entirely unaccountable, but it was very largely so; enough to give some substance to Cobden's complaints, and to the idea that was current (and may be still) that really diplomacy was a thing on its own, conducted on an altogether higher plane from other state activities, and divorced from the ordinary life of the nation.

None of this was fortuitous. The foreign policy-makers defended their privileges and their immunities tenaciously. Some of them may have clung to them out of pure prejudice. Hidebound reactionaries who deeply deplored the eroding away of old values in other areas of government drew comfort from the knowledge that here at least was one place where the rot had not yet set in, like a gentlemen's club left standing in a street of office blocks. But there were much better reasons for it too. Diplomacy after all was a special skill, which it was not everyone's good fortune to possess. Aristocrats were supposed to have it peculiarly. They were also supposed, by virtue of their special position in British society, to be peculiarly detached from the enthusiasms – especially the moral enthusiasms – which animated the newly dominant classes in that society, and which, however laudable they might be intrinsically, if they were allowed to intrude here might spoil one's play. Diplomats, like chess masters, could not risk being emotional. The games metaphor was the nineteenth century's own. It was ubiquitous in diplomatic circles. Diplomats all the time were 'dealt hands', 'played their cards', raised or lowered their 'stakes'. The allusion clearly indicated the kind of activity diplomats liked to picture themselves engaged in. Not that it was in any way a low or frivolous occupation – quite the reverse. In a way it was the most elevated of callings, elevated by virtue of the special skills required for it, the distinction of its participants, and the issues at stake. It was an entirely different level of activity from mundane domestic politics – 'poor-law questions, sanitary rules, railroad bills' and the like, whose *aficionados* (claimed the novelist Charles Lever, who was himself an intimate of diplomats) could not possibly appreciate the heady excitement generated by 'this great game played by about twenty mighty gamblers, with the whole world for the table, and kingdoms for counters'.[12] It was a game of chance, but also of calculation and bluff, whose fortunes depended very largely on the skills of its players. Those players were restricted to the élite of European political society, in whose hands alone (and also, Lever suggested, their women's) rested the fate of nations. So it was all a matter of personalities, of individual character and wit and nerve. How then could these qualities possibly be measured, asked the permanent under-secretary in 1870, by the crude device of a 'competitive examination open to all comers'? How could they be sure that a mere meritocrat was 'a fit and proper person to be entrusted with the affairs, often delicate and confidential, of the British Foreign Office'?[13] In this field there was no substitute for personal acquaintance with a man's family and background and character: no substitute, therefore, for patronage. If this meant that only unrepresentative men got in, then so be it. It was justified by the nature of their task, which was seen as a skill rather than a function; a field for expertise more than for principles, and for able men, therefore, rather than representative ones.

So the foreign service preserved its distinctive quality and character; and preserved also its values, which were distinctive too – distinct, that is, from the values of the dominant middle classes. While those classes for example looked down on Europe for retaining so long the 'feudal' structures and conventions of the past, the aristocrats who ran their foreign policy tended to envy her for them. While the middle classes concerned themselves with imports and exports, and foreign markets and foreign investments, the Foreign Office – judging by the low esteem it accorded its own 'Commercial Department' – thought nothing of these things at all.[14] For the Foreign Office it would have been vulgar, for example, to measure a country's importance by the amount of trade done with it. Nowhere in the world was more important than Europe: Europe *was* the world. The rest was periphery. Bright young diplomats regarded other ministries than European ones as mere stepping stones to greater things, and Paris or Vienna as the ultimate prize. Foreign diplomacy, as it was conducted by the Foreign Office, meant European diplomacy nine times out of ten. The rest of the world scarcely mattered. Trade scarcely mattered. All that did matter was a kind of *haute politique* which appeared to have very little to do with ordinary, everyday life in Britain, and with the real material interest of the dominant classes in society. One or two diplomats saw this as a failing, like Sir Henry Bulwer, who once admitted to Lord John Russell his concern that the diplomatic classes did not have a more 'thorough acquaintance with the spirit and interest' of their own country.[15] To others it was the virtue of the system. With themselves at the helm, whatever was happening down below the ship could be trusted to sail a straight course. But once let the bourgeois on to the bridge, and there was no saying into what perilous and deviant channels they might be led.

It will have done them no harm to think this – that they were the masters of events – if it encouraged them to perform their duties soberly and responsibly. But was it entirely true? Clearly there were some limitations to their freedom of action, which they were all aware of. Even the most experienced and respected foreign secretary, for example, was likely quite often, on big issues, to have to trim his sails to winds from around the Cabinet table. Some less respected foreign secretaries were mere cyphers in the hands of their prime ministers. Others found themselves continually harassed by the Queen, who was very prone to interfere in foreign affairs and whose precise constitutional role in them was never quite settled beyond doubt. As for the middle classes: the ways for them to influence foreign policy were less direct, but could occasionally be effective. They may have been especially effective in the 1850s, for example, when Parliament was independent and a force to be reckoned with. At other times 'popular' pressure could usually be resisted, as it was for example by Disraeli over the Eastern Question in the 1870s. (You should never give in to public opinion, Disraeli advised his foreign secretary then; 'they won't respect you for doing it'.[16]) Very rarely can 'public opinion' be shown to have positively diverted policy away from paths which the foreign-policy-making élite was intent on following otherwise.[17] Which is not to say, however, that 'public opinion' was not a factor that was sometimes taken account of by the élite when it formulated its policies in the first place; and is not to say either that the formulation of foreign policy was not quite often affected by other kinds of pressure, quite apart from 'public opinion', which were rooted as much – or more – in the domestic and economic situation of the time.

For middle-class *opinion* did not necessarily reflect middle-class *interests*. The two should not be confused. Middle-class interests were (for the time being) immutable and rational; middle-class opinion was fickle and often inconstant, blind to its own interests, or otherwise confused in its appreciation of them. Often in the earlier part of the nineteenth century, for example, middle-class opinion seemed (we can never be certain – opinion at this time cannot be quantified) to clamour for war with Russia:[18] which at most times would have been inimical to middle-class interests, though the clamour itself may have indicated a real threat to them. Public opinion in this way might symptomatise a need, but irrationally: like a diabetic calling for water. At other times a particular expression of public opinion might run entirely counter to the real interests of the middle classes, even though it was consistent with a system of values which in a broader sense helped to uphold those interests. It was not surprising, for example, that the moralism which so sustained mid-Victorian capitalism should sometimes spill over and affect popular feeling over foreign policy, where it was generally inappropriate and inimical – if it were acted on – to the best interests of the system. It was perhaps fortunate, therefore, from the middle classes' point of view as well as from anyone else's, that cooler heads should be in charge of foreign affairs, and shielded as they were against influence from that quarter; though it is likely that if the middle classes had been able to infiltrate the diplomatic élite more they would have conducted policy very little differently from the aristocrats. For the real restraints imposed on the conduct of foreign policy in the mid-nineteenth century, and afterwards, may have been imposed neither by the predilections of the aristocracy nor by 'public opinion', but by the *facts* of Britain's economic and political situation; the logic of which made a foreign policy which conformed to that situation unavoidable, and very largely determined the role which Britain played in the world. Public opinion was one possible manifestation of these restraints: but there were others.

In fact when it came to it every foreign policy-maker was fully aware that his options were limited to an extent, even a considerable extent, by external factors. The 'games' analogy itself allowed for one kind of factor, which was the pressure put on a player by the hand he was dealt, and also by the hands the other players were dealt and the ways they would play them, both of which were unpredictable. No card player is entirely the master of his own fate and fortune. British diplomats were always complaining of weak domestic cards they were dealt: like for example the British army, which was probably the weakest. They often grumbled too at the way their counsels were ignored and the national interest flouted by politicians concerned only for cheap popularity and the safety of their seats – which was another way of regarding 'accountability'. This is one small sign of the efficacy of some sort of pressure from 'below'. The question however is how efficacious it was. Diplomats appear to have believed that it could be resisted – otherwise what was the point of complaining? Their masters had a choice: if they liked they could defy the elements, lead opinion rather than cravenly bowing to it, and take control of the destiny of their nation – as Disraeli for example was supposed to have done in the 1870s. The same opinion is shared by those modern historians at whose hands the reputation of the fifteenth Earl of Derby, for example, has suffered so much in recent years.[19] Derby is blamed for having weakened Britain's international position and prestige in the 1860s. Clearly if he was culpable, he must have had a choice. And in Derby's case the argument is strengthened by the fact of Disraeli's imposition against his will in the mid-1870s of an alternative policy which was 'stronger'. Disraeli's alternative was Derby's choice. Similar choices can be seen to have existed for foreign secretaries at other times. But were they really significant choices? In Disraeli's case there is no way of proving that those of his actions which differed from Derby's made any great impact on the course of events. An attempt will be made in the following chapter to show that they did not. The differences were all 'show'; the reality underneath remained the same. It is sad, and perhaps depressing for those who would prefer to believe in the power of individuals to control events: but it may be so. Even Disraeli may have been irrelevant.

In a way, therefore, the élite were important. In so far as international events were affected by decisions, they were the men who took them. But that does not settle it. Possibly 'decisions' were not really so important as they were thought to be. Possibly also the decisions these men took were not entirely – or even at all – a matter of real choice. The problem cannot be settled empirically. No one will ever be able to prove one way or the other whether the Crimean War, for example, or something like it, would have happened independently of decisions taken by the British government and the Russian tsar. Nor will anybody be able to prove that it was ever open to these men – though they might have believed it was – *not* to go to war. History's options are always hypothetical. Because they are hypothetical it will always be possible to put up a fair case for stressing the importance of the actions and motives of individual men. But maybe the Crimean War would have happened anyway – if not then, perhaps later. Or if it did not, then maybe the results of it – whatever *they* were – would have been achieved some other way. And if *that* did not happen – well, what was the difference anyway, in the longer term, when the situation changed again, and the ripple in history that 1854 had caused was smoothed over once more. It is a slippery argument, but it does not follow that it is an invalid one.

And if it is not, then it makes a difference. It means in effect that it was immaterial who was steering the boat. Their broad course was set for them by factors outside their control. If the men on the bridge tried to venture more than a little way off course, they were soon blown back, or else grounded and the ship returned to more compliant hands. They were at the mercy of the winds and the currents, and the trim of their vessel.[20] If they seemed not to be it was only because the course they had plotted – whether they realised it or not – was where the winds and the currents were taking the vessel anyway. This happened more often than not, and it was the source of the impression that prevailed, that statesmen were in control of events generally. Where there was conflict, and governments could be seen to have been deflected from preferred courses of action by outside pressures, the efficacy of those pressures was clear. Where there was no obvious deflection – where the sailing was plainer – the pressures will not have been so clear: but they may none the less have been as decisive. It depends on how one looks at it. A man may choose, for whatever reason, to travel in a certain direction; and so long as he keeps to that route he may not ever be made aware of the fact that other ways are closed to him. In that case it is a moot point whether the *cause* of his going that way is or is not identical with his *motive* for going that way. The question is a philosophical one: but it opens up the possibility, at least, that the view from the bridge might not be so significant as a study of the winds and the currents, as a way of accounting for Britain's foreign relations in the nineteenth century.

The aristocrats who conducted Britain's diplomacy were in any case by no means entirely out of sympathy with the prevailing current. Their 'bourgeoisification' in the nineteenth century may not have been complete, but it had gone some way to neutralise old prejudices. The Tory Party, for example, with its Derbys and Salisburys – all of the bluest blood – was won over quite early to free trade; and the third

Viscount Palmerston was sent to school in Edinburgh under a pupil of Adam Smith to steep himself in political economy before he was let loose on affairs of state. Beyond this there were always some restraints put on the Foreign Office by Parliament, and by a general awareness of public feeling outside. That the foreign-policy-making élite was perfectly clear where it could *not* go is indicated between nearly every line of any of its despatches, and sometimes more explicitly. All this constituted a fairly tight rein, for any Foreign Office thoroughbred who might, on some particular issue, take it into his head to bolt.

This being so, it did no harm at all to have them there. In some ways it was a real advantage. Diplomacy *did* require special skills which, whether or not they were in its blood, did seem to be cultivated by the aristocracy in particular. Their social class was an intrinsic advantage too: after all most of the men they had to deal with on the continent were aristocrats themselves, who it was thought were likely to get on better with their own sort. The aristocracy's monopoly of foreign affairs may also have given it a sense of importance, a feeling that as a class it was respected and involved in British public life still. Possibly this was one of the factors helping to reconcile the aristocracy to the more general usurpation of its old powers by the bourgeoisie, so preventing a bloodier confrontation between the classes – perhaps in an odd kind of way this was even the *purpose* of it, a peculiarly British way of softening the blow of revolution. To make the aristocracy feel that it counted still, Britain's real rulers gave it foreign affairs to play with: but on sufferance only, and subject to rigid, if unspoken, conditions.[21]

And anyway there was nothing the middle classes required of foreign policy at that time that could not quite easily be squared with a moderately flexible aristocratic conscience. This was the decisive factor. The middle classes did not require diplomats to tout for trade for them, which would have been distasteful, or to go to war for trade, except in situations where such wars could be justified on higher and purer grounds. A young, vigorous, dynamic economy like theirs, almost without serious competitors in the markets of the world, could get along very well on its own, without help. Some things they might have wished to have changed. It would have been nice for example to have free trade everywhere: but even free trade was not worth having at the cost of a major war, which would (it was thought) be more damaging to British trade than anything. For this reason there was no question but that the middle classes' primary and abiding material interest in Europe was peace: which was not an objective so alien to the aristocracy's interests (though Cobden sometimes feared otherwise) as to render it impossible for an aristocratic Foreign Office to pursue.

15

They may have had different values and objectives, but they were not incompatible ones.

Britain's foreign policy in fact was very firmly rooted in her economic situation at that time: not each single policy *specifically* – searching for 'economic motives' in the details of mid-Victorian diplomacy has never been a very fruitful activity[22] – but generally, and very pervasively. This was one of the things which most distinguished her policy from the continentals'. For other countries trade was always a marginal activity; for Britain in these years it may have been vital. It was certainly an activity she pursued much more vigorously than they did. In 1860 for example her share of the world's trade was 25 per cent, which was more than double that of her nearest competitor.[23] Most of her staple industries depended very heavily on foreign trade both for raw materials and for markets: about a third of her woollen manufactures in the 1860s were exported, for example; more than 40 per cent of her iron and steel; and two-thirds of her cotton goods.[24] For millions of men and women in Britain, therefore, foreign trade was the source of their livelihood – of their jobs and wages. For no other country of the world were industry and trade so prominent in their national lives: which was bound to make a difference to the ways they looked at the world. Britain, when she looked at it, tended to see it in market terms – to see the world *as* a market. This had important implications. In a very general way it was a liberating factor, helping to free Britain from all those prejudices about 'prestige' and territory which still entrapped continentals. The 'cash nexus', after all, transcended national boundaries; the laws of supply and demand were blind to race and culture and even – with the invention of the steamship – to distance; older-fashioned loyalties and conventions came to mean nothing, in the light of the beautifully simple facts of political economy, and the natural laws of production and exchange which that new science had revealed. The whole game was different: the rules, the counters, and even the board.

The board for a start was a much wider one. Most countries' diplomatic interests in the mid-nineteenth century stayed close to home – for European countries (except Russia) for example, in Europe. Even if trade had been as vital to them as it was to Britain the position would not have been greatly different. Two-thirds of France's foreign trade in 1860 was with other countries in Europe, two-thirds of Holland's, 86 per cent of Belgium's.[25] Britain by contrast did only two-fifths of her trade with the continent, and less later on. The rest was scattered all over the world: 21 per cent in North America, 9 per cent in South America, 15 per cent in Asia, 6 per cent in Africa, 5 per cent in Australasia.[26] Her interests therefore were spread much wider.

16

Of course her European interests were important, but they were less important than other European countries' European interests were for them. They were diminished still further by the fact that Britain had no territorial ambitions on the continent, for which geography – the Channel – was as much responsible as political or economic principle. Britain therefore was drawn inexorably away from Europe by the sheer pull of her interests outside. It was a situation which continental Europeans were hardly likely to understand, and which some Euro-centred diplomatic historians like Henry Kissinger, for example, have been unable to understand since.[27] It was this which underlay what has been called Britain's 'isolation' from Europe in the second half of the nineteenth century. Why after all should Britain have been expected to commit herself to Europe, in the kinds of ways the continental 'despots' continually craved, when the whole world was before her, offering material opportunities, and also a vision of better things, which were quite beyond the purview yet of a continent too primitive to grasp them? To the continentals themselves, when Britain's defection from Europe became clear to them in the middle 1860s, it looked as though Britain had sacrificed national greatness for mere mercenary gain. Britons however knew that true greatness was not to be measured by the kinds of qualities the continentals set so much store by, but consisted *in* mercenary gain: the pursuit of which, wherever it was to be found, would eventually give rise to an international politics which would entirely supersede the continentals' more parochial kind.

This it was that made the foreign policy of mid-Victorian capitalism so intrinsically internationalistic: truly internationalist, dedicated to eroding the barriers between all nations, and not just a few, which was how later the term came to be distorted by imperialists and then by Europeanists for their own ends. Isolationism and internationalism were the same creature: the shunning of close and binding and essentially exclusive commitments to specific nations merely another aspect of that more open and inclusive and undiscriminating involvement in the whole world, which was the mid-Victorians' purer strain of internationalism. Of course it was a very nationalistic kind of internationalism in a sense. It was internationalism on Britain's own terms, terms which the rest of the world often had to be persuaded or compelled to accept, which was why, as we shall see,[28] the international amity which it was widely assumed should accrue from it often did not. Nevertheless the intention was there, the belief that if only other countries *could* be brought to see it there was no real way in which the interests of any of them need conflict. It coloured too the mid-Victorian brand of 'imperialism', which has been more than a

17

little calumniated by being labelled as such, and by being associated –
for a good reason, but still unfortunately – with bedfellows the
mid-Victorians themselves would vigorously have disowned. When
the mid-Victorians hawked their wares abroad, opening up new
markets by force sometimes, and occasionally by annexation, they did
so not for Britain's exclusive benefit but as a kind of international
duty, to police unruly parts of the world for their own good and for
every other nation's. The distinction between this and what the
mid-Victorians preferred to call imperialism may appear suspect to a
modern cynic (as it did also to contemporary cynics like Bismarck),
but it was a genuine one. Anyone could do business in one of Britain's
colonies: that was the important thing. Britain bore the cost (in men
and – if local sources failed – in money): for that the world should be
(and often was) grateful. There was no cause here for foreign jealousy.
Nor was there any necessary conflict with her internationalism, or any
of her liberal principles: so long as she did it only in the last resort, and
in 'trust', so to speak, for others. If this was imperialism it was not
imperialism in Napoleon's sense (which was the sense in which the
word was used then), or in Joseph Chamberlain's sense at the end of
the century. Its lack of exclusivity made all the difference.

It fitted in too with the main broad imperative behind Britain's
foreign policy then, derived from the particular situation of her
national economy, which was the nurture of her trade in the world and
also – less directly – of her industry at home. Both depended on a low
level of taxation to flourish, and a low level of taxation required,
among other things, that Britain have only the smallest of armies – of
standing armies anyway – to support. The ubiquity of the military on
the continent was one of the features of life there which was most
disapproved of in Britain at the time, chiefly because of the use it was
thought could be made of it against civil liberties. This was a long-
standing prejudice in Britain, which tied in neatly too with the
middle classes' fiscal obsessions. As well as being potentially oppress-
ive standing armies were expensive, and consequently a drain – human
as well as financial – on industry. Britain after all had to have a navy:
her worldwide commitments saw to that. A navy was expensive
enough – between £5 million and £10 million a year was normal in the
1850s and 1860s; but for that price she could have a navy which was
the biggest and best in the world, and a match for all comers. Armies
came much dearer, even in the days when officers more or less paid
their own salaries. In the 1860s Britain's army cost her £15 million a
year – nearly a quarter of her total budget[29] – and the return in this
case was not nearly so good. Not only was the British home-based
army during most of the nineteenth century considerably smaller than

Raises good points

continental armies – 100,000 regulars was a normal peacetime complement – but it was also notably less efficient. For most of the century its prestige rested, with steadily diminishing effect, on the memory of Waterloo. After Waterloo its main glories were some ponderous victories against ill-armed savages, and some gallant fiascos. It went through the Crimean War scarcely winning a single battle of note,[30] to the irritation for example of the Queen, who resented the way the French had somehow managed to score all the runs for their side, and had then decided to declare before the British had the chance of a decent innings.[31] But to most other people in Britain this did not seem to matter greatly. Their lack of concern about their army was attributed by one American observer to their 'insular position, and the security from invasion afforded by a powerful navy'.[32] They did not need soldiers for defence while their navy was there to prevent foreign soldiers landing. They did not need them for offensive purposes either, because they had no offensive ambitions anywhere (like in Europe) where there were armies that could stop them. That was one way of looking at it: but the argument could just as well be turned on its head. There were times when Britain could have done with a bigger army than she had. The Schleswig-Holstein crisis of 1864 was one: how could Britain contemplate war, asked Palmerston, with a force of only 20,000 – 'and more could not be got together' – against 'the hundreds of thousands which Germany, if united, could oppose to us'?[33] Clearly in this case it was her military capacity which determined her policy, and not the other way around. That military capacity, or lack of it, rested on more than mere expediency. In the middle of the nineteenth century a small army was a domestic necessity, vital to the political and economic structure of Victorian society. The alternative, though it was sometimes canvassed by military alarmists, was virtually unthinkable – for Britain to get herself an army on the scale of France's or Prussia's. It was more than just a question of numbers. Britain fitted out with a continental-style army would become a continental-style state, qualitatively different from what she was now. Taxes would soar, the labour supply would shrink, military habits would spread, and the people would be living perpetually under the shadows of the garrisons. The nature of Britain's liberal–capitalist society could not abide this.[34] Consequently her governments had to make do with an army which was little more than token, and adapt their foreign policies accordingly.

From this it followed too that British interests were set very firmly against war. War after all was the most 'exclusivist' of all kinds of international relationship, and the one most inimical, therefore, to the interests and ideals of the industrial and commercial middle

classes. How uneasily the two coexisted was illustrated right at the
beginning of the century, during the Revolutionary and Napoleonic
Wars; much of the opposition to which in Britain came from manu-
facturers who resented the damage they did to them in a dozen ways —
war taxation depleting their capital, the militia ballot and the press-
gang draining them of labour, food shortages disaffecting their
employees, blockades and Orders in Council and the fighting itself
cutting them off from their markets: for as one critic put it, encap-
sulating the whole contradiction in a sentence, 'Every impoverish-
ment to them [the enemy] is a loss of a customer to us.'[35] For some of
them, following the logic of this through, it made sense to sell
military uniforms and even arms to Napoleon, so long as he paid
promptly for them:[36] for not to do so would only impoverish and
therefore weaken England more. That was the commercial view,
which was clearly incompatible with any orthodox military view, and
in fact with the whole ethos of war. Of course there were profits too to
be made from the wars, which at other times might have been
considered more than fair recompense for all the disruption. At the
particular stage of its development that British capitalism was enter-
ing then, however, war was coming to seem more and more inappropriate. The best that could be hoped from it economically was to
stimulate certain industries, temporarily, and possibly to gain a few
new colonial markets. But how could that possibly compensate for the
taxation and the drain on labour and the shortages of raw materials and
markets, and for the social unrest and the political repression which
wars inevitably brought in their train? To the early Victorian commercial middle classes it came to seem almost self-evident: that
capitalism meant the death of war, like a crucifix to the devil. Which
was what, for its high priests like Richard Cobden, gave it its lofty
moral tone, and gave Britain her abiding interest in peace.

Her pacifism therefore was not — and was never claimed to be — a
policy of self-denial, any more than her anti-annexationism was; nor
was it a political absolute, a fundamental principle of policy, whose
contravention on any particular occasion implied any kind of betrayal.
Britain was pacifist because it was in her material interest to be; from
which it followed that if ever peace was not in her interest she could
quite happily resort to war, and did. The occasions when she did, after
1815, were generally occasions when the expense and the risks of war
seemed worth it: when a large market was at stake, for example, and
her opponents merely naked Africans, or ill-organised Chinese. Her
enemies called this bullying — picking fights with the weak, grovel-
ling before the strong — which it was: but it also made solid actuarial
sense. Losses had to be weighed against profits, risks against possible

20

gains. In China war might very well be worthwhile; in Europe, surely, it could never be. Britain might be beaten; or if she was not then the expense of victory – economic, human and political – would very likely vastly outweigh any advantages she might gain, which in any case, because of the damage her victory would do to her enemies as consumers, would be negated by the very fact of it. To work and earn and save, and then to spend it all killing your customers, was worse than immoral. It was bad business too.

But what if your customers threatened to kill *you*? That surely was a different matter entirely. European peace was not guaranteed simply by willing it. Britain had no interest on the continent that was worth a war – but she might be forced to have an interest there if events on the continent threatened either her security, or her trade. The Royal Navy was a comfort: in most situations it might prove to be a sufficient defence against either. But what if it was not: if the French did manage to land on the Kent beaches, for example, or if Russia could cut off Britain's trade routes by land? Of all the problems that faced British diplomatists in the nineteenth century, this was always the most intractable. In a sense it was insoluble, because the only way really to solve it would defeat its whole object, undermine what was being safeguarded. Britain could have achieved a pretty good degree of security had she been prepared to reconsider her prejudice against large armies, and to intervene more actively in European affairs: but what would be the effect of this on the society – low taxation, *laissez-faire*, liberal, capitalist – that was being defended? It was like a bee's sting, but without the bee's ultimate (social) rationale. Fit out commercial England with an effective army, and she no longer was the commercial England she was before. There would be nothing left worth defending.

In the long run they could perhaps count on good sense prevailing abroad, as the continent came to see – as surely it must – the error of its 'feudal' ways, and the hollowness of the fears and ambitions which *made* it a threat. For it was almost an article of Liberal faith in the mid-nineteenth century that conflicts between nations were really unnecessary, and that when other nations came to see this there would not be any. Most causes of conflict were trivial, compared with the enormous advantages to be gained from peace and co-operation. 'Prestige', for example, which was supposed to be a cause of war, was a chimera. Territory was profitable to the country which possessed it only if that country exploited it to its own advantage exclusively, and to exploit territory exclusively was never in the long run advantageous because it acted as a restraint on the omnibeneficent growth of world trade. Security was less trivial, but would become less likely to provoke conflict once the reasons for threatening it dissolved. Peace was mankind's natural state, and so in time it would prevail. The idea sounded visionary, and in a way it was; but it was never so 'unrealistic' as to forget, for example, that heaven on earth had not been achieved yet, or to engender policies predicated on the assumption that it had. So it hardly answered the present situation. It could be borne in mind for the future. In the mean time however there had to be some way of providing for the present: a way – if not a perfect way – of protecting the plant without deforming it.

This was where diplomacy came in: but a diplomacy which for Britain was always conducted from a position of weakness. Because, as Palmerston put it as early as 1836, 'England alone cannot carry her points on the Continent', she required 'allies as instruments to work with';[37] and alliances could be double-edged. Allies might not have quite your interests. Policies pursued in harness with others might be diverted by others; in extreme cases help from a country might only be secured in return for a commitment to give help *to* that country, perhaps in a war from which Britain had nothing to gain at all. Britain's continental alliances in the first fifty years after Waterloo, therefore, had to be cautious, limited affairs, less effective than some British statesmen – Castlereagh and Wellington, for example – would have preferred, and less whole-hearted than many continental states-men wanted. 'It is to be observed', as Lord John Russell reminded the Queen in 1851, '. . . that the traditionary policy of this country is not to bind the Crown and country by engagements, unless upon special cause shown, arising out of the circumstances of the day.'[38] Open-ended alliances therefore were ruled out, as a means to preserve the peace.

There was however another device which was supposed to do the job better. The idea of the 'Balance of Power' went back to the eighteenth century, but it was revived again at the Vienna congress as a means to contain European conflicts. Its working principle was that if the four or five leading powers of Europe were all roughly equal in strength, then no one of them could be stronger than the others combined, who *would* combine against any of them who tried to get stronger or who aggressed. It was seen at first as a positive, active principle of policy, which required a vigorous commitment from its participants. Some of its continental participants saw it too as a means of maintaining what they called 'legitimacy', on the grounds that challenges to that legitimacy themselves constituted a threat to European stability. Throughout the middle years of the nineteenth century this was a source of great suspicion to British liberals, and of ill-feeling between Britain and the continent. Continentals, especially the 'Northern Courts' of Russia, Prussia and Austria, believed it was incumbent on all the powers in the interests of European stability to co-operate to ensure the security of their established regimes from internal subversion as well as external aggression. This involved for example mutual aid against dissidents and revolutionaries who operated across national frontiers: collaboration between police forces, extradition for political offences, denial of asylum to refugees, and the like. This kind of thing the British could not stomach. Asylum was a revered national tradition; political policing of any sort was supposed to have no place in Britain; continental regimes were very widely disapproved of anyway, and their opponents rather sympathised with. So in 1849–50, for example, Britain encouraged Turkey to resist Austrian and Russian demands for the extradition of Hungarian refugees there; and whenever she was asked herself to join in concerted continental measures against 'subversion' she nearly always refused, to the irritation of her allies, who regarded her attitude as less than *communitaire*.[39] These little incidents fundamentally arose out of – were a rare visible sign of – those essential differences between British and continental societies which were described at the beginning of this chapter; and they tended to bear out British liberals' suspicions of any kind of general European arrangement designed to maintain the peace. Some liberals saw in the Balance of Power nothing more than a new 'Holy Alliance' in sheep's clothing: a barrier against liberal progress on the continent, a tool of reaction, and a mere 'pretence', as Cobden put it, 'for maintaining standing armaments'.[40] This latter charge too seemed to have some foundation, in the preamble to the annual Mutiny Act, for example, which until quite late gave the preservation of the Balance as the reason for the army's existence. Britain's problems therefore were not solved by the Balance: not at any rate by what was made of the Balance abroad.

From Canning's time onwards, however, Britain steadily disengaged herself from any military commitment to the Balance; so that by 1850 the reference to it in the Mutiny Act was generally regarded as anachronistic.[41] And yet the Balance itself was not dropped, but continued to figure large in British policy. What happened was that the idea of it was adapted to Britain's peculiar situation. People 'came to think that it worked automatically, like the law of supply and demand or any other of the famous economic "laws" that the Victorians imagined they had discovered'.[42] It could be left to function on its own, like a self-regulating mechanism. If one country attacked another, all the other countries would leap to the victim's defence. This could be depended upon. It was a seductive notion. The joy of it, from Britain's point of view, was that it took much of the weight of her own security off her shoulders. If she did have to intervene in Europe in the interests of peace, it would not be alone. Consequently it would be neither dangerous nor expensive. Conversely, if she were attacked herself she would not have to defend herself alone. She did not need a large army, therefore, or to take any measure which was inconsistent with her fundamental national interests. It was a policy tailor-made for her: and, she believed, for everyone. Herein lay – for those who were genuinely taken in by this – its strength and its appeal.

Herein also lay the explanation for a lot of policies pursued by Britain during the 1840s and 1850s which seemed illiberal at the time, but really were not. The Balance of Power made them right. Without the Balance there would be no European peace, and peace was a prerequisite for the growth and expansion, not only of commerce, but of liberal enlightenment too. So if Austria's continued possession of Hungary, for example, was essential to the Balance – to maintain Austria's weight in it – then it, too, was ultimately consistent with liberalism. This is what Palmerston used to tell those of his Liberal followers who cavilled at what they saw as the incongruity of supposedly Liberal governments bolstering up illiberal regimes in Europe. Palmerston's attitude towards the Habsburg Empire was quite clear. He was critical of its internal administration, and sympathised with those who rose against it in 1848, like Kossuth's Hungarian nationalists. The Hungarians sensed this, and consequently felt let down when Palmerston did nothing effective to support them: to them it merely demonstrated his hypocrisy. But for Palmerston sympathy and support were entirely different things. Palmerston sympathised with the Hungarians because they were ruled illiberally by Austria, and for this he continually berated the Austrians, who misunderstood his position too. It was because they were ruled illiberally that they had been turned into nationalists – as others elsewhere, for example, were turned into socialists and democrats; but it did not follow from this at all that he must therefore support their nationalistic aspirations, any more than he could support the others' democratic ones. Liberalism and nationalism[43] (like liberalism and democracy) had very little to do with each other. They are not, indeed, inseverable; nationalists are not always – not often, even – liberals, and sometimes may be far less liberal than the 'oppressors' they wish to supplant. Later in the nineteenth century the two ideas came to be associated together in Britain, under Gladstone; but in the middle years of the century nationalism found very few champions, and few men who even understood it, on any government's front bench: not Palmerston, for example, and not even Lord John Russell, despite his famous ratification of Italian unification in October 1860, which came very late in the day, and was more an act of political realism than of principle. In fact no principle was involved here at all, no reason why Britain should, even if she was able to, go to the aid of any nation which was 'struggling to be free'. The question of principle involved liberalism, which was different, and was entirely consistent with Austrian territorial integrity (at least north of the Alps – Lombardy and Venetia were different), and with the Balance. The solution to Austria's Hungarian problem was not for her to stop ruling Hungary, but for her to start ruling Hungary more gently,[44] and this was the policy Palmerston constantly urged on her. Austria, because she believed gentleness only encouraged rebellion and separatism, inferred from this that he wished to destroy her and the Balance, but the opposite was the truth. The misunderstanding arose, again, from the fundamental ideological difference which existed between the two countries. Austria believed that freedom was a source of weakness, Britain believed it was a source of strength. Consequently Palmerston held that the Habsburgs could only do themselves good by giving in to liberals (not nationalists) in Hungary, and to secessionists (again, not nationalists) in northern Italy, whose possession by Austria, unlike Hungary's, he believed was a source of weakness to her.[45] The argument was involved, but entirely logical – and of course highly convenient. Playing Sir Galahad to oppressed continental nationalists had little to be said for it on grounds of self-interest either. It was nice therefore to have something to justify one's national indifference: a liberal principle which saved one the bother of having to act on other and more dangerous ones.

Most of the 'principles' of Victorian foreign policy were, in this way, clearly rooted in national self-interest. From which it followed that if that national self-interest ever appeared to be in conflict with a principle, then that principle could very often be bent. 'Non-interventionism', for example, was a policy dictated chiefly by the practical risks and dangers of intervention. But what if intervention carried no such risks? Or what if those risks themselves appeared justified, in the light of a larger national interest – a commercial interest – which intervention could be regarded as furthering? In these circumstances the principle no longer had any material rationale, and so might be suspended. Palmerston for example had little compunction about intervening, often clandestinely, in the domestic affairs of second-rank and peripheral states like Spain and Greece and Naples, to further (in their own interests as well as Britain's) the cause of 'constitutionalism' there.[46] This is what gave him his reputation as a meddler. Neither was the British prejudice against intervention sufficient to prevent Britain becoming involved in – perhaps even provoking – a major war in Europe in 1854: dramatic proof, surely, of her continuing commitment to the continent? But the Crimean War was not really, from Britain's point of view, a European war at all. Chiefly it was a war to check Russian expansion towards Asia and towards Britain's trade routes there. There is no other way of making sense of it (for which reason many Eurocentred contemporaries and historians came to regard it as senseless).[47] As soon as Britain's position as a world trading power was threatened, the non-intervention principle cut out, overridden by another higher principle, or interest. True there was some doubt as to whether Britain's interests really did require such a major commitment to safeguard them. The issue was very finely balanced. The war itself was vigorously opposed by many of the leading representatives of commercial opinion, who in a way needed the experience of the war to point the non-interventionist lesson. One effect of the war was to make another one like it unthinkable in Britain for many years afterwards. What it did, therefore, was to test and endorse Britain's interest in European isolation and non-intervention. She needed to dip a toe into the water sometime, to confirm how cold it was. It might have been on another issue than the Crimean one. But whatever issue it was on, it could not have happened more than once. Or is this too ingenious?

There were other occasions too in the mid-nineteenth century, especially before the Crimean War, when Britain appeared to come close to provoking a war through too much meddling on the continent. Most of these occasions were when Palmerston was foreign secretary. Palmerston had a knack for rubbing up foreign governments the wrong way: unnecessarily, felt many of his colleagues and superiors, and at bottom merely with a view to winning a cheap popularity among the *hoi polloi*. His critics constantly worried that Palmerston's abrasive style might bring disaster: but it never did. However close to the wind he sailed the vessel never capsized. Attitudes were struck which appeared to threaten war, but it never came to it. Sometimes the crisis just passed over. On another occasion (and on another pretext, in December 1851) Palmerston may have been removed from office just in time. At other times the continent climbed down; or *he* climbed down. This happened for example over Poland and Schleswig-Holstein in the early 1860s, when he was expected to intervene but did not, because the risk to Britain's interests of a war in Europe, even with French help, was just too great. On those occasions his bluff was called, and so Britain's reputation as a European power was shattered. Before 1863 it survived, but resting only on Palmerston's word for it, and on the misleading precedent of the Crimean

War. Palmerston's word was not tested then, because domestic problems made it inadvisable for the European powers too to risk war over, for example, Don Pacifico or the Hungarian refugee issue in 1850, so soon after 1848. But if it had been, would it have stood any firmer than in 1863? And if he *had* stood firm, how long would Palmerston's public have stayed with·him in a war which could be seen to further no conceivable material British interest? Palmerston is supposed to have been popular for his bluster. But it may be that his popularity, and also his success, rested not so much on this alone as on his very fine, almost uncanny judgement as to exactly how far he could *afford* to bluster without bringing on a war. 'He exults', wrote one famous German newspaper columnist in 1853, 'in show conflicts, show battles, show enemies. . . . What he aims at is not the substance, but the mere appearance of success.'[48] This may be the key to the contradiction. In the 1840s and 1850s as well as in the 1860s, and despite appearances to the contrary, Britain was never likely to become involved in a European conflict, unless she was attacked directly herself or on her commercial frontiers. To this end she scrupulously avoided binding alliances and treaties with continental powers, except over the Eastern Question. For the rest she relied on bluff, and the Balance of Power; and then, when these failed, on nothing at all.

In the later 1860s Britain seemed to pass from a foreign policy of 'meddle and muddle' – Lord Derby's phrase[49] – to one of retreat and isolation; but the transformation was more apparent than real. What made it apparent were the débâcles over Poland and Schleswig-Holstein in 1863–4, which in turn were rooted in the collapse of the old Balance of Power idea; which while it had lasted had seemed to suit Britain's interests perfectly, but by the 1860s was clearly suiting no one else's. In order to work it required a majority of the great powers to be broadly satisfied with the territorial status quo, which in 1860 only Britain and perhaps Austria were. With more than half the great powers sharing at least a conflicting interest in upsetting the status quo, the balance was bound to wobble. What if France and Russia, for example, agreed to tolerate and to co-operate in furthering each other's territorial ambitions (on the Rhine and in the Balkans): what kind of counterbalance could be exerted against *them*? And even if just one of the powers aggressed alone: how could Britain trust any ally she might call on to resist it not to take advantage of the situation for her own ends? This in fact was the problem Britain had with Russia over the Polish affair, and with Prussia and Austria over Schleswig-Holstein. The French were willing to join with Britain to resist them, but only – in all likelihood – to gain territory for themselves. For Britain this would defeat the whole object of the exercise; between

Prussian or Russian aggression and French there was little to choose. The Balance of Power consequently was at an end, destroyed by its own contradictions, and Britain was left without even an illusion to cover her nakedness. In the great European events which followed – the unification and consolidation of Germany – she took no part at all, beyond securing from the main participants a guarantee over Luxembourg which even at the time was acknowledged to be a sham, and another over Belgium which (to the chagrin of the foreign secretary) was not.[50] Her isolation then was revealed for what it was, and for what – in view of her fundamental and vital interests in the world – it was bound to be.

In the world outside Europe those interests could in their turn be seen for what *they* were, stripped of illusions and pretences. In the main they were economic interests, but not necessarily disreputable or even particularly selfish for that. Of course her trade abroad was profitable to Britain, maybe even vital; but it did not follow at all that it was profitable to her alone. Trade between nations was supposed to benefit everyone, particularly the way the British chose to do it – 'freely and fairly', as the saying went at the time. No one was forced to buy from them, or sell to them, or even prevented from competing with them: where was the harm in this? For this reason too British trade was not supposed to involve diplomacy at all, for there was nothing it required diplomacy to do. For the Foreign Office to have pushed British trading interests abroad, even if it had been willing to, would have smacked of favouritism: the kind of favouritism which in the middle of the nineteenth century British commerce was supposed not to need, and was anyway (and probably for that reason) against the Victorians' commercial principles.[51] All that kind of thing had passed with the passing of the bad old ways of the eighteenth century – tariffs and colonial systems and naval wars and the rest; all things which economic doctrine now frowned on and Britain, it was thought, had outgrown. Her interests in the wider world therefore could be left to look after themselves. It was better that way, not least because it was cheaper.

It was just like at home, with capitalism being left free there too to flourish without state assistance or control: except that at home capitalism had a general framework of public law to operate within, which in the wider world was, for obvious reasons, lacking. This it was that upset the theory a little, and caused Britain in certain situations to compromise her principles, or to seem to. The problem was not so much that some countries refused to trade with her. When that happened she generally accepted it. Unwilling customers were not worth having – not at any rate while there were plenty of more amenable ones around. The real difficulties arose with customers who were willing, but unreliable: who broke faith, contravened treaties, defaulted on debts, and the like. Trade could not be carried on in such conditions. Most of what Britain characterised as the 'civilised' countries of the world accepted this and did their best to provide reasonable conditions for trade – security for merchants, facilities for credit, redress against fraud, and so on. They did this because they realised the mutual advantage of it. Other countries however did not, and these included many of the countries British merchants saw as some of their most promising markets. The prime example was the Chinese Empire. China's practice for decades had been to have no kind of contact at all with the 'barbarians' of Europe – no normal diplomatic relations, for example – with just one tiny exception, which was to prove a fatal one: that European merchants were permitted to ply their trade at certain specially designated enclaves on the coast, subject to rigid conditions. The trouble was not the rigidity of the conditions, so much as their mutability. If they had been adhered to by the Chinese – if the merchants had known where they stood – there would have been little ground for resentment. Too often however the conditions were flouted quite capriciously. Agreements were reneged on, European 'factories' burnt down, lives endangered, goods confiscated: and with the civil authorities refusing even to listen to the resulting complaints. To those civil authorities the 'barbarians' were there on sufferance, allowed to carry on their business not as a right but as a privilege, and subject therefore to quite arbitrary treatment at any times. Agreements stood so long as the authorities wanted them to; treaties were binding only while they were compelled to abide by them. The Chinese may have had good reason and ample provocation for this behaviour; for the 'barbarians', however, it was patently unjust.[52] And it created a situation into which even the most non-interventionist of governments might therefore be drawn, in the ordinary course of its basic diplomatic duty to protect its subjects overseas.

What would happen then depended on the circumstances, and the way they bore upon Britain's economic interests generally. Whatever was done would need to make economic sense; it could not be costlier than the material gains that could be expected to come out of it, for example, or undermine Britain's commercial position in any other way. China was a particularly tricky case, where the wrong kind of action might easily provoke the Chinese government to revoke her trading concessions altogether – for this reason many of the most hard-headed British merchants there believed submission was the wisest course; or it might so undermine its authority as to reduce the Chinese Empire to chaos, which must be worse for trade even than the tyranny of the Manchus, or for Britain, if she was thereby dragged into China as she had been earlier into India, to her enormous cost and maybe peril.[53] Action in China therefore was limited and 'punitive' in nature: seeking to coerce her government into restoring favourable conditions for European trade – including the lucrative but demoralising trade in Indian opium – without involving Britain in more responsibility than it was worth. On the way she picked up one new colony, Hong Kong, in 1841: not with any great enthusiasm or sense of gain, but as the price she had to pay to achieve her main object. Elsewhere in the world she gathered some others too in these mid-Victorian years: parts of west Africa and the Malay peninsula, Labuan off the coast of Borneo, New Zealand, Natal in southern Africa, the Kingdom of Oudh in northern India, and one or two more. In every case it was done with a sense of reluctance, of necessity; annexation of territory chosen as a last resort means of safeguarding existing and 'legitimate' British interests there or nearby.[54] Some of those interests were trading ones, as in China. Others arose out of British settlement in what later were to become the 'white dominions' of the empire, and where the action taken was in the interests of the native inhabitants against the settlers as much as of anyone – or of the British taxpayer, perhaps, who if the settlers were not controlled from the beginning might have to foot enormous bills to put down native wars provoked by them. Others still grew out of colonial responsibilities the nineteenth century had inherited from the eighteenth, like India, which could not be abrogated now even if anyone had wanted it. Most people in Britain in the mid-nineteenth century were probably in two minds over whether they would like to get rid of India or not; in a way it was a considerable ideological embarrassment, though an exceedingly profitable one. Very few people however wanted or thought they could afford to take on another colonial responsibility of the same size. If there were any doubts about this the Indian Mutiny of 1857 soon dispelled them. This was their reason for caution; together with the prime fact that in general Britain could get what she wanted – the markets her economy needed – without such commitments. If annexation were essential – if even the very minimal conditions for the rule of law, as she saw it, could be established no other way – then, after weighing the costs, she might do it. But she much preferred to exert her influence in the world more 'informally': more cheaply, therefore, and so more consistently with her overall national interest.

Mid-Victorian foreign policy is sometimes presented as an uneasy amalgam of idealism, or pretended idealism, and sheer cynical self-interest. This is really not to understand it at all. For the Victorians there was no inconsistency between the two: no way in which Britain's interests in the world – which lay at the bottom of her foreign policy – ever should conflict either with other countries' interests, or with any of her own ideals. She believed the same should be true for other countries too, and that the fact that they did not realise it yet – which was the root cause of all the trouble that went on in the world – was another sign of her elevation above them. She was encouraged in this view, of course, by the knowledge that her own interests did not in fact conflict with other countries', partly because those interests were of a different kind – mainly commercial; partly because they were so widely spread in the world; and partly because she had the Channel as a barrier between herself and her nearest neighbours. For these reasons her ideals fitted in very well (and very conveniently, as Bismarck once remarked[55]) with her own special material circumstances; which does not however necessarily mean that those ideals were either spurious or invalid. It is a very mercantilist attitude to take, to believe that one nation's advantage is always another nation's loss; and Britain had grown out of mercantilism. The point about free enterprise capitalism, and the foreign policy of free enterprise capitalism, was that self-interest and the general interest were one: so long as both were calculated aright. This was the Victorians' big discovery in this field, and it coloured everything they did.

Specifically, what Britain's material circumstances and her ideals both demanded of foreign policy in the middle years of the nineteenth century was that it be as *inactive* as possible, which surely could do little harm to anyone. Even economic motives – particular economic motives – were to play no part in it. For ambassadors to give special assistance to capitalists would have been out of character, and inconsistent with the general requirements of capitalism then. Capitalists could look after themselves. In the wider world the opportunities for them seemed to be boundless, and to require only the minimum of state agency to make them available. The Royal Navy provided a general security; in very exceptional circumstances it might be called on to help more directly. Otherwise there was no need for foreign policy – no call for it. In Europe the commercial opportunities were more restricted, by tariffs and the like. Time would bring the Europeans eventually to their senses, but nothing else would, short of war, and so there was nothing much that capitalists required of foreign policy here either. It went without saying that war in Europe could do them no good at all, what with blockades and customers being killed and war taxation and the rest; and even a readiness for war, in the shape of a large standing army, was commonly believed to be detrimental both to industrial progress, and to the political liberties which were tied up with it. The inescapable logic of all this was disengagement from Europe: from commitments, that is, which might involve Britain in wars – even 'preventive' wars – for European reasons.

This disengagement from Europe, or 'isolationism', was the central fact of British foreign policy from the 1830s onwards, though before the 1860s it tended to be obscured by Napoleonic memories, and Balance of Power myths, and Palmerstonian bluster, and a haze of rhetoric from every quarter. In the middle of the nineteenth century Britain was scarcely in any sense at all a 'European' power. It would have been impossible for her to be so: impossible, that is, without changing her social and economic structure and her political nature fundamentally. It would have been impossible for Britain as she was then to become part of the continent as *it* was then: a different world, with different interests and values and priorities; full of tadpoles still, with not a frog in sight.

2

Doubts and Fears
1870–95

None of the special conditions which had determined Britain's foreign relations in the middle of the nineteenth century could last for ever. By around 1870 very few people in Britain can have expected that they would. Some of the auguries were plain. The collapse of the Balance of Power in the 1860s – or of the illusion of Balance – had left an ominous gap in Britain's diplomatic defences. The peril of the situation was highlighted by the events which had contributed to that collapse. The map of Europe was transformed, a new pattern of nationalities and allegiances created whose implications were unknown, and the old conventions of international diplomacy – respect for treaties and the like – overturned. With the Europe of old Britain had at least been able to reach a kind of *modus vivendi*, an understanding which was fragile, and on Britain's side rooted more than a little in wishful thinking, yet which enabled them to coexist. But how could one coexist with chaos? The answer of course was to fit oneself out for chaos too: but the implications of this for Britain's whole way of life in the 1870s were almost too depressing to contemplate. There were other signs too of a rougher passage to come. Economically for example other countries were beginning to catch up with Britain's levels of industrial production and trade. In the 1850s she had been the one advanced capitalist economy in the world: by the 1870s she no longer was. Some of the tadpoles were sprouting legs. This was bound to affect her position in the pool.

Theoretically, of course, 'foreign competition' was not supposed to matter. Most political economists positively welcomed it. Prosperity abroad created new markets for everyone and so stimulated industry generally. Ideally too it should give foreign countries common interests with Britain, especially in free trade and peace. Initially the facts seemed to confirm this. The continent's very rapid industrial development in the 1860s did no harm at all to Britain. Germany's output of pig-iron, for example, increased more than sixfold between 1850 and 1869 – from 212,000 to 1,413,000 tonnes; Britain's obviously could not expect to expand so greatly, starting as it did from a much higher level, and yet it still managed to double itself, from 2·25 million to 5·5 million tonnes.[1] Europe's growing prosperity, therefore, was not at Britain's *expense*. British commerce, too, thrived in the new conditions. In the 1860s exports from Britain to the continent increased by two-thirds, which was more than the rate of increase (53 per cent) of her exports to the rest of the world. During the next few years, from 1871 to 1873, her European trade flourished even more, exports for example increasing by 43 per cent in only three years.[2] The Franco-Prussian War had a lot to do with this, but the point was that the British economy appeared to be doing just as well in competition with others as it had before on its own. It was as the theorists had always said. Free enterprise capitalism was seaworthy in any waters.

From 1873 onwards, however, things began to look just a little different. Industrial growth faltered, profits fell, and trade got sluggish. People called it a 'depression', even 'the Great Depression', which was puzzling to free marketeers because theoretically free economies should not get depressed. Some of them refused to believe it was happening (Liberals for example who boycotted a Royal Commission set up by the Tories to enquire into it): but something clearly was. In retrospect this period can be seen as the start of Britain's long decline as an industrial and commercial power in the world. For British capitalism the times would never be as gilded again.

The trouble though may have started much earlier, when British capitalism was flourishing, and its very success made it impossible that it could ever be rooted out. Capitalism had perhaps had it too easy then, and so lost its competitive edge. Easy profits took away the incentive to innovate. In a way British industry in the 1850s and 1860s was in any case still living on the inventive skills of a previous generation. What may not have helped either were the strong traces of older social values which still remained in the new capitalist Britain, diverting its energies away, especially in the second and third generations. Landed wealth still carried status, for example, which may have diverted capital from industry. Successful businessmen or sons of businessmen felt the need to assert their success in traditional, non-capitalist ways. The 'public' school movement, which to all intents and purposes started in the 1860s, catered for this and by doing so further undermined Britain's industrial virility. The love of money – the root of all progress – became overshadowed by the love, and purchase, of status; and so the system was constantly drained of the men and the capital that might have carried its dynamic momentum forward further still. Perhaps Britain's bourgeois revolution had been too gentle, not drastic enough to remove all the old feudal roots, which now began to flower again in the liberal soil the bourgeois had prepared for them.[3]

This was the new moneyed class. For those who still needed to make their money, finance was coming to be a more promising and slightly more prestigious way of doing it than manufacturing and trade, which also had an effect on the economy, diverting capital and talent into banking, for example, and insurance, and investment abroad. Foreign investment especially came to play an increasingly important part in Britain's economic life as the century wore on, though the exact amount of it cannot be known. The latest estimate is that about £500 million of British capital was invested abroad in 1870; it used to be thought to be much more.[4] Of course this was beneficial to her, even vital; for Britain could never have balanced her budget without the interest these investments paid. They also, in the natural course of things, generated demand abroad, much of which was supplied by British goods. But they may also have helped dig her grave as an industrial power, not then perhaps but later, by starving her own industry of capital while at the same time developing that of her competitors.[5] At the time this would have been an unspeakable heresy, but it may all the same have been true.

And none of this could possibly have been prevented; for the simple reason that it could not have been foreseen. By the time the damage began to show, it had already been done. The thing that caused it was also the thing that hid it. To have stopped it early enough would have meant stifling the very factor that was at the root of Britain's prosperity then: free enterprise. Free enterprise capitalism meant allowing capital – and by extension men – to flow wherever the market called. To have stopped capital going abroad where the interest was higher, or capitalists buying country houses and sending their sons to public schools, would have been unthinkable: a negation of those very freedoms which were the foundations of Britain's present success, as well as of her future difficulties. This may have been the fatal flaw in the system: that it did not – could not, by its very nature – look to the long term. Or it may be that capitalism was bound to become less and less prosperous anyway: even at the time there was a respectable school of economic thought which saw a natural tendency in it for profits to diminish.[6] In which case the decline of British capitalism – Britain's economic decline, therefore – was capitalism's own fault, and went back before 1873. 1873, however, is the most convenient point to date it. After that the seas got noticeably choppier, and Britain's voyage in the world much rougher.

Yet she stuck to her course — as again she was bound to. She stuck to free trade, for example, because there was no *pressing* need for her to throw it over: nothing yet to make the cost of throwing it over seem worth the price. There was no absolute decline, no real industrial depression, no great shrinkage of markets, no convincing opposition at home to the economics or the politics of capitalism. There were, as we shall see, some adjustments made: but these were mostly responses taken to obstacles found in her way in the ordinary course of her journey, and not in any significant way changes of direction. In foreign policy too she kept to her old course of isolation and non-involvement in Europe, because the alternative was too daunting. For Britain to have taken on any more active European role now, in fact, was more out of the question than it had ever been. The stakes had been raised much too high. With her regular army of a mere 130,000, and about the same number of reservists, plus another 60,000 in India but *needed* there, how could Britain sit at the same table with Germany's and France's and Russia's new *millions*? And was the game worth it anyway? What could Britain gain from it? Some security, perhaps; but even this was questionable. If she kept her navy in trim and her neighbours divided it was arguable that she was secure anyway. Whether her intervention in the affairs of the new *real-politischer* continent would make her more so was highly debateable: would it not be more likely to drag her into others' wars, which could be of no conceivable benefit to her? Then again: it might do wonders for her 'prestige' on the continent, which after the diplomatic disasters of the 1860s stood pretty low. There were some who cared quite a lot for this: Disraeli, for example. But for others, including both his foreign secretaries, prestige was nothing if you could not eat it: a relic of a backward age, as immaterial to Britain's real interests as 'morality'. To make any sacrifice at all for such a chimera would have been foolish, inconsistent with Britain's fundamental principles and interests as they were seen then.[7]

In any case the adjustment would need to be very drastic indeed. Britain's swords had been ploughshares for a long time now. It would take more than just a few extra millions on the army estimates to beat them into swords again. Isolationism had by now become woven into the fabric of her society: into its whole free trade, low taxation, liberal, anti-conscription, wider-world orientated structure. It was no simple matter to abandon it: the ramifications of such a course would run too deep. It needed a different kind of society to be able to do it: that, or a strong sense of crisis. And things were not that bad yet. In 1870 one had to be very alarmist, or very percipient, to sense a crisis. Not all the events of the past dozen years, after all, had been to Britain's detriment. Palmerston if he had been alive would have been delighted with some of them: like Austria's banishment to north of the Alps, and the measure of self-government she gave to Hungary in 1867, which were exactly the kinds of things he had been pressing on her for years, and showed that the old rogue had more sense than he was sometimes credited with. Gladstone too found considerable cause for optimism in the way the principle of nationality, which he saw as a stabilising influence in Europe, had come recently to be so widely accepted and knitted into international law. Everywhere it was coming to be acknowledged that people should choose their own allegiances: in Italy, in Romania, in the Ionian Islands, and even in Savoy and in Schleswig-Holstein, where a rather cruder way of proceeding did at least seem to fit in after the event with local desires. The exception was Prussia's annexation of Alsace-Lorraine, which consequently agitated Gladstone greatly, not least because of its likely adverse effect (in his view) on Europe's future stability. But Gladstone was wiser than most men. Few of his contemporaries could discern any immediate danger to Britain. If anything recent events could be seen as having alleviated any threat there was, by taking France – Britain's more likely future enemy – down a peg. Diplomatically, and economically too, little harm seemed to have come to Britain from the war: too little to tempt a nation grown fat so long on liberalism and capitalism and isolationism to turn readily to any sparser kind of diet. The whole weight of circumstances was against it.

Sometimes it did not appear to be like this at all. Gladstone and Disraeli both had their moments of non-isolationism: Gladstone for example when he itched to do something to stop Prussia taking Alsace and Lorraine, Disraeli when he marched right into Europe (figuratively speaking) and smashed the *Dreikaiserbund*. Like Palmerston's continental meddlings in the 1840s and 1850s these are sometimes taken to indicate a new interventionist course in British foreign policy. But as in Palmerston's case, appearances are deceptive.

Gladstone's itches were one thing: Disraeli's were quite another. Gladstone would have liked to intervene in 1870, partly because the annexation of Alsace-Lorraine offended his principles and partly because he thought it was making for trouble later on: but he never did. The only kind of intervention he advocated anyway was 'moral' – a simple protest – and even that was overruled in Cabinet on the grounds that it would be a waste of breath.[8] Nothing therefore ever came of it; nothing more material than a few posturings. With

Disraeli it was different. In the first place his motives were different. His leading one appears to have been to reassert Britain's influence and prestige as a European power again – to reverse in other words the whole isolationist trend of the past decade or more. In the second place he was prepared to go much further to achieve this aim: as far even as threatening European war, which was as far removed from isolationism as it was possible to go. In the event it did not come to war; but the gesture seemed to succeed. By 1878 Britain was back there in Europe again, at the front of the stage, where Disraeli wanted her. History had been seized by the scruff and turned right around. Alone Disraeli had done it.

Diplomatic victories are not often so dramatic as was this one over the Eastern Crisis of 1875–8, and Disraeli should not be grudged his moment of glory. But it was only a moment. It had three broad results, none of which was quite so impressive as it looked at first glance. It kept the peace, and it kept Constantinople and the south-eastern Balkans out of Russia's hands. It is likely however that both these objectives could have been achieved earlier and more easily had Disraeli been willing in the early summer of 1876 to go along with the other European powers' concerted policy towards Turkey. The reason why Disraeli refused to do this was that he objected to being treated 'as if we were Montenegro or Bosnia',[9] and asked merely to tag along with the continent, instead of leading the pack. His concern, in other words, was not with the Eastern Question itself, so much as with the part Britain was to play in solving it. So he scuppered the 'Berlin Memorandum', and sought thereafter to use the Eastern Question as a means to assert British prestige. And it worked. The third and to Disraeli the most satisfying result of his Eastern policy was that the *Dreikaiserbund* of Germany, Austria and Russia, which before 1878 was dominating the European scene, was both weakened and upstaged. Austria and Russia, who had conflicting interests in the Balkans, came out of it at loggerheads with each other, resentful against Germany for not helping them more, and all of them pushed into the background by Britain. Disraeli wrote jubilantly to the Queen that she was now 'the arbitress of Europe'.[10] But it was not to be so for long.

This of course may have had something to do with Disraeli's death, which happened in April 1881. A year before this his government had been defeated in an election at the hands of Gladstone, who was dedicated to a different line of foreign policy from Disraeli's. Maybe Disraeli if he had lived and got back into power could have maintained his European momentum, but it is difficult to see quite how. The *Dreikaiserbund* did not remain in disarray very long. By the end of

1879 Bismarck had his alliance with Austria back, and by 1881 all three 'Kaisers' had their full league in working order again, and no less dominant in Europe. There was little Britain could do to stop this, short of joining a continental alliance herself, which even Disraeli seems to have jibbed at. His Eastern settlement was hardly more permanent. The treaty on which it was founded was persistently infringed, and it was not long before the position it had been designed to reverse in the Balkans was restored, when Bulgaria's absorbtion of Eastern Rumelia in 1885 effectively did what the Russians had been prevented from doing at San Stephano. Perhaps if he had lived Disraeli could have stopped this; but his successors, Conservative as well as Liberal, thought not.

In any case it was questionable, even in the 1870s, whether Britain really needed in her own interests to maintain so much of the Ottoman Empire's integrity; and Disraeli himself gave the impression sometimes that he was contemplating breaking with it: in November 1874, for example, when his purchase of an interest in the Suez Canal was widely taken to presage a partition of the empire between Britain and Russia, and in June 1876 when he hinted as much to the Russian ambassador. The opening of the Suez Canal in 1869 had in a way altered the whole near-Eastern situation for Britain; Suez was now the only route to the east, out of three or four overland ones which had been mooted before, and the only part of the Ottoman Empire therefore which had any direct bearing on Britain's national interest. There were other reasons for defending Constantinople and Turkey-in-Europe, but none of them so pressing as they had been before. Russia already (since 1870) had warships in the Black Sea; if Britain was worried about them getting through to the Mediterranean it was unlikely that Turkish integrity would stop them. Russia at Constantinople of course was nearer to Suez than was Russia on the Danube, but still the distance was enormous; and she had never shown any signs of wanting to venture so far south. Turkey-in-Europe in any case was becoming harder and harder to defend, morally as well as materially. The whole Eastern Crisis of 1875 had arisen out of armed rebellions in the Balkans, which by now were a chronic feature of life there. The barbarity of the Turkish reprisals against them may have been exaggerated by the anti-Disraeli lobbies in Britain, but they were an indication that the chances of Turkish 'reform', which Disraeli's predecessors had used to pin their hopes on, had by now worn pretty thin. The signs were that the Ottoman cause was lost, as well as being no longer necessary in Britain's interest. Surely therefore the realistic course was to recognise this?

One of the remaining problems was that Turkish integrity was generally supposed to be a point of honour with Britain, so that her prestige might suffer if she gave it up. Prestige was a consideration to the 'jingo' mobs who backed Disraeli in the country, and to the Queen, and to Disraeli himself; but not to Lord Derby, for example, who in December 1877 complained rather bitterly to Lord Salisbury about Disraeli's obsession with it: 'He believes thoroughly in "prestige" – as all foreigners do, and would think it (quite sincerely) in the interests of the country to spend 200 millions on a war if the result was to make foreign States think more highly of us . . . . These ideas are intelligible, but they are not mine nor yours.'[11] For the sake of 'prestige' Disraeli had risked a European war, committed Britain secretly to defend Turkey alone if she were attacked in the future, and encumbered her with a new quasi-colonial commitment, the island of Cyprus, which was always more trouble to Britain than it was worth. It was a high price to pay for an advantage which was at best intangible, and soon to be made redundant by events.

For in 1882 Britain took over the government of Egypt: which was what the logic of her international situation had pointed to for some time now. Why defend the whole Ottoman Empire when all your interests required was this part of it? With Gladstone so squeamish about the Ottomans anyway, and a partition of their empire on the diplomatic cards since at least 1844 (when Lord Aberdeen had approved the idea in principle), and the Straits not really (as the Admiralty finally admitted in 1892)[12] defensible any more, the time had clearly come for Britain to cut her losses and concentrate on Egypt. A final and probably decisive factor was that she was deeply involved in Egypt in any case, financially rather than politically, but with finance and politics getting harder by the month to keep apart. In July 1882 a British naval squadron bombarded Alexandria, and a little later the country was occupied by British troops: to save it, and the routes to India, from the threat posed to them by a national uprising which in its turn had been provoked by British and French financial interests there. From then onwards, apart from a little Disraelian flurry by Lord Salisbury over Bulgaria in 1887, Egypt became the main focus of Britain's eastern policy, and her influence in Turkey and at the Straits was allowed slowly to seep away. The kink which Disraeli had put into the fabric was finally ironed out, and events returned to their 'natural' path.

The occupation of Egypt was a way of securing Britain's essential interests in the area without involving her too deeply with its European great power neighbours; a way therefore of maintaining her traditional isolation from the continent. On the surface it is a curious thing to find Gladstone of all people doing: Gladstone who in the first place disapproved of annexations against the wishes of the annexees, and secondly professed a deep commitment to what he called the 'concert' of Europe. Of course he had a solution to the paradox: which was to point out to his critics that if they looked carefully they would find that he had not really 'annexed' Egypt at all, and did not want to. As soon as Egypt's financial and political affairs had been put in order he would bring the troops back. In the mean time the country would continue to be ruled by Egyptians, but with British 'advice'. Put like that it seems disingenuous, but it was not. Neither was his insistence that Britain in this instance had acted not for her own exclusive advantage, but on behalf of the European 'concert'. He had tried to interest the other powers in a co-operative scheme to secure the Canal before he had intervened. When he did intervene it was in collaboration initially with the French – indeed partly at their behest. That the French had backed out at the last moment was hardly his fault. In the end Britain had gone in alone – but as the agent, so to speak, of the whole of Europe. True, she had never been formally mandated by Europe, but that made no difference to her intention. That intention was to settle the Egyptian question for the benefit of everyone. That was what she was doing. The Egyptian affair therefore was a genuine exercise in common European action: no less 'European' merely because the rest of Europe was not consciously involved.

Of course this could have been sheer hypocrisy, a convenient but unconvincing cover for what was really a policy of pure national aggression. It is interesting, and maybe suspicious, that in this instance as well as others Gladstone (unlike Disraeli) never let 'ideals' come between him and a highly realistic awareness of where Britain's solid material interests lay: that his idealism, such as it was, was so practical. On the other hand this surely was the essence of Victorian liberalism: to believe that 'interests', properly perceived, were not mutually exclusive but were common and complementary, so that what was ideal and what was practical really were the same. From which it followed that it was perfectly possible for one power to act to its own advantage, and yet at the same time be furthering the advantage of all: of the 'concert of Europe' even though no such 'concert' formally existed, and of every other country in the world too. (For it was an important feature of Gladstone's Europeanism that it was not an exclusive kind of Europeanism: a feature which distinguished it fundamentally from most other visions of European unity both at the time, and since.) This in fact was what Britain had been doing in the world for years now: acting on her own initiative but as everyone else's agent, to bring about conditions of stability and free trade in which any nation, if it wanted to, could share.

Egypt, therefore, was of a piece with all that had gone before. So were the rest of Gladstone's activities in Africa, which are often supposed to have inaugurated a new era of 'imperialism' in the history of the world, and may in a way have done so, but were never intended to. What is called the 'scramble for Africa' in the mid-1880s, when much of the continent was partitioned between the European powers, was entirely consistent with traditional British policy, even with traditional British 'anti-annexationism'. From Britain's point of view the important clauses in the Berlin Africa Treaty of 1884 which shared west-central Africa out were those which imposed free trade throughout the area. It did not matter much apart from that which pieces of Africa Britain got or did not get; she did not hanker after more than she got, and did not do much, officially, with the bits she did get until very much later. Most of them she called 'protectorates' or 'spheres of influence', which was supposed to indicate a relationship with them that was less than colonial – a negative title, rather than a positive one. As long as other countries did not interfere politically in Nigeria, for example, where she had an established trading interest, or in Uganda, where she was supposed to have a strategic interest, or indeed in Egypt: then she was satisfied. This was why the 'scramble' was such a relatively friendly affair between Britain and her 'rivals'; why this stage of the partition of Africa was expedited so painlessly; and why Gladstone was able to come out of it all with his anti-imperialist virginity – in his eyes at least – still intact.[13]

And in a way it was intact. The word 'imperialism' in the 1880s was usually associated with a national desire for territorial expansion, and neither Gladstone nor Salisbury, who was the Conservatives' prime minister in the 1880s, had any such ambition. Disraeli may possibly have had; though what strikes one most immediately about his style of imperialism is the importance that was attached to that 'style' itself: to the propaganda benefits, domestic and foreign, that were thought to accrue from the lesson he taught the Abyssinians in 1867, for example – without Britain taking an acre of their territory – or from his elevation of Queen Victoria into an 'Empress' in 1876.[14] If he had wanted to do more, to extend the boundaries of the British Empire to meet future exigencies which he may have seen more clearly than most, he did not get the chance to, outside Cyprus; and the reason for that was that the time was not yet ripe. Actual territorial expansion involved armies and bureaucracies and attitudes which were still totally inconsistent with Britain's fundamental interests as they stood then – which was roughly where they had stood for the past thirty years. What was happening under Gladstone was entirely different. In

Egypt he had taken temporary action to stabilise the country. In central Africa he had made an arrangement which enabled him to avoid colonising it. In southern Africa he even gave a colony away, to the Boers in 1881. None of this was at variance with Britain's interests, or with her old ideals; or with the idea, which Gladstone held to firmly, that even in the real world there was no call for empires, because empires meant exclusiveness, and exclusiveness worked to the detriment of all.

So the events of the mid-1880s, despite their apparent novelty, did not indicate any great change in the direction of British foreign policy: not at any rate in its motives and aims. What it may have indicated, however was another flaw in the theory which underpinned this policy; which in its turn reflected a flaw in the system which underlay that. The flaw – the mistake the Victorians made – was to assume that the expansion of European commerce in the world naturally conduced to international peace, and so was consistent with minimal expenditure on armaments; which was on a par with that other assumption of theirs, that on the domestic level the free operation of market forces naturally conduced to public tranquillity, and so was consistent with (even essential to) a liberal and unrepressive society. Economic and political freedom went together. It was a natural assumption, and it may have held true in some circumstances. By the 1880s, however, certain signs were appearing – not yet indisputable signs, but disturbing all the same – that it might not be quite the immutable scientific law many Victorians imagined. The system was beginning to fail, to throw up contradictions which seemed to threaten its whole basis, and which eventually (in 1914) were to land Britain in precisely the situation which it had been that system's whole object to avoid.

The problem fundamentally was this: that the kind of free market capitalism the Victorians favoured, with its strong emphasis on financial retrenchment and therefore on non-intervention not only in economics but in politics too, depended upon a degree of voluntary acquiescence on the part of everyone who became involved in it which could not in fact be guaranteed. The reason why the Victorians had believed that it could be guaranteed was that they believed that men, being rational, would see that the system worked to everyone's advantage. The reason why in the event it could not be guaranteed was that some men failed to see that it worked to *their* advantage: either because it did not, or because they were not rational enough to see that it did, or possibly because it was not being allowed to work properly – the free and beneficial play of market forces being obstructed, perhaps, by protectionism, or welfarism, or whatever. This last possibility was always a way out, and a plausible one, for free marketeers who if they had allowed themselves to accept either of the other two must have had their faith shaken a little; for the clear implication of *them* was that capitalism might require help, which was like saying that gravity needed a push occasionally: it undermined the whole principle of the thing. Nearly as bad, for those who were not so much concerned for theoretical consistency, was the unhappy prospect it opened up of more and more government intervention being required in order to keep the system going; which intervention in the long run threatened some of the Victorians' fondest ambitions. On the domestic front, for example, the growing social unrest which was a feature of the 1880s, accompanied as it was by the quite sudden re-emergence of a vigorous native socialism on to the political scene, seemed to indicate a need for measures to suppress it or assuage it or both, which were bound to implicate the government and therefore the taxpayer more than was supposed to be good for either of them, or for the principles of political liberalism. And the same was true of Britain's relations with the outside world. If what was going on now in Egypt was to be a normal feature of Britain's commercial and financial dealings abroad, then it had implications for her foreign policy which were deeply worrying.

For the occupation of Egypt went on and on. It was supposed to be temporary, but it did not turn out that way. Once he was in Gladstone found he could not get out again, despite all his efforts, and Lord Salisbury's after him, to come to some arrangement with the Egyptians and the great powers which would allow Britain to evacuate the country while still ensuring the Suez Canal's security. Egypt remained a British colony, in fact if not in name, for half a century or more. And the reason for this was that the Egyptian 'problem' was a general and fundamental and endemic one, arising out of Britain's economic position in the world, and essentially incapable of solution in any of the ways liberal Victorians would have liked.

The point was that the Victorians' commercial and financial penetration of the world was bound to provoke reactions. They liked to think not, because they liked to think that trade was beneficial to all. Hence the association that was assumed to exist between free trade, peace and economy. Free trade benefited everyone, therefore it was acceptable to everyone, therefore it would not need to be fought for, therefore it would not cost. But it did not always work out that way. Customers sometimes complained and even rebelled. This is what had started the trouble in Egypt: a rebellion of the people provoked by the stranglehold over Egypt's finances which foreign bondholders had exerted for some time now, after a series of bankruptcies or virtual bankruptcies had given the country into its creditors' hands. Bankruptcy was always a possibility, when the European money-market became entangled – as it was bound to, at the rates of interest it could command – with economies which were too weak or unsophisticated either to handle debts responsibly, or to repudiate them with impunity; and then the natural consequence was for the bondholders first and then their governments to be dragged in politically. But bankruptcy was not the only situation that could lead to this. Even a normal thriving trade, in capital or goods, between an industrial and non-industrial economy could produce economic and social tensions and provoke resentments in the latter which might eventually give rise to political intervention in much the same way. It had happened many times before 1882, so the Victorians knew it was possible. What they did not know yet, however, was that it was normal.

It had not been normal before 1882 because one vital factor had been missing: a convincing European challenge to Britain's interests outside.[15] Continental countries generally were not interested in those parts of the world where these problems arose. Britain therefore was given a clear run to cope with them on her own, which usually meant that she could do it cheaply and informally. What was different about Egypt was that other European countries were interested in her too. Consequently Britain's interests there had to be secured against them as well as against the natives. That, as it turned out, could only be done 'formally'. The same thing was to happen later in other parts of the world. Wherever it did happen it spelt the end for Britain's traditional method of extending her influence, with the minimum of responsibility and expense. European colonial rivalry acted as a catalyst for the transformation of a commercial empire into a territorial one. In this way free trade capitalism, for its own preservation, quite naturally metamorphosed into a full-blooded imperialism, or just the kind that earlier in the century had been widely regarded as its very antithesis.

And that was not all. Full-blooded imperialism also required full-blooded imperial governors. Colonies needed to be ruled, and ruled more directly than the United Kingdom, for example, was thought to need at that time. So men had to be trained up to be rulers; which further nourished some of those older values – like public service – which we have seen were beginning to flourish again in Britain (especially in her public schools) in any case. India especially was a magnet for what earlier in the century had been commonly reviled as 'functionaries' and would later come to be called bureaucrats: men whom it was difficult to see as creators of wealth in any way. The ethos of these men had little to do with liberal capitalism. In some ways it could be regarded as directly inimical to it: by diverting talented men from more productive pursuits, for example, or encouraging bureaucratic ways of thought in Britain,[16] or obstructing – protecting their subjects from – the full capitalist exploitation of the colonies themselves. This was a strong tradition in India, for example, going back at least as far as 1833 when the East India Company's commercial functions were curtailed, and reiterated by Queen Victoria's proclamation of 1858 when the country was taken over by the Crown: that native interests were to come before European wherever they seemed to conflict. Later on the same thing was found, albeit patchily, under the Colonial Office: the colonial bureaucracy acting as a buffer between the natives of west Africa, for example, and the demands of capitalist enterprise. To a great extent therefore this was the effect of the extension of formal imperial rule, and rulers, in the later nineteenth century: an anti-capitalist as much as a capitalist effect, which was ironic if it was true that it was the needs of capitalism that had created the demand for these men. It was another way in which liberal capitalism conjured up its own antithesis: by setting up breeding-grounds for the very leeches that were eventually to suck its life-blood – *free* enterprise, *minimal* government – dry.

These apparent contradictions between liberal capitalism and territorial imperialism led some critics of the latter, a little later on, to attribute it to some kind of perversion or betrayal of the former, and others to see it as a manifestation of capitalism at a different and higher 'stage': but really it was neither. All the evidence suggests that 1880 is far too early to be talking of a higher 'stage' in the development of British capitalism; and in any case the territorial imperialism of the 1880s, such as it was, is perfectly explicable in terms of the older kind of capitalism, without having to hypothesise any significant internal change. There were changes, but they were minor ones. There may have been some shift in the balance of Britain's economic interests abroad in the 1880s away from trade and towards investment, for example, but it hardly shows up in the (imperfect) figures that are available. The British economy was encountering difficulties at this time, but they were far from being desperate ones. Not all capitalists accepted this: but then capitalists do not always see things very broadly. When trade started sagging for any particular group of them they sometimes behaved as if things *were* desperate – petitioning governments to stop 'dumping' or to secure colonial markets, for example, to get them out of trouble;[17] but then when things got sunnier they forgot all about it, and governments never took very much notice. So far as they, the government, were concerned they were doing no more than they had always done to secure as inexpensively as possible a free and fair field for trade (everyone's trade) in the world. Nothing had greatly changed; the policy was the same, arising out of an economic structure in Britain which was also essentially the same as it had been for years.

This was why the full implications of these events did not percolate through at the time. How could they? Egypt did seem exceptional; being part of the 'Eastern Question' made her so. The continental powers always had been involved in the Eastern Question; it did not follow at all that they need involve themselves in any of Britain's other worldwide problems. The German challenge in tropical and southern Africa was not taken very seriously by British statesmen, and indeed may not have been meant very seriously: Bismarck's whole conduct during the Berlin Africa Conference and afterwards suggests so. Britain's own actions hardly seemed to indicate a very sharp break with the past either: temporary in Egypt, negative in west-central Africa, devolutionary elsewhere. There was very little here to indicate, without the benefit of hindsight, the nature of the storms that were to come, or to justify changing the boat's trim to meet them. Consequently the government's broad course in foreign policy remained the same in these years, obeying (as it was bound to) economic requirements which were broadly the same too.

In Europe this meant supping with a long spoon still. This was inevitable, in view of the continuing disparity between Britain's interests and the continent's. Economically that disparity was as wide as it had ever been, or wider. In 1880 only 36 per cent of Britain's exports went to Europe, compared with 44 per cent in 1860: as a market for British goods therefore the continent was shrinking relative to the rest of the world. For France, Holland and Belgium, and probably for Germany too, the trend was the other way.[18] That was one indication of the gulf. But it went much deeper than this. In 1860 a treaty of commerce concluded between Britain and France had given rise to hopes in England that the continent was moving towards a liberalisation of trade: which it was thought would bring British and continental interests closer together than anything. For a short while this had appeared to be happening. The Anglo-French treaty was followed by others. But then in the 1870s the brakes were put on, and the movement went into reverse. France, Germany and all the other countries of the continent scurried back into their protective burrows, and left the position by 1890 worse than it had been before. This was an enormous blow to Britain, ideologically as well as materially. It closed the door on that vision of theirs, of a society of nations prospering together freely and peacefully, more firmly than if the door had never been opened in the first place. From now on it was clear that the continentals were not going to join the international community on Britain's terms. And the continentals' terms, from Britain's point of view, were still too high.

It was not as if she was not invited. The trouble was that the invitations she got from the continent were not the kind that could possibly appeal to her. She wanted openness, freedom; a natural form of association predicated still on the liberal assumption that national interests did not need to be *compromised* in order to harmonise them, and that harmony between partners did not necessarily involve the exclusion of others. The 1860 commercial treaty had been based on that assumption: the key feature of it, said Gladstone, was that it was not exclusive; 'that, in concluding the Treaty, we did not give to one a privilege which we withheld from another, but that our Treaty with France was in fact a treaty with the world'.[19] Gladstone's 'concert' idea was rooted in precisely the same idea: not that European nations should sink their differences for their mutual benefit, but that there *were* no differences of substance to be sunk, between any nations of the world at all; which is what makes it so unsuitable a precedent for later forms of European association whose bases are the very antithesis of this. What Britain was offered from Europe was not this, but something far different: an *alliance* with one or more of the great powers of the continent which by its very nature must be exclusivist, and even dangerous. There were two alternatives. One was to revive the Anglo-French *entente* in some form or another. The other was to come to some kind of understanding with Germany, who repeatedly in the 1870s and occasionally later put out feelers to Britain to this end.

There were particular difficulties in the way of each of these options. The French option was probably always the likeliest one; and indeed Britain and France did manage to work together on a number of occasions before 1882, when they started to co-operate over Egypt but then fell out. Thereafter however, and for the rest of the century, Anglo-French relations were continually poisoned by this Egyptian affair: by France's resentment (though it was her own fault) at Britain's eventual unilateral action there, and her use of the financial powers she retained in Egypt afterwards to thwart Britain's plans for the country. This long-running Anglo-French grievance was seen by Germany as a way to attract Britain over to her side, together with her sudden new African initiative, whose main purpose may have been to impress on Britain the advantages of coming to an arrangement with Germany. But that scheme foundered too, on British suspicion of Germany's intentions in Europe, which had been aroused by Bismarck's aggressions in the 1860s. The last European statesman to behave as he had behaved then had been the first Napoleon, and it was Napoleon's image that came to many people's minds now: he was, said the British ambassador in Berlin in 1875 when Bismarck was rumoured to be on the point of attacking France again, 'really another old Bonaparte again, and he must be bridled'.[20] Fears of German aggression may have been unfounded. In the 1860s Germany had been disunited and incomplete, which was perhaps what had made her aggressive. Now she could be seen as a 'satisfied' power, with no further territorial ambitions in Europe, and an interest therefore in preserving, not upsetting, the status quo – an interest therefore which fully complemented Britain's. But this could not be banked on. And besides, any association with Germany after 1873 meant an association too with the *Dreikaiserbund* (or one of its successors), which for Liberals reeked too strongly of the old reactionary Holy Alliance to be popular, and for Disraeli's taste was rather too domineering. So nothing came of Germany's overtures to Britain either; to the great disgust of Bismarck, for example, who was reported to have said that he had 'lost five years of his political life by the foolish belief that England was still a great power',[21] and from then on was going to have nothing more to do with her.

But of course Bismarck's measure of 'greatness' was not Britain's; and what he could offer Britain in the way of 'greatness' could not possibly justify the risks she would run if she did consent to involve herself in the continent in the way the continentals wanted. Britain and Germany together, thought Bismarck – the British navy and the German army – could dominate Europe and the world: but Britain did not want or require to dominate the world that way. Nor did she want to get involved in the next Franco-German war which nearly everyone thought was bound to break out sometime, mainly because France wanted it to in order to exact revenge for 1871, and the prospect of which was the main obstacle to any proper continental commitment by Britain. Britain (as ever) could gain nothing from a war, and would only wish to ally with another power in order to prevent a war. In this case the possibilities looked fairly well balanced, but still it looked more likely that any alliance Britain joined would drag her into a war, than that it would deter one. And it made no kind of diplomatic sense to board a bus hurtling towards a cliff edge, merely on the off-chance that your weight in it might slow it down.

Possibly it would have slowed it down. If Britain, for example, had responded positively to Bismarck's first overture in 1870 it might have pre-empted the *Dreikaiserbund*, created a formidable enough obstacle to deter France from reopening the war with Germany, and allayed the fear of 'encirclement' which *may* have been Germany's reason for provoking that war later: but there could have been no certainty that any of this would follow, and it would have required a phenomenal degree of foresight on the part of statesmen even to see that it might. Lord Salisbury, who was probably the most 'realistic' of all British foreign secretaries in the nineteenth century, believed that foresight like this was unrealistic anyway: that the future was essentially unpredictable, because it could *alter*, and that only the short- and possibly the middle-term could ever be planned for. He also believed that in 'democracies' like Britain governments were not free ever to commit *future* governments, which made it difficult for her to accept the kind of commitment any of her putative European partners required. Under Salisbury therefore Britain's diplomacy in Europe remained cautious, short-term, and limited in its scope. In the main it was limited to that part of Europe which touched on her interests beyond Europe: the Mediterranean, Constantinople and the Balkans.

The 'Mediterranean Agreements' of 1887 were the only significant European treaties Britain concluded in the 1880s, and her liability under them was very strictly limited indeed. Like similar arrangements in the past they were directed against Russia, who in 1886 again seemed to be on the move in the Balkans. For reasons mentioned already in this chapter this was not so serious a matter then as it would have been earlier, but it still had to be taken seriously by Britain, chiefly because she was *expected* to take it seriously. The agreements were concluded, secretly, with Austria and Italy, with Germany's support for them being hinted at but never declared (she could not declare it without endangering her Russian alliance), and they worked. Russia thought better of her designs in the Balkans, and Britain was left with an involvement in the European treaty system which was just deep enough to serve her own particular and very localised interests in the area, and no deeper. She was a kind of associate of the Triple Alliance (of Germany, Austria and Italy), but with her commitments to it kept to a minimum. It was a good arrangement from Britain's point of view but less so from Germany's, especially after 1890, when the Kaiser's failure to renew Bismarck's 'reinsurance' treaty with Russia, and the Franco-Russian flirtation which inevitably followed, made Germany's diplomatic defences that much shakier and made a proper British alliance therefore more necessary. So when the Mediterranean agreements lapsed in 1896, Germany and Austria insisted that if they were renewed it would have to be in a more binding form than the old ones. By this time however (just after a new series of Turkish massacres, in Armenia) people had got used to the idea that Turkish integrity was not an object of British foreign policy any more, and certainly not an object worth making sacrifices for. So the agreements, and Britain's tenuous connection with the Triple Alliance, were dropped.

In the middle of the 1890s, therefore, Britain's isolation from Europe was as great, and as necessary to her, as it had ever been. Yet there were signs that it might not remain so for long. One of the signs was Germany's sudden irruption into Africa in the 1880s, which it might be felt later gave her a common area of interest with Britain for the first time – something worth coming to an arrangement about. But there were other signs too, of a different kind and on a different level, that perhaps the gulf between them was narrowing just a little. They came in an area of policy which is not usually dealt with in conventional histories of diplomacy, presumably on the ground that it had little bearing on the essential relations between countries.[22] But in a way it had a very great bearing. The question of extradition, for example, affected very intimately the ordinary, everyday relationship between countries; as also did the problem of 'foreign enlistment', which was to do with the obligations of governments to prevent their citizens making war privately against friendly states. In both these fields changes took place in Britain between 1870 and 1890 which may be highly revealing. What they reveal specifically is the beginning, at least, of a shift in official and public attitudes in Britain, on matters which in the middle of the nineteenth century had lain at the heart of the difference that was supposed to exist between her and the continent. They mark therefore a very slight closing of the gap between them; the start of what can perhaps be called the 'Europeanisation' of the British.

Possibly the British needed to be Europeanised. The situation before 1870 with regard both to extradition and to foreign enlistment was widely acknowledged to be unsatisfactory. In 1868 Britain had only three extradition treaties with foreign countries, compared with France's fifty-three.[23] Even those three were very imperfect instruments, particularly the French one, which French criminals in England usually slipped through with ease.[24] The pre-1870 Foreign Enlistment Act was hardly more effective. It was frequently evaded, notoriously by the *Alabama* in 1862 and the *Ward Jackson* the next year,[25] and it was shot through with holes. By the terms of it guns and bombs could be shipped abroad, for example, and even warships, so long as while they remained in British waters their guns were not actually wheeled into place. This was being less helpful to foreign states than they felt was reasonable; as also was Britain's persistent refusal during those years to co-operate with them to put down left-wing subversion and terrorism, much of which, as the continentals pointed out, was hatched in the shelter of Britain's asylum.

But then of course Britain was not aiming to help. One of the reasons why she refused to co-operate more with foreign countries over these matters was that she believed they did not merit it. Criminals were not extradited to France because English magistrates did not trust French judicial procedures. The Foreign Enlistment Act was lax very largely because the British tended to sympathise with the people – the Italian and Polish and other freedom fighters – it was generally directed against. Co-operation over 'subversion' was disapproved of because it was felt that foreign regimes deserved subverting. The whole situation with regard to these very sensitive points of contact between Britain and continental states arose from her strong feeling of ideological separation from them, which grew out of the economic disparities between them, and was expressed in a popular radical patriotism which most governments were forced to defer to even when they did not entirely share it. Mid-Victorian Englishmen, superior and secure in their liberal freedoms, were not going to prostitute their own domestic laws merely to satisfy the convenience of foreign despots.

After 1870 this changed a little. A new Foreign Enlistment Act was passed that year, clarifying and tightening up the old one.[26] A general extradition Act was passed the same year,[27] which formed the basis of a number of new treaties negotiated with foreign countries soon afterwards, which by 1887 included all the five great powers of Europe.[28] By the end of the century Britain had extradition treaties with thirty foreign states in all,[29] which was a total transformation of the picture of just a few years before. Britain therefore was quite suddenly much more amenable to the continent in these matters. There was nothing particularly sinister in this – nothing, for example, 'political'. None of Britain's extradition treaties allowed foreigners or anyone else to be extradited for political offences. A clause was written into the 1870 Act (section 7) specifically excluding them. It was even doubtful whether murderers could be extradited if their motives were political. Governments stood quite firm on this; and also on the question of international co-operation to combat terrorism, a proposal for which Gladstone turned down in 1881 (after an outbreak of terrorist acts on the continent) on the ground that it ran counter to British tradition.[30] For Scotland Yard to connive with foreign police spies was still unthinkable. Nevertheless the other measures which were taken to help the continent (and of course Britain in return) indicated that the prejudice that had prevented this kind of thing in the past was waning. The outer fortifications had been taken down, which brought Britain and the continent just a little closer together in spirit.

What was happening was that the pure milk of mid-Victorian liberalism was becoming diluted a little; not getting weaker necessarily, but changing its mix. The growth of bureaucracy in Britain and of bureaucratic notions by some Liberals was one sign of this, and another way in which Britain's administrative practice was creeping closer to the continental norm.[31] On the political level there was a clear shift in Liberalism's priorities, as some enthusiasms waxed and other older ones grew dim. 'Nationalism' for example (in the sense of 'nations struggling to be free') was a new priority, one which had hardly been a Liberal priority at all in Russell's and Palmerston's time; as was Gladstone's special brand of liberal–Christian moralism. Liberals were more sensitive to foreign yokes than they had used to be, and to sin. But they were less sensitive in other areas, as if certain of their old antennae had been cauterised. They were less sensitive, for example, on the issues of freedom of speech and freedom of the press. An early illustration of this is the prosecution and conviction of the German socialist Johann Most in 1881 for a newspaper article he wrote applauding the assassination of the Russian tsar. Thirty years before no government, least of all a Liberal government, could have risked such a thing; especially to gratify (as seemed to be the case here) a foreign power. After this affair the Home Office started spying on the activities of foreign refugees again, which they had not dared to do for more than twenty years.[32] There were other indications too that the British authorities were becoming slightly less solicitous of certain 'English liberties' than they had been before. It was at about this time for example that the 'Special Branch' – a political branch – of the police was first set up, initially for duties in Ireland. The police also came in for criticism for some rough tactics at socialist meetings, which more than one observer at the time thought presaged a move towards continental methods of policing in Britain.[33] All these may have been straws in the wind; indications that one particular difference between Britain and the continent was slowly being eroded away.

One of the roots of this lay outside England; in the uncomfortable fact that, however liberal Liberal governments tried to be at home, abroad they were forced to act in illiberal ways. India and Ireland, especially, were living betrayals of almost all the leading liberal political principles of the time; whose implications most Liberals tried to ignore as long as they could, but which inevitably came to exert an insidious and corrupting influence (as Northern Ireland still does) on British liberalism from without. ('Belial', wrote Robert Lowe in 1878, 'is a divinity who will not be served by halves, and no nation can ever cast away the principles of just and fair dealing in its relations with others, without speedily feeling the recoil in its domestic

affairs.'[34]) Another more obvious and immediate reason for this convergence between Britain and the continent was that, on a domestic
level too, they were now sharing experiences they had not shared
before. One of those experiences was what today is called terrorism. In
the 1850s Britain could not really sympathise with continental
measures against terrorism while she did not have any terrorism of her
own. Bombings and stabbings and other similarly unsporting
dissident activities, at least on a regular basis, were virtually unknown
there.[35] Even socialism was almost unknown, except as a peculiarity of
a few ineffective foreigners who had made their temporary home in
England. The conclusion which tended to be drawn from this, as we
have seen, was that Britain was protected from these things by the
liberality of her laws. When therefore Britain was suddenly afflicted
by these things *despite* the liberality of her laws it was a shock. For the
first time she was faced with problems the continent had been faced
with for decades. A Fenian campaign of bombings in England in the
early part of 1881, for example, may have shocked the government
into its prosecution of Johann Most. The Phoenix Park murders the
next year, and the quite violent demonstrations that took place all over
England but especially in London in the middle and late 1880s, all
tended to confirm the notion that maybe Britain was not quite so
happily different from other countries as she had thought. The new
measures were a response to these new challenges, which were beginning to create a kind of community of sentiment between her and
them.

They may also have been symptomatic of something deeper, which
has been touched on already. The ebullient libertarianism of the 1850s
had reflected a particular moment in the development of the British
economy then. That moment was just beginning to pass. As it passed,
much of the old confidence in free enterprise capitalism seeped away.
The seepage was reflected in the current revival of socialism and of
protectionism: neither of which however presented a real challenge to
orthodox dogma yet. Very few people seriously doubted that it was in
Britain's interest still to trust to market forces. What was beginning
to be questioned, though, was the assumption that it would take no
effort to keep the country trusting to market forces: that free enterprise
capitalism did not require to be defended. Consequently the relationship between economic and political freedom, which in the special
conditions of the middle of the century was very close indeed, was
starting to break down. British capitalism was becoming less self-
confident, and consequently slightly less liberal. Continental capitalism, on the other hand, which was making great strides now, never
was associated with the degree of liberalism it was associated with in

54

Britain (partly, perhaps, because the weather for it was never quite so fair). So there was a kind of convergence between them: between a British capitalism slightly less liberal than it had been because it was in the earliest stages of its decline, and a continental capitalism less liberal than it might have been, in view of the fact that it was approaching its maturity. The distance between them was still great; but the moment when it had been greatest had passed.

The Liberal vision, too, which had sustained Britain's sense of difference before, was beginning to fade. This was sad, because it was a beautiful vision while it lasted. Capitalism and the spread of capitalism were supposed to usher in an age of domestic tranquillity and international peace, but they did not. The reason for this probably lay in the system itself. In certain privileged circumstances it did make for tranquillity and peace, and was compatible therefore with political freedom, a small army, and above all with economy. But circumstances would change. They were beginning to in the 1880s. The mid-Victorians' chickens were coming home to roost. Their economy was faltering, despite – perhaps because of – the healthy freedom it had been allowed to develop in. Resistance to the system it rested on was not withering away as it should. Consequently measures might need to be taken to combat it: measures which undermined that very important link which had been forged in the 1850s between capitalism and political liberalism. Abroad a similar contradiction was emerging. Britain's markets were looking less secure than they had been in the days when no one was challenging her for them. The less secure they looked, the more effort and force and responsibility and expense it took to maintain them. What the wider implications of this would be could not be predicted. Formal empires, which is what all this was leading to, required quite different military and diplomatic defences from informal ones. They might also require a different political and social base. How would Britain's new territorial responsibilities abroad square with her traditional anti-militarism, for example, or her liberalism, or her European isolationism, or indeed with a form of capitalism which in the past had always been supposed to require a very low public expenditure for it to flourish? These were quite fundamental problems; but they were problems that were not going to be solved yet. While the need for Britain to adapt was not immediately pressing, it was unlikely that she would adapt. This accounts for the continuity of her foreign policy in these years. A lot was staked on the old policy; it would need a crisis therefore to shift it. That crisis came shortly afterwards, at the very end of the century. Then the contradictions inherent in Britain's position really emerged, and with them the possibility, at least, of change.

3

Crisis
1895–1914

By the middle of the 1890s Britain's position in the world was far from comfortable. Diplomatically she was 'isolated', which meant that she had no ally in Europe she could count on in a crisis, even for a limited purpose. The three major powers of the continent all seemed threatening, for different reasons: Russia out of ambition, France out of resentment, Germany out of jealousy. Lurid scenarios could be painted, and were,[1] of Britain attacked and overrun by one or another of these rivals, or even by all three together. This last, for example, was a real fear during the South African War of 1899–1902, and with fairly good reason. But the problem was not merely that Britain was threatened. A threat, once known, can be provided against: if this had been the sum of the difficulty there would have been little to worry about. Britain after all was still an island, which gave her enormous defensive advantages at that time over all her likely enemies. What made the threat especially dangerous was that if it ever did materialise (and for the moment there might be diplomatic ways to prevent that), then it could not possibly *be* provided against, without repercussions that would be immensely damaging. The problem at bottom was this: that the only way Britain could adequately safeguard her vital national interests against external dangers was by undermining those same interests from inside. It was like a man threatened with burglary having to sell his valuables to buy protection against the burglar. To defend herself and her assets in the world properly Britain needed to strengthen her armed forces, extend and fortify her empire, 'modernise' her domestic institutions, and seek alliances abroad: all expedients which in the past had been thought to be fundamentally incompatible with the principles that lay at the very root of her national interest. It was a kind of catch-22 situation. Fail to fortify the citadel and it would be stormed from without. Fortify, and

56

it would collapse from within. There was no way through this
paradox, and no way, therefore, that British foreign policy from the
1890s on could possibly 'succeed'.

Not all of this — not even the threat — was widely perceived at the
time, partly because of the fit of 'jingoism' that came over Britain
then, and to a great extent obscured it. This 'jingoism' was associated
with the expansion of Britain's empire, which was going on apace, and
was treated as a sign of her growing power in the world. The British
Empire was already more extensive than any empire ever known to
history, and getting bigger every day. By one traditional way of
measuring national 'greatness', therefore, Britain seemed to be
approaching the apogee of hers. Her national mood reflected this.
Britons took a noisy pride in their achievements: turning royal
jubilees for example into celebrations of their national might, and
demonstrating in the streets to affirm it. The literature and music of
the time were shot through with imperial pomp and circumstance.
Even Britain's most apparent weaknesses were turned to account, like
'isolation', which the Colonial Secretary Joseph Chamberlain insisted
in 1896 was 'not an isolation of weakness, or of contempt for our-
selves', but was 'deliberately chosen, the freedom to act as we choose in
any circumstances that may arise'.[2] The impression given off was one
of immense national self-confidence, in Britain's ability to defy and to
dominate the world on her own. But it was a false impression, and well
known to be false by many of its purveyors. Chamberlain for example
was not nearly so unconcerned at Britain's 'isolation' as he made out,
and beneath the euphoric surface of many of jingoism's other mani-
festations in the 1890s and 1900s there was a clear undercurrent of
uncertainty and apprehension. Elgar is full of it, for anyone with an ear
for it — even Pomp and Circumstance No. 1;[3] and Kipling also had his
moments of doubt. The jingo mobs may have done too. It is significant that the most notorious of these — the crowds that took over the
London streets on 'Mafeking Night' in May 1900 — were celebrating
not a real victory but the relief of a beleaguered garrison; and they may
have been expressing a *sense* of relief too. Things might have been
worse. That they could still become worse was many people's fear —
especially politicians' — at the time.[4] The jingoism was all a show, a
brave face put on a worrying situation, for the sake of morale. Some
were fooled by it, but many were not. There were cracks; and in the
cracks the foreboding showed through.

Even the empire was not much of a comfort, for two reasons. The
first was that not much of the new colonial territory Britain took in the
1890s was a real gain. On paper it looked to be all gain, with only one
tiny island in the North Sea — Heligoland — given up (to Germany in

1890), and a dozen or more new acquisitions taken, including Uganda, the Sudan, Weihaiwei on the China coast, and the Transvaal, as well as extensions to existing colonies elsewhere. What seemed on paper to be a highly profitable exchange, however, was not necessarily so. This was not because Uganda and the rest were worth less to Britain than Heligoland – of course they were not – but because, in the first place, they might be worth no more to Britain *as colonies* than they had been *before* they were colonies; and secondly, because they were worth less to her than her 'informal' interests elsewhere, which were diminishing at the same time that her formal empire was expanding. Very few of the annexations Britain made in the 1890s were in areas where she did not have interests already, and none of them compensated adequately for the slow attrition that was taking place, year by year, at the outer edges of her former, if undeclared, domain.[5] They were a partial compensation, and that was all: some scraps of influence salvaged from a deteriorating situation. It was in fact the situation that was at the root of it all. With other nations coming to menace Britain's vital interests more and more, and old ideas about international co-operation looking more fanciful every day, there was nothing left for it but to play safe, prepare for the worst, and secure by force what in former times she had preferred to secure more subtly. Her motives therefore were defensive, and the effect of this new 'imperialist' surge was not to increase her power in the world, but only to preserve some of it. Some people may have found this hard to credit, like for example the Sudanese and the Transvaal Boers (especially their dead): but it was how Britain saw it. She was not extending her frontiers but defending them: defending them by formalising them, which is what created the illusion of expansion, when all that was really happening was that certain patterns of dominance which had been invisible before were now becoming *revealed*. At the same time others were abandoned. Britain could not afford to defend all her 'informal' interests in the world; some therefore she had to give up, if the effort of defending them seemed more than they were worth. So, in a way, what appeared to be an expansion of her power and influence in the world was actually a contraction. It was a reflection of Britain's new adverse situation in the world; and it may also, in a kind of vicious circle, have made that situation worse. As her formal empire grew, in response to threats to her informal empire from other powers, it left her less capacity to defend her remaining informal empire; which consequently fell away from her, into other powers' pockets. She consolidated, and at the same time shrank.

If this process had really made Britain more secure the sacrifice might have been worth it: but it is arguable that it did not. This is the other reason why the empire was less of a comfort than it seemed. Just as an empire is not necessarily a sign of a nation's strength, so neither is it necessarily a source of it: least of all Britain's kind of empire. Scattered widely as it was, with interminable frontiers, enormously extended supply-lines and large patches of potential disloyalty, it clearly posed defensive problems of some magnitude. These problems were bound to weaken Britain in some ways. They were a test of Britain's military capacity, for example, which she might not always pass with credit.[6] They diverted troops from the home front, weakening her there; and they provided enemies with other weak points to attack. In certain circumstances this could be dangerous. What if Britain were at war in Europe, for example, and her adversary persuaded her colonies to rebel? This was a constant fear, and a well-founded one, for it occurred to her adversaries too: in 1914 when Germany exploited to the full any unrest she found in Africa, India and the Middle East, and in 1940 when Japan did the same in India. Or what if Britain were at war in a colony, and a European power used that opportunity to invade *her*? This was the big worry during the Boer War, when at one stage it looked as though not one but a very frightening combination of several continental powers might attack. Of course it was not all debit. The traffic of military forces in wartime, for example, went both ways. Colonial troops came to help on the western front, and in the Boer War, as well as British troops being drawn off to defend colonial frontiers. Some of the troops that defended colonial frontiers were found locally. The British were very good at this: putting much of the burden of defending and policing and also administering and paying for colonies on to colonial shoulders. But this device could not always be depended on: the Indian Mutiny had taught them that. And the help Britain got from her colonies in other war theatres did not usually come from the colonies that needed to be defended, so that it was not a true recompense for the *effort* of empire. Britain's dependent empire, the empire she effectively ruled, was still a military burden overall. In this sense the fact of her imperial 'power' in the world was no advantage to her at all.

This should not however be taken to imply that Britain was significantly weaker with her formal empire than she would have been without it. To a great extent her vulnerability at this time arose, not from her new colonial responsibilities, but from the national interests which lay beneath those responsibilities, and which would have needed to be defended whether they had been formally colonised or not. Even if Britain had not ruled Egypt in 1914, for example (and there was a sense in which she did not), she would still have needed to commit troops there when war broke out. These same problems anyway had beset Britain for years before 1890. All the time she had India she had a potentially vulnerable flank, and when that flank had mutinied in 1857 it had occurred to more than one British statesman how insecure this made her position, not only in India, but also in Europe. What made her especially vulnerable in the 1890s and 1900s was not really the extent of her empire, but the new threat which the continental powers were posing then to *all* her interests — imperial and 'informal' — overseas. Their new-found enthusiasm for colonies — the 'scrambles' for Africa and China — was one aspect of that threat. Another was their sudden interest in naval power, which started with the French and Russians who both began large naval building programmes around 1890, and then took hold of the Germans in 1898.[7] By the turn of the century Britain had nothing like the same naval lead over the rest of the world that she had used to have, and so was now highly vulnerable, even at sea, to a combination of two or more foreign powers. This was the key factor. For almost the first time in a hundred years Britain had powerful enemies where it mattered to her — in the wider world; and hardly a friend at all in Europe.

To some extent it might be said — and was — that this friendlessness, her isolation, was itself a reaction to this new 'imperialistic' phase of her foreign policy, especially her war against the Boers, which was almost universally deplored outside Britain and her colonies at the time. It was her 'aggression' that turned the continent against her. But this is unlikely. Nations do not generally complain of other countries' 'aggressions' unless those countries are regarded hostilely anyway: Cambodia in 1970 and Afghanistan in 1980, for example, were reacted to entirely differently by British governments, though they were closely similar, and similar too — similarly 'defensive', for example — to most of these exploits by Britain in the 1890s. Britain found herself isolated from the continent not because of her new imperialism, but because of her old extra-Europeanism, which was a very different thing, and which as we have seen had divided them for many years now. Imperialism therefore was not the source of her difficulties, though it did little to meet them. What it was was a symptom of them: of the fundamental weakness of her position in the world.

For some men, however, it meant more than this by far. These were the men who called themselves 'imperialists', and saw in the expansion of Britain's empire at the end of the century a possible solution to the problems that beset her. They were not the only ones to call themselves imperialists — the name was much in fashion then. What distinguished these 'new' or 'visionary' imperialists from the others, however, was that they did not merely accept the empire as a necessary expedient of British foreign policy, but wished to build upon it a whole new order of things, which was to be fundamentally different from what had gone before. These men became very prominent politically in the 1890s, and were to remain prominent for another fifty years. Their analysis of Britain's international situation was in many ways more perceptive than anyone else's in those years, and illustrates clearly the essential dilemma the country now found itself in.

Their argument went like this. Britain's traditional foreign policy was based on assumptions about international amity which had been demonstrably falsified recently, and which it was dangerous for Britain, with her widespread interests and responsibilities, to put her faith in. Nations were natural enemies. If they did not always show their enmity it was because they were deterred from doing so. If they were not deterred from doing so, then they would act to get all the advantages they could at the expense of weaker rivals, quite un-conscious of – or perhaps indifferent towards – the old liberal axiom that the best advantages of all were not to be got at the *expense* of others, but in collaboration with them. If there was any truth at all in this it was merely theoretical: in the real world nations behaved differently. It followed from this that it was naïve to expect them to behave towards Britain's interests in the wider world in a way which would allow her to ignore, as she had in the past, the proper defence of those interests. Sooner or later there would be an onslaught – it had begun already. Consequently Britain had better prepare herself for it.

The empire, the 'new imperialists' went on, was one essential agency by which this could be done. Empires were the thing of the future anyway. Soon there would be no patch of fertile earth left in the world that was not part of one. It followed that to try to defend any of Britain's interests that lay outside the area of her own empire would be hopeless: 'informal' empire, that convenient limbo between in-dependence and real empire, would no longer exist. Britain therefore had to start thinking imperially: to start regarding empire not as incidental to her worldwide interests, but as central to them. The two things eventually would be identical, the area of Britain's influence conterminous with the area of her empire. That was the way the world was moving.

While it was still moving – while there were still some vacant plots left – Britain had to make sure that she got as many of them as she could. That was the first priority, but not the most important. More important than this, said the imperial visionaries, was to see to the defence of the whole. That would involve all kinds of things: re-armament, for example, and possibly conscription; social reform, in order to make fitter defenders of the empire out of undernourished proletarians; perhaps some adjustments to the political structure at home, which surely in these ominous days was too free and open and divisive to be efficient; and so on. These were some of the ideas that were canvassed and debated among the 'new imperialists', though they were never a coherent programme, because there was never any agreement among all of them on any of this. What they did all agree on, however, was that the empire itself could help: if it were properly 'developed' economically, and rationalised, and above all brought together as a political and economic and military unity; by means of a common tariff, for example, and a co-ordinated defence strategy, and even – some imperialists fondly thought – a federated, empire-wide Parliament, which really would give to the whole that coherence and sense of identity which at present it seemed to lack. Thus united, the British Empire would be able to face an unfriendly and predatory world, and the challenge of the other rising world powers of Germany, Russia and the United States, confident in its security and strength. But first the empire had to be put to the forefront of things, regarded not as a mere by-product of Britain's foreign policy but as the base of it; and on it built her whole international strategy for the future.

Or nearly her whole strategy. For in a hostile world even this degree of 'imperialism' might not be sufficient for Britain to survive by, let alone the very much lesser degree of it the new imperialists might hope actually to achieve. The situation was already ominous – new imperialists tended to see the ominous side of it more vividly than others – and so Britain needed special help, which some of them believed could come from an alliance with another great power. Germany, for example, could be a great support. Some new imperial-ists felt a natural affinity with the Germans anyway, on racial or religious grounds or because of the Germans' refreshingly no-nonsense approach to domestic politics. Germany too had often shown herself amenable to a liaison in the past. These were some of the consider-ations that lay behind the imperialist Joseph Chamberlain's initiative for some form of Anglo-German alliance in the summer of 1898, when his less imperialist chief, Lord Salisbury, was ill and away from London, and Chamberlain thought, presumably, that he could set the wheels rolling fast enough to make an alliance irresistible in the end. Chamberlain's European policy was the other side of his imperial policy, his wish for Britain to become involved again with the con-tinent closely related to his ambition for her to consolidate and capitalise on her empire, and to a particular reading of the international situation of the time which lay beneath both. Imperialism and 'Europeanism' in this instance were not conflicting alternatives, but aspects of the same policy, and of the same way of looking at the world.

It was a way that made rather more sense of the world than some others did at that time. Faced with the clear contradiction that existed between Britain's global interests then, and the means that were coming to seem necessary to secure those interests, these new imperialists resolved it quite tidily. How they did it was by redefining the interests. Free trade for example went out of the window, superseded now by Chamberlain's plans for a protectionist imperial *Zollverein*. So did the avoidance of entangling alliances, which had always been assumed to be a primary British interest in the past; and a low military budget; and even, for some imperialists, the most sacred shibboleths of Victorian political liberalism: all of which appeared to them to be incompatible with national security. It was pretty drastic, but it accorded with a more sensitive awareness of the relationship between foreign policy and domestic structure than some of their contemporaries had. The existing domestic structure could no longer be defended adequately, and so it would have to be changed. The new imperialists grasped this nettle. To make Britain safe, her old, weak heart was to be torn out, and a new one put in. It was logical, but it was likely to be difficult for older-fashioned Britons to digest. This was one reason why it did not catch on widely yet.

New imperialism

For it is important to realise that it did *not* catch on, either as a public ideology or as a determinant of government policy, despite one or two signs to the contrary. The voices of the 'new imperialists' seemed to carry far in the 1890s, but only because they were shouting more loudly, and raising echoes which seemed to give strength to them, but did not. Popular imperialism, or jingoism, was one thing; popular support for the whole panoply of 'new imperialist' policies was quite another. Chamberlain saw the difference, if some historians after him could not. Public backing for his South African policy in the late 1890s was gratifyingly widespread and vociferous, but it had taken him all manner of tricks of persuasion and propaganda to win it, and even then it was little more than skin deep. It was a reaction to the spectacle of empire,[8] and it palled as the spectacle faded. What Chamberlain had wanted was a really deep-rooted imperial sentiment, to sustain a consistent and determined imperial strategy between the adventures as well as during them, and this he was never able to achieve.[9] If Chamberlain did not know this then, he was made aware of it afterwards, when he tried to promote the more solid side of his imperial scheme – colonial development, his *Zollverein*, imperial federation – and failed. The people were not interested. Neither by and large were the politicians, most of whom treated the new imperialists' enthusiasms with a great deal of suspicion. As a consequence both Chamberlain and the Liberal imperialist Rosebery eventually, in the early 1900s, found themselves ploughing lonely furrows[10] outside the main bodies of their political parties. They and their soul-brothers in the field, men like Alfred Milner and Lord Curzon, were – to use a convenient if treacherous expression popular today – 'extremists' in British politics, out on one of its wings. They never represented, or managed to capture, the middle ground.

But of course, as sometimes happens, they did achieve a moment of power without capturing the middle ground. Chamberlain and the rest were not voices in the wilderness in the 1890s, but politicians in positions of authority. They held those positions of authority at a time when the empire was expanding: from which it is natural to assume that they were responsible for the expansion – that the new imperialism therefore made its mark. And some of the expansion may indeed have been their responsibility: Uganda for example Rosebery's doing, and the Transvaal Chamberlain's. It is possible to argue, however, that they were able to do these things only because circumstances and older priorities called for them to be done anyway. The interests, economic and strategic, that were secured by Britain's annexation of Uganda and the Transvaal were no different from the interests that had been secured by dozens of other similar colonial annexations that had been made over the course of the previous fifty years. The threat to them may have been new, but the acquisition of both these territories fits easily into a pattern of imperialism and a conception of Britain's place in the world which long predated Chamberlain's and Rosebery's. In any case they only completed the building, most of whose fabric had arisen before them and so had nothing to do with their kind of imperialism at all. If they were not responsible for this, they were not responsible for much else either. Chamberlain was able to do something while he was at the Colonial Office to 'develop' his 'imperial estates', but not nearly as much as he wanted.[11] Overall the new imperialists' achievements, when they were measured against the full extent of their ambitions, came to really very little. They failed for example to federate the empire. They failed to establish their imperial common market. Britain's domestic political institutions remained totally unmarked by their sallies. And so, as we shall see, did the broad tendency of her foreign policy. In the election of 1906 their programme – or some of it – was part of the debate, but was spurned. Thereafter, so far as the realities of politics were concerned, it was as if they had never been; until wartime, when the conditions came to suit them again.

All of which illustrates once again the wide gulf that quite often existed in nineteenth-century foreign policy between rhetoric and reality – between what people were saying and what was happening; which gulf in its turn arose from the more important fact that what happened was influenced very little by what people said, or wanted, but depended much more on the economic and political circumstances of the time. In the economic and political circumstances of *that* time no visionary of any kind, not even one as strong-willed and as formally powerful as Chamberlain, stood a chance if his vision did not happen to be consonant with the current: which the new imperialist vision was not. New imperialists themselves tended to put the blame on a 'public opinion' which they believed was blind to its own national interests.[12] This was natural. The franchise after all had been widened to embrace most of (male) 'public opinion' only very recently, and conservatives in particular were bound to worry about the effects of this on policy (before they came to realise how easily it could be managed). But that was not the half of it. In this instance 'public opinion' only reflected a real need, an imperative which ran much deeper and had firmer roots than the new imperialists could hope to replace just then. Britain's continued broad adherence in these years to traditional lines of foreign and domestic policy may have owed something to other factors, like sentiment – a sentimental attachment for example to old liberties – but had much more to do with solid material interests. She kept to the old lines because she was bound to; and she was bound to because of the state of her economy then.

Quite simply, Britain's economic situation was just not bad enough yet to make any of this new imperialism – federation, the *Zollverein*, conscription, a German alliance, and the rest – worthwhile. It was different from what it had been: but not in its demands on policy. This has to be emphasised, because some historians have got it wrong. British capitalism may have been changing quite fundamentally in the 1890s and 1900s. The industrial sector – certainly the older industrial sector – was declining. Finance was taking on a more central role. The patterns of trade were shifting, and Britain's exports in many of the world's markets being undercut by rivals. All this was happening: but the effects of it had not yet percolated through to foreign policy. The new state of the British economy had not yet created new political needs. The imperial expansion of the 1890s, for example, was not an expression of new sorts of capitalist need but, as we have seen, of the old capitalist needs under new external pressures. The fundamental requirements of British capitalism were broadly the same as they had been throughout the second half of the nineteenth century, and were to remain the same for some years yet. So far as Britain's external policy was concerned those requirements were that its interests abroad be safeguarded, and liberally. These were the two desiderata which underlay British foreign policy now, as they had in the past.

During the 1890s and 1900s Britain's foreign economic interests grew enormously. By 1913 her exports had come to be worth £525 million in the year and her imports £769 million, compared with £263 million and £421 million in 1890.[13] Of this trade, 61 per cent was done outside Europe.[14] In addition the amount of capital she had invested abroad came to about £4,080 million in 1914, compared with about £1,625 million in 1885; and 95 per cent of this investment was outside Europe.[15] Other countries had economic interests abroad too, especially Germany, whose trade figures by 1913 were nearly as high as Britain's, but none of them had anything like the same economic stake as Britain *outside Europe*. Germany for example did £354 million worth of trade outside Europe compared with Britain's £791 million, and had £663 million invested outside Europe compared with Britain's £3,867 million.[16] Britain's economic interests abroad therefore were still very considerable, and still very extra-European; which gave her, as it had in the past, a different perspective on world affairs from her continental neighbours. Yet that perspective was far from being exclusively an imperial one: for if only a minority of her trade in the world was done with Europe, an even smaller minority (25 per cent)[17] was done with her empire; which made Chamberlain's scheme, for example, of an imperial customs union no more sensible for her, on simple economic grounds, than a European customs union would have been, if it had ever been mooted. Consequently it may not be true to say, as it sometimes is said, that what drew Britain away from Europe in these years was her empire. Of course for very many Britons the empire did have an attraction of its own, to do with the sheer excitement and exoticism and glory of it, and the *Britishness* of it compared with anything that was to be found on the continent; but that may have been incidental to the more fundamental national interest that lay beneath and extended beyond it. The empire may have pulled opinion away from Europe; what pulled *governments* away from Europe however is likely to have been a more inescapable gravity, which was the pull exerted by her material interests overseas, not only in the countries of the formal empire but also in the Americas and the East and a dozen other places too. To have sacrificed or risked *these* for Europe – if the choice were ever as stark as that – would have been just as irrational (by conventional economists' ways of regarding 'rationality') as to have sacrificed them for empire:

irrational, and therefore unlikely. Britain's true interests lay in neither of these directions alone, but in preserving her right and her capacity to trade and invest anywhere and everywhere in the world: as indeed they had done for many years now. The whole pattern of them was set against exclusiveness or preference of any kind; or any foreign policy whose effect might be to undermine the conditions (peace, economy and the rest) which favoured them. It would take more than a mere sense of foreboding to cut across the logic of that.

And the sense of foreboding after all was only a very vague one. Nothing very dreadful had happened to Britain yet. This was another factor discouraging change. The main fears that were expressed at the time were for Britain's economy, and her security, but neither was showing any obvious signs of damage. The economy was undoubtedly 'declining' in a sense, but not absolutely, and not in a way which seemed to be affecting people greatly. This has always been one of its chief problems: that its weaknesses have not always been clearly seen at the time they set in. On this occasion they were obscured by a very healthy national balance of payments surplus (of £81 million in 1905, for example, and £224 million in 1913),[18] whose health however derived largely from the huge income Britain was earning now on her overseas investments, and her flourishing trade in the relatively un-sophisticated markets of the wider world. Now it is clear that this was a sign of sickness, but at the time it did not have to seem necessarily so. The trend might have been temporary, and even if it was not, it might have been 'natural' and therefore good: a normal manifestation of the classical principle of the international division of labour, whereby Britain now concentrated on investment rather than manufacture because it was what she did best. Consequently, however much British industry was falling behind Germany's in some sectors, and however overshadowed Britain's exports of goods to European countries already were by Germany's and France's and even Holland's,[19] it did not show: not enough, at any rate, to require any wholesale abandonment, of the kind the new imperialists advocated, of the general principles which were supposed to have been the foundation of Britain's prosperity in the past. The military threat too was rather a notional one. The continental powers after all had had their chance to invade Britain during the South African War, and had not done so; which Lord Salisbury for example believed was far more significant than the fact, which the new imperialists had stressed, that they *could* have done and put Britain in the fat.[20] To give up the known and tested and valued advantages of Britain's present way of doing things for such phantasms was more than could be expected of British society then. Perhaps this was shortsighted of it: so the new imperialists said. But it was hardly avoidable. We have noticed before that it is not in the nature of free market economies to have much regard for the morrow. Which may be why so many of the new imperialists were a little ambivalent, at the very least, in their attitudes towards liberal capitalism at this time.

So Britain remained by and large a 'liberal' society in the 1890s and 1900s; and while she was still liberal there was no hope at all of any significant change in the direction of her foreign policy. It was not nearly as confident a liberalism as it had once been. It was coming under attack from many directions: from imperialists, from socialists, and even from some Liberals themselves. Imperialists regarded it as inefficient, socialists as inequitable, and Liberals as illiberal — illiberal in view of the inequalities of power and opportunity in any 'free' society, which negated the real freedom of choice of many of its members.[21] As well as ideologically liberalism was coming under attack practically too, from a state that was tending to intervene more and more as time went on to protect its 'weakest' citizens from the misfortunes that were visited on them by the system, or by themselves, according to one's point of view. So in 1906, for example, the state started providing free school meals for needy children (possibly for political and imperial reasons as much as humanitarian ones — to improve the stock from which soldiers were recruited);[22] and a little later some other 'welfare' measures;[23] all of which were considered by priests of the old religion like A. V. Dicey[24] to run counter to the pure canons of liberalism, and did. At the same time there were signs of decay elsewhere: like the trade union legislation of 1906 which protected unions against ordinary legal liability for contract-breaking, the 1905 Aliens Act which undermined a principle, of free immigration, which had stood in Britain for nearly a century, and the use of the troops against civilians at Tonypandy in 1910 which violated a taboo which was nearly as ancient: all in different ways offences against traditional liberties, and signs, perhaps, of the enormous pressures — external and internal, and partly arising from its own intrinsic contradictions — that the structure of British liberal society was coming under at that time. Yet on the whole that structure still stood, and that is the significant fact. Its economic wing stood very firm indeed. There was never any state direction of industry, for example, and no commercial protection. Britain's loyalty to the principle of free trade in fact was quite touching; and yet natural, for as we have seen there seemed to be no convincing reason yet to adopt a new set of commercial manners entirely, and a dearer loaf, which was the slogan that sank Chamberlain's campaign for tariff reform in 1906. Political liberalism too was preserved, including the whole paraphernalia of the parlia-

mentary and party systems, and most of the old individual legal
liberties, including liberty from military service in peacetime.
Liberalism in the 1900s was possible still, and necessary still: possible
because capitalism could still maintain itself with it, and necessary
because people were not yet ready to be without it.

Despite the pressures on it therefore from the outside and from
within, and whatever the force of the argument that it was sapping
Britain's capacity to survive, liberalism remained entrenched, which
meant that the priorities of foreign policy which in the past had been
associated with liberalism were entrenched too. For liberalism just
could not carry the weight of any other kind of foreign policy: of a new
and more whole-hearted imperialism, for example, or of the sort of
European commitment the new imperialists were calling for too. It
found it enough of a strain carrying Britain's existing imperial
responsibilities, which some contemporaries believed were already
reacting harmfully on her situation at home. The Liberal J. A.
Hobson, for example, worried about the political effects which
authoritarian viruses, picked up almost as a matter of course in the
colonies, might have when they were carried back to England.[25]
Others were concerned at the way the rapidly expanding bureaucracy
the empire was spawning diverted talent and energy away from the
industrial pursuits which had provided the basis for Britain's success
in the past, into fields which according to the old philosophy were
essentially unproductive and consequently an incubus on the economy. The empire, and the service of the empire, was where all the
status and the glory and the adventure were now: Henty's imperial
heroes, for example, quite displacing Smiles's engineers as objects of
aspiration for the young middle classes. Formal imperialism still sat
uneasily with the liberal capitalism that had unwittingly engendered
it; enough to make liberal capitalists pause before taking too much
more of it on board. Similarly liberalism could not easily live with
continental alliances: partly because they were bound to be with less
liberal regimes than Britain at that time considered herself to be,
certainly less peace-loving regimes; and secondly because, arising out
of this, they were likely to involve Britain in wars which it was still
very much British liberalism's – and British capitalism's – interest to
avoid. It also baulked against great continental-style armies, which
were necessary for any country which wished to have a continental-
style policy, but which British liberals regarded as inimical both to
freedom – conscription clearly, but also in the more insidious effect on
the ethos of a society a large military sector was likely to have – and to
prosperity, through the public cost of them. Britain's fundamental
national interests therefore – the interests of political and economic

liberalism – had hardly changed at all from what they had been earlier; and so she was stuck too with a traditional foreign policy, whatever the difficulties and the incongruities of it in these very different new times might be.

And the incongruities were really very serious. For the truth was that, whatever there was to be said in favour of Britain's traditional foreign policy, there was one thing to be said against it at that time: which was that it was impossible. It had two broad aims: a worldwide commercial one and a liberal one; and those aims were contradictory. They had not been in the past, when Britain had been able to safeguard her commercial interests in the world 'informally'; but now, in order to safeguard those same interests, she seemed to be driven increasingly towards expedients which clearly did violence to her liberalism. If her liberalism were not violated, then her commercial interests would be sacrificed; that was the new imperialists' analysis of her dilemma, and it was a true one. It was made the more unbearable for liberals themselves by the strongly held idea that these two interests were connected: that her world trade was necessary to her liberalism and her liberalism to her world trade, and that both were essential to Britain's prosperity. Yet one of them, surely, had to give. And one of them probably would have given; if Britain had not found one or two ways of papering over the dilemma, and of getting by for the time at least without seeming to sacrifice either. This was another reason why she was able to cling to the same policies for so long.

One of the ways she found was to delegate authority in her colonies to others. The colonies were a problem to her, because they needed a lot of policing. If Britain had had to police them all herself the military and financial burdens would have been (from a liberal point of view) insufferable. So she did not try. Instead she gave control of many of her colonies to groups of men who could be trusted to do it, and raise money for it, in their own interests. In the 'white dominions' this was usually the majority of their populations. Elsewhere it could be local traditional ruling élites, or settler minorities, or even commercial companies, like the one which ruled Southern Rhodesia. This had been a favourite Liberal dodge for years. It was sometimes dignified by being called 'home rule', or 'indirect rule', or something else; but its main advantage was that it reconciled the new demands created by Britain's extra-European interests with her liberal interests. 'Indirect' rule seemed to be somehow less 'imperialistic' than direct rule. It also obviated the need for Britain to have a military establishment commensurate with the extent of her empire. She could have her cake and eat it. There was of course a disadvantage: which was that a great deal of her power in the colonies, her freedom of action, was lost.

Delegation is a two-way process: collaborators will only collaborate on conditions. Those conditions made Britain's empire a far less tractable entity than it would have been otherwise (as Chamberlain, for example, found when he tried to get it federated); but it meant also that it could be kept on without too serious repercussions – the sorts of repercussions J. A. Hobson for example feared – at home. There were other things too that could be done. In certain situations a treaty with another power, so long as it were framed very carefully so as not to compromise Britain too greatly, could ease the burden of her imperial defence, as the treaty which Lansdowne negotiated with Japan in 1902 did, for example, in the East. Such solutions were not perfect; they did not prevent both prongs of Britain's dilemma bending a little. Overseas interests were sacrificed, as we have seen, because they had to be; elsewhere Britain's colonial and military commitments expanded regardless. Neither principle therefore was preserved intact. Each of them however was preserved sufficiently to disguise the inherent contradictions between them, and to maintain them therefore in uneasy harness with each other, as the dual determinants of British foreign policy in the 1900s.

Consequently the responses that British governments made to the succession of international crises that faced them in the twenty years leading up to the First World War were not founded upon any significant re-thinking of their foreign policy objectives, but on older ideas and priorities, which were the only ideas and priorities that were effectively open to them at the time. The position was hopeless. Britain's interests in the world just could not be defended any longer in the ways they had been defended in the past. Yet to try to defend them any other way – with a programme of constructive imperialism or an alliance – would have involved political, economic and social upheavals so great as to be inconceivable. It would be a little like expecting the frog to turn back into a tadpole again. So Britain stumbled along in the old way: trying to avoid colonial annexations, for example, but failing; resisting still the blandishments coming from the continent for her to join in the great alliance-system that was forming there, but being sucked into it all the same; making adjustments all the time under the pressure of events, aware of their implications perhaps, but never capitulating to the logic of them. It was a muddled sort of policy; and it was probably bound to fail.

But so probably was any other kind of policy too. The alternative that was most often canvassed at the time was the alliance one; and it is difficult to see how it could ever have been to Britain's interests in any circumstances to join a continental alliance, even to prevent a war. It was questionable whether alliances did prevent wars anyway. Britain believed that the present system of alliances on the continent, with Europe split into two armed camps each vying for security against the other, was far more likely to provoke one: and who now can say she was wrong? It was sometimes called a 'balance' of power; but this was misleading if it was meant to imply continuity with the old multi-lateral balance, which was a totally different animal. No one partner in the old balance *could* dominate the rest, either alone or in combin-ation, unless it were to repel aggression: that was (in theory) the beauty of it. There were no permanent combinations, and so no one felt threatened. In Europe now, however, everyone felt threatened: France, for example, by the triple alliance, Germany by the dual *entente*; and was not this as likely to stimulate their propensity to fight as anything? By joining this system Britain would only increase the fears of whichever side she did not join, and so add to the chances of war. Even if not it would add to her chances of being *involved* in war, which Salisbury believed was a compelling reason for staying out: 'Isolation is much less danger than being dragged into wars which do not concern us.'[26] Security was all very fine, if it meant security against the threat of war. In this instance however security appeared to mean, if it meant anything, security against being beaten in a war, which was not the same at all. Britain did not need to win wars: she needed to avoid them.

The main object of her diplomacy during these years, therefore, was to avoid being involved in, or damaged by, a European war. To this end she negotiated a number of treaties and conventions with con-tinental powers in the 1890s and 1900s, each of which was designed to remove a particular cause of friction between them: a potential flash-point or a potential weak point. The fewer quarrels she had with other great powers the less likely she would be to find herself in conflict with them — less likely, at any rate, to *need* to conflict with them. Most of her quarrels with other great powers then were about colonies, which was why most of her settlements were about colonies too. There was a series of them, starting in 1890 with a convention between her and Germany which delimited their spheres of influence in east and west Africa and gave to Germany the formerly British possession of Heligoland in the North Sea. Though eleven of its twelve articles related to Africa it clearly had a European purpose — 'to maintain terms of amity with Germany', said Salisbury[27] — and was part of a general policy which is fairly described as 'appeasement'.[28] Some people, including the Queen, objected to it on these grounds. But there had to be some appeasing if Britain was to continue to balk at alliances, which were the only other way of maintaining her security. If she was to have no special friends, she must make sure that she had no special enemies either. And usually at this stage this could be done without giving away too much. Germany especially was quite easily satisfied, possibly because she was still not really as interested in colonies as she sometimes made out. Usually Britain did not need to give any actual territory away, but something less tangible. In 1898 for example she 'obviated' one particular set of 'international complications'[29] by secretly conceding to Germany the title (at some future unspecified date) over a large part of Angola and Mozambique, which were not hers to concede in the first place, but Portugal's. Later, in 1911, she helped defuse another potential crisis with Germany by persuading France to do a colonial deal with her. In China all the appeasement she did seemed to be at the expense of the Manchus, and to be balanced by gains she made herself – Weihaiwei, Kowloon, and a 'sphere of influence' in the Yangtze valley. This obscured the fact that really she had conceded much more: a general access, or potential access, to the whole of the Chinese market. But she could not hold on to everything: not if holding on to it created reasons, or pretexts, for continental European powers to go to war with her.

One reason why she did not have to concede more than she did was that the European powers themselves were almost as anxious as she was to avoid a breach between them, so as not to push her into an opposite camp. Germany for example needed a British alliance quite badly, at least for a time; one whose 'indispensable condition' for her was, in von Bülow's words, 'its extension to Europe, in plain language the guarantee of our territories'.[30] There was a good chance of this eventually, she believed, because of Britain's very real conflicts of interest with France and Russia, so long as Germany did not do too much to upset her.[31] (Despite this she did upset her once or twice: perhaps to impress upon Britain the harm she might do to her if they did not ally, or because her need for an alliance, or hope of one, waned.[32]) France was less solicitous: partly because she felt safer in her particular camp, with Russia, than Germany did in hers with Austria and Italy; and partly because her colonial quarrels with Britain, unlike Germany's, were genuine ones, and only exacerbated by the concessions she was occasionally forced to make – like the humiliating one at Fashoda in the Sudan in 1898. It was the Anglo-French colonial sores which festered, therefore, and threatened the whole appeasement strategy: whose idea was to preclude the need for an alliance by minimising the chances of war. If France refused to be appeased it meant that the chance of war remained, and the need therefore for an alliance. This indeed was the main hope Germany had that Britain would join hers.

But the hope did not last long. For in 1904 France herself felt sufficiently threatened to make the idea of a colonial arrangement with Britain more attractive to her than it had been in the past, and so – in April – was concluded that famous series of agreements between them which came to be known as the Anglo-French *entente*. They were to do with colonial matters only, and were hence very similar in their nature to those other treaties that had been signed with Germany before, as part of Salisbury's general policy of colonial appeasement. So far as Britain was concerned this was their great attraction. They were limited commitments only – hardly indeed commitments at all; and yet they seemed to offer as much security to Britain where she needed it as any of the arrangements the Germans for example offered, and at much less risk and expense. They followed therefore the pattern of the past: eliminating causes of conflict rather than preparing for conflict. But there were some important differences. In the first place these Anglo-French agreements were much more comprehensive than any in the past: a general settlement of the colonial differences, or potential differences, that existed between the two powers nearly everywhere: Africa, Canada, the Pacific, the East. More important were their European implications. These were not explicit in the written agreements, but they were none the less clear. The purpose of them was to eliminate friction between Britain and France: but the effect of them would not stop there. Friction between Britain and France had been a positive and very far-reaching factor in European diplomacy for twenty years now. Once it was removed, then all kinds of things were bound to follow.

Lord Lansdowne, who negotiated the *entente*, seems to have regarded it as primarily a colonial arrangement and not – what some people at the time had hoped for – a full-blown Anglo-French alliance in disguise. Sir Edward Grey, who succeeded him as foreign secretary in December 1905, was always at pains to emphasise to the French government that there was no commitment on Britain's part arising out of the *entente* to do anything for France in Europe, and to other governments that her French arrangement by no means precluded similar arrangements with them too.[33] The *entente* made war less likely between Britain and France: that was all. But it was not all. The fact that war was less likely now between Britain and France made it more likely between Britain and Germany. Germany before this time had depended upon Anglo-French hostility, especially over Egypt, to keep Germany safe from the most dangerous of potential combinations against her. Whether the *entente* was intended as a combination against Germany or not, the possibility of such a combination was now there. The *entente* also put paid to any idea of a combination between Britain and Germany. That project had always foundered in the past on Britain's unwillingness to countenance as close and as 'European' an alliance as Germany wanted. Germany had felt however that if she waited long enough the pressures on Britain would force her to reconsider. But the *entente* lifted those pressures, by removing the threat from her main colonial rival.[34] Consequently Britain was relieved of the need to join a European alliance, and that one in particular. This was splendid for Britain, but ominous for Germany. At present Germany had as allies Austria-Hungary, who was not the force she had once been, and Italy, who never had been much of one and was anyway unreliable. France had Russia, and this kind of proto-alliance with Britain. Later, in 1907, the third side of that triangle was pencilled in when Britain and Russia came to an understanding over Persia, Afghanistan and Tibet which was very similar to Britain's arrangement with France. 'Politics', Bismarck had once said, 'reduce themselves to this formula: to try to be one of three, so long as the world is governed by the unstable equilibrium of five great powers.'[35] Germany was now one of two – Italy could not be counted – with the three powers left over less likely than ever to make up the weight. She therefore felt 'encircled' and insecure. Insecurity has been a contributory cause of more wars in modern times than any other single factor. It may have been a cause of the First World War, which came of course to involve Britain too. In this sense it might be said that the ultimate effect of the Anglo-French *entente* of 1904 was to achieve just that 'full commitment' to Europe by Britain that it was intended primarily to avoid. Such are – or may be – the ironies of history.

Be that as it may, war was surely not inevitable as early as 1904, and no British government behaved as though it were. Grey's efforts throughout his long tenure of the Foreign Office were consistently directed towards the avoidance of war. Like other foreign secretaries before him, however, he was hamstrung. He was hamstrung by two things: firstly by the economic and political pressures on him, which have been described already; and secondly by the intentions of the other powers, which may have been directed to completely different ends, and in any case were unfathomable. If it takes two to start a war it does not necessarily take two to *want* a war to start one; and if Germany, for example, was all the time set on war, or on a course of action that was bound to risk war, then there was little Britain could have done to prevent it. It has been claimed that Grey in all these affairs was 'his own master',[36] but in any significant sense he was not.

He was the slave of pressures and of circumstances. For that reason he cannot be held fully responsible for a policy whose failure he felt deeply. The failure, or rather a failure of some kind, was inherent in Britain's situation at that time. It arose out of contradictions which Grey, or anyone, was powerless to affect.

Not that he resented, or even perhaps was aware of, the restraints on him. Those he was aware of he showed little sign of chafing at. He had his battles with his Cabinet colleagues, and lost some of them – over naval estimates, for example, and over a pledge of support for France in the week before the outbreak of war in 1914 – but overall his chosen course seemed to be with the currents, and not against them. This was why he lasted so long in high office: longer for example than either Chamberlain or Rosebery, who were more at odds with their times. Before he became foreign secretary he was closely associated with Rosebery and the 'imperialist' wing of the Liberal Party, but so too were many other Liberals then who were never really imperialists in Rosebery's mould. For Grey the empire was something to be valued and defended, but not to be 'slobbered over',[37] and not a thing to be allowed to deflect Britain from her traditional and still very pertinent priorities in the world. When imperialism became a 'fad', he instinctively turned away. No ideologist himself, he was always reluctant to give ideas – his own or anyone else's – precedence over his feeling for what was 'practical politics'.[38] As a result his political sensitivity was less clouded than other men's by strong opinions: which made him unusually responsive to the pressures and the political realities of his time. This accounts for the illusion of his 'mastery'. Grey was seldom thwarted or diverted, but only because he rarely chose a fundamentally contentious path. In nothing which touched the essentials of Britain's external relations did he run counter to the accepted liberal wisdom of the time. He never questioned for example, as Chamberlain did, that Britain's commercial interests in the world still required free trade.[39] He did not seek continental alliances, which he often pointed out (and with no sign of regret) were 'not in accordance with our traditions'.[40] Neither did he complain against the prevalent British prejudice against large armaments, which certainly weakened his diplomatic hand, but which he shared. He battled against it on occasion, in the interests of 'preparedness', but he always retained the classic liberal view of great armies and navies, that they must be detrimental both to peace and to prosperity.[41] These were the basic principles, arising out of Britain's material interest, that fired her foreign policy then. If Grey had offended against any one of them, it would have been interesting to see how real his mastery was. He was effective, in fact, only within rigidly

76

limited bounds, which were the bounds set by the economic and political circumstances of his time. For what happened, therefore, the circumstances were more responsible than was Grey.

The main circumstance was the ambiguity of Britain's relationship with the rest of Europe, which arose directly out of the discrepancies that still existed between her material interests and the material interests of all the continental countries before 1914. At the risk of repetition it is worth spelling out the differences once again, for they lie at the root of everything. Britain at this time was a mature capitalist economy, older in her capitalism than any other country, uniquely dependent for her prosperity and even her life on the wide spread of her commercial and financial interests overseas, and wedded to a far greater degree than any continental state, and for solid practical reasons, to the principles of free trade, low public expenditure and political liberalism. These things all set her apart from continental Europe, and set her foreign policy apart too. The gulf between them was maybe not so wide as it had used to be, but it was still fundamental. Whatever 'advances' the continent had made recently towards Britain's situation – however capitalistic and prosperous it had become, for example – and however much Britain on her side may have been forced to adapt, still their underlying priorities remained different; and it was this difference that accounted for many of Britain's European diplomatic difficulties then.

It affected her relations with her allies as well as with her rivals and enemies. France was a witness to this, though she never seemed quite to understand the reason. This was why there was so much bad blood between them.[42] France accused Britain of bad faith, which was partly justified, but was also based on a misconception. She distrusted the strength of Britain's commitment to her, but without fully appreciating her very different circumstances. Sometimes it was put down to Britain's infatuation with empire, which was not quite fair. France did not allow *her* empire to turn her head in this way: but then France's empire was never quite so valuable as Britain's was, and her broader pattern of trade and investment in the wider world, which empire was just a part of, never so vital. France therefore was always liable to expect more of the British than they could deliver. So far as she was concerned, situated as she was in Europe with a vulnerable frontier which had been violated in the very recent past, the first priority had to be security; Britain's first priority, however, arising out of these interests overseas, was bound to be peace. The two priorities were not entirely complementary. France was prepared to risk war in the interests of security, but Britain could not. This was the source of their mutual mistrust and just possibly – if it could be shown that a firmer alliance between them would have deterred Germany – a contributory cause of the war.

But that is unlikely – or no more likely than the contrary assertion, that Germany was provoked into war by the belief that the *entente* was firmer than it was. There may have been other provocations from Britain's side too. The dominance of her navy, for example, was one in a way: Germany saw it as a challenge, and it was her efforts to emulate it that gave rise to most of the underlying tensions between them in the prewar years. Here again Britain's attitude and policy were governed by her fundamental interests. Her rationale for her own navy was that it was necessary to defend those interests; from which it followed that any nation without similar and commensurate interests was not entitled to a similar and commensurate navy. By this way of looking at things Germany's naval building programme was quite clearly a proof of aggressive intent; added to which the fact of German *military* superiority made it especially ominous. As Grey pointed out in 1908: 'If the German Navy ever became superior to ours, the German Army can conquer this country. There is no corresponding risk of this kind to Germany: for however superior our fleet was, no naval victory would bring us nearer to Berlin.'[43] For this reason Britain insisted that before she would budge on the question of a political arrangement with Germany, like a pledge of neutrality, Germany must budge over her navy: which price, for reasons of his own, the Kaiser was unwilling to pay. Possibly this intransigence was another cause of the war; but it was unavoidable. Everything pointed to Britain's naval superiority – or what there was of it left – being her sticking point: not only the fact of her overseas interests, but also the unattractiveness of the alternatives. 'Whatever the cost may be,' commented Lord Esher in July 1912 after a Cabinet wrangle over naval expenditure to keep pace with the German challenge, 'it is cheaper than a conscript army and any entangling alliance.'[44] Armies and alliances were directly inimical to her way of living; naval spending was less so. It was the least evil of several, therefore: the one that did least essential damage to Britain's interests in the world, and to the principles of policy that upheld them.

It was almost the only positive thing Britain did stick on. On the question of colonies, for example, which were thought by some radicals at the time to be the root of the quarrel between her and Germany, she was accommodating up to the last. During the Moroccan Crises of 1905 and 1911 she did all she could to try to appease Germany's colonial demands, albeit at someone else's expense. On other occasions she seriously contemplated appeasing her at her own expense – Zanzibar for example was mentioned, and Walfisch

Bay – if only Germany would moderate her naval ambitions in return.
Just before war broke out she made some real concessions to Germany,
in treaties covering the control of the Baghdad railway in Asia Minor
and the Portuguese colonies in Africa. That none of these moves
succeeded in placating Germany is of course no proof at all that
imperial rivalry had nothing to do with her antagonism, just as
Britain's willingness to make colonial concessions is no proof of
colonial apathy on her part. Rich men can afford to be generous, to a
point; and poor men with ambitions to be rich men are not likely to be
satisfied with crusts. What it does show however, if it needs to be
shown, is that on Britain's side her actions were not at all motivated by
a need for colonies. If she ever had positively desired further territorial
expansion in the world, she had long ceased doing so now. If the Anglo-
German rivalry of the 1900s was about colonies, then it was about the
colonies Britain already had, and was concerned only to defend.

The colonies had to be protected because they (as well as the navy)
protected a more fundamental and vital British interest: which was her
freedom and ability to trade and invest in the world. This was at the
bottom of everything, as it had been for decades now. It was not a new
objective – the fruit of a new kind of imperialism or stage of capitalism
or whatever – but a very old one, and pursued in the old way. Every
other one of Britain's diplomatic aims and strategies in the 1900s
followed from it: her reluctant yet positive response to foreign naval
competition – reluctant because of the cost; her relative neglect of the
army, because of its irrelevance to her extra-European priorities, and
the cost again; and her European isolationism which, despite the
entente, was nearly as strong as ever it was in the nineteenth century. So
far as Europe was concerned, in fact, her aims were very much rooted
in her interests, and very clear: to avoid the damage and expense of a
war, while at the same time avoiding the damage and expense, and
also the risk of provoking a war, that preparing *against* a war would
involve. This was why she remained so determined to shun European
commitments and entanglements, which in her view were only too
likely to involve her in wars which did not really affect her interests,
and unlikely to prevent a war which did. Until it was plain that any
likely war was going to affect her it was, from where she stood,
obviously sensible to keep clear. For it was never absolutely certain,
right up to the last moment, that she would not be able to keep clear –
in Grey's view not until Germany's ultimatum to Belgium, without
which 'we should have kept out of it'.[45] Though the likelihood of war
was in the air for many years before that, no one could be sure what
kind of war it would be. Grey's repeated advice to the French,
therefore, that Britain's part in it could not be settled before the event,

was realistic. It reflected the feelings of his electorate,[46] which derived from Britain's fundamental interest in peace with Europe, which was greater than most other European nations', and derived in its turn from the difference between their material interests in the world and hers.

It was a difference however which it was rapidly becoming impossible on Britain's side to sustain. Her difficulties had begun, as we saw, much earlier. Already by 1900 many of the interests and principles which had used to distinguish Britain's external policy in previous years had taken a battering. The new empire she had accumulated in the 1880s and 1890s was one of the bruises. The Anglo-French *entente* in a way was another: not perhaps in its original conception, but in what developed from it thereafter – tacit understandings between the partners which the public was not allowed to see, but which were strongly suspected to compromise Britain's 'isolation'. Her entry into the Great War in August 1914 was a further and much more serious blow. In a way the danger of defeat was the least of the problems it brought. Even if she won it was likely to damage her irreparably: to damage, that is, the essence of what she had been before. She had nothing to fight for in Europe beyond her own security, and her security in the most literal sense only: the inviolability of her territory. Britain however was more than a patch of territory, or even a territorial empire. She was a mesh of interests and principles, the greatest of which were especially vulnerable in the situation she found herself in now: vulnerable not so much to Germany, as to the means that would need to be taken against her. All her resources now would have to be pulled in and directed to the war effort, mainly in Europe. At home the structure of her economy and her society might have to be adapted to cope. Everything was under threat: her world trade, the basis of her economic life, even her liberalism. The war therefore, whatever its outcome, could mark the destruction – perhaps the final destruction – of most of what Britain had stood for and prospered by in the previous sixty or seventy years of her history. It was no wonder, then, that this outcome had been so much dreaded before.

By some people it was dreaded so much that they continued to oppose the war even after it had begun. Two members of Asquith's Cabinet, Morley and Burns, resigned on the grounds that the circumstances still did not call for Britain's participation in the conflict yet. During the course of the war the level of 'conscientious objection' to it was always remarkably high, considering the extremity of Britain's situation and the violence of the reaction to the objectors from the 'patriotic' side. This may have been symptomatic of the seriousness of Britain's dilemma: though it was not necessarily a sign that she had indeed taken the 'wrong' decision in August 1914. Peace may have been a fundamental desideratum to her, well worth paying a high price for; but it was not really a choice open to Britain then, unless she was willing to sacrifice all the advantages to her that peace was supposed to bring. Britain went to war not because she was committed to France, or in defence of 'gallant little Belgium', though the latter made an evocative slogan and a good reason for some to fight. If she was bound by treaties, then she could have wriggled out of them, as she had done often in the past. She went to war because her survival was threatened in a way it had not been for a hundred years before. It was threatened by an expansionist Germany whose hegemony on the continent (if it had been achieved), combined with her new navy, would surely create a world environment, and not merely a European one, in which Britain would very shortly be unable to breathe. This was the difference between 1914 and 1870, for example, when the implications of a Prussian victory over France in the immediate term had not been anything like so ominous for Britain's interests in the world. Consequently she was bound in this instance to act, though the action she took was likely to lead to her ruin. There was no way out of it. Her problem was insoluble, in any satisfactory way.

Whether *before* August 1914 the war could have been avoided by Britain is beyond the scope of this book to decide. It depends on how vital other countries' contributions were. Grey, it has been argued here, was restricted in the response he could make to the European crisis of the prewar years by material factors over which he had no control; which factors may have directly contributed to the crisis, by provoking Germany, for example, or by encouraging her. Britain's own separate crisis – the crisis caused by the growing mutual incompatibility of her various vital interests – was similarly determined by material factors which were unalterable. So far as Britain was concerned, therefore, the crises were inevitable; which is not to say, however, that the transition from crisis to war was inevitable too. The crisis was one thing; the war may have been another – one possible culmination or resolution of the crisis, out of a number. If a car is faulty it is likely that something adverse will happen to it, but it does not follow that what happens to it is bound to be a head-on collision with a bus. That will depend on the disposition of the bus and the way the car is driven. Maybe if Grey had driven the car differently it might merely have stopped, or run into a ditch, rather than into the First World War. There is no way of telling. For this reason it cannot be said for sure that the war for Britain was unavoidable. But her fundamental dilemma, which conditioned her response to the crisis that preceded the war, was.

4
Holding On 1914—45

In view of all that has been said so far about the inherent weaknesses and contradictions of Britain's situation before the First World War, it may be thought surprising that that war did as little damage to Britain's international position as it did. Of course it did damage her, in many obvious ways; not least in the horrifying human slaughter it was responsible for. Three-quarters of a million British lives were lost in it, and hundreds of thousands of others blighted and maimed. To most people who took any part in it at all it was, by nearly all accounts, the most searing experience of their lives. Individually and socially, therefore, Britons suffered greatly from it; and yet not, apparently, the nation's role in the world outside. Britain as a nation was affected, as we shall see; but she was not reduced as a result of the war either to a petty tyranny or to the status of a minor power. The prognostications of prewar liberals, therefore, seemed not to be borne out; war had not turned out to be the absolute disaster it had appeared to them. Perhaps Britain was more resilient than she had been painted. Or alternatively, she may really have been damaged severely, but for some reason the damage did not yet show.

While the war was still going on, of course, the damage showed up very clearly, and not only on the bloody banks of the Somme. For a start there was the enormous drain on the national exchequer it involved, with nearly £4 billion spent on it, which was nearly twenty times Britain's entire budget in the last full year of peace. As well as this her trade balance was knocked right out of kilter by the war, with imports doubling during the course of it and exports plummeting down.[1] Her political life too was shaken by the war, with a coalition government for the first time in sixty years,[2] no general election for eight years, and the executive arm taking on extensive new powers. Several cherished British liberties were sacrificed to it, as well as economic *laissez-faire*. The most dramatic curtailment of individual freedom was military conscription, which was brought in for single men in January 1916 and for married men in May; but there were others too. Press censorship was one. Another was the Aliens Restriction Act of 1914, by which foreigners in Britain were more strictly regulated than they had been for a century, and interned if they were Germans and of military age. Even trial by jury was suspended for a period in some cases, for civilians as well as troops. Industry and trade became subjected to what in peacetime would have been an unthinkable degree of state direction, with ships requisitioned, land compulsorily purchased for growing food, coal mines nationalised, wages and prices fixed by the state, and strikes and even changing jobs prohibited in certain industries: all to facilitate the war effort. These measures went right to the root of Britain's national life, reversing nearly every principle she had been thought to stand for before. They will have confirmed the old liberal feeling that war was the most hurtful thing that could happen to Britain, whatever its result. Nothing in fact so much justified the priority Liberals had given before the war to avoiding it, than the outcome of it when it came.

The purpose of it all, of course, was to save Britain from defeat and dispossession, which would make the sacrifice worthwhile. This it did in the end; but not before Britain had had one or two frights, and it had become plain that the *entente*'s survival could not be guaranteed by its own efforts – however illiberal – alone. It needed allies; and the problem with allies from Britain's point of view was that they were unlikely to defend her interests, particularly her imperial interests, out of philanthropy alone. Britain therefore was forced during the course of the war to make, or promise, concessions: in order to enlist and then retain the support of allies, and also the loyalty of those of her colonial subjects who might otherwise be tempted to exploit an awkward situation for themselves. The consequence of this was that large parts of her empire, and her enemies' empires, became pledged to others in a way that threatened to attenuate Britain's world role seriously, if the pledges were ever redeemed. In one notorious case she pledged the same piece of territory to two rival nationalities simultaneously, so desperate was she for the support at that stage both of Palestinian Arabs and of European and American Jews. Whether she ever intended to fulfil either of these promises if she could avoid it, or any of the others she made (to India, for example), may be questioned; but the fact that they were given is indicative of the weakness of her position at that time. As well as this she found she had to make other kinds of concessions to the United States, whose help Britain needed urgently when the war turned against her in 1916, and who demanded a great deal in return. What America demanded was not territory but a moral commitment: first of all to a negotiated peace before the war had been fought to a finish, and then later, when she entered the war herself (in April 1917), to all kinds of idealistic conditions which the more hard-bitten and war-worn British regarded as damaging to their own national interests, as they were. What the Americans wanted in particular was a statement of liberal war aims, to reassure themselves that they were fighting not an old-style European war of conquest, but for the bright new principle of freedom in the world. So far as Britain was concerned freedom was all very well for Serbia and Belgium and Germany's other victims, but needed to be thought about when it came to the Middle East and her own colonies beyond. But beggars, for the moment, could not be choosers; Britain's army was close to exhaustion, her merchant fleet being torpedoed out of the seas, and the most pressing need was for some fresh young blood from across the ocean to help her hold the line. Consequently she was forced to agree – with as much fudging as she could get away with – to go along with the Americans' terms.

All of which had grave implications for Britain's future: or would have done, if America had continued to exert after the war the strength that the war demonstrated she now had. For America gained enormously from the war, much as Britain had gained from the Napoleonic Wars a century before, and for the same reasons: because she was anyway economically on the rise, and because her participation in the war had been distant enough for it to have profited her at the other allies' expense. The result of this was that she had now become what it had been long and widely predicted she would become: the richest, and therefore potentially the most powerful, nation in the world. This gave her the means to pull the plug on Britain's pretensions, if she wanted to. In the event, however, she did not, probably for the good economic reason that as a flourishing capitalist economy she had no cause – any more than Britain had had when she had been a flourishing capitalist economy – to waste money imposing her will on the world. This was one of the reasons – the defeat of her main prewar rival was another obvious one – why Britain was given a further lease of life as a world power. While America kept aloof, she had a chance of staying top dog; for as long, that is, as the other dogs took to recuperate from their own efforts in the war.

The result was that whatever territorial losses Britain seemed to have suffered during the war she made up immediately afterwards, and more. Her empire remained intact, and was augmented by the addition of Palestine, Transjordan, Iraq and the Persian Gulf in the Middle East, Tanganyika, South-west Africa and parts of Togoland

and Cameroon in Africa, and western Samoa, the Solomon Islands, New Guinea and some smaller islands in the Pacific. These new acquisitions were not called colonies, but 'mandated territories' – mandated that is by the new League of Nations to be run for the benefit of their inhabitants; but the difference was not supposed to matter much. In effect Britain's overseas possessions were vaster by far now, after the war, than they had ever been before. For this Britain had to thank the indulgence of the Americans, who had been expected to take over a mandate in the Middle East but cried off, and seemed content to let their anti-imperialist scruples be allayed by this new form of words.

Nearer home, too, things appeared after the war to return very quickly to the prewar norm. A general election was called, for example, immediately after the armistice, which was a good start; and the government that took power as a result of it, though it was not a normal peacetime government – not a *party* government – behaved in many areas as if nothing drastic had happened and things really could be taken up again just where they had been left off before. Almost the first thing it did was to lift all the old wartime controls on industry, to the disappointment of some who had hoped they might furnish the basis for a kind of planned economy afterwards; but a planned economy was not felt to be necessary any more. Things were back to normal, and in normal times *laissez-faire* had not failed Britain yet. Consequently the lapses of the past, or some of them, were put behind her, and the country returned again to her chaste old ways.

In some ways the prospects for Britain looked even rosier than they had been before. The skies were no longer being blackened by the German threat, for example, and no other European country was in any position to pose a threat of a similar kind. Russia's revolution posed a new problem, as we shall see, but for the moment her internal difficulties had clearly put her out of international commission, and had released the Dardanelles, which would have gone to Russia if she had not withdrawn early from the war. Most important of all there was a chance now that a system of permanent world peace might be constructed, probably through the League of Nations Covenant which was signed, with great expectations, in January 1920. Peace, of course, was as ever what Britain needed most of all, in order to maintain her material interests in the world. If that could be achieved then all the shocks and sacrifices of the 'war to end wars' would really have been worthwhile. Britain could then look forward to a new national and imperial golden age, happy in the knowledge that her possessions and her interests were secure.

But it was unlikely to last. Britain did manage to hold on to most of her possessions and interests after the war, but with increasing difficulty as time went on. This was partly because of events in the world outside, and partly because the contradictions which had bedevilled her foreign policy for years now were pulling tighter, and so preventing her from responding effectively to those events. The main contradiction was the one between her responsibilities and her capabilities: between her need to safeguard her widespread commercial and financial interests, and the restraints which those interests placed on the resources she had available for safeguarding them.

Her responsibilities were, if anything, more widespread now than they had ever been. So far as her colonial possessions were concerned this was certainly so. The additions to her *de facto* empire which the war had bequeathed to her stretched her terribly, especially in the Middle East, where in 1920–21 a series of local rebellions forced her to retreat and compromise. She had to retreat and more than compromise in Ireland too; and elsewhere in the empire the difficulties of governing it increased from year to year. This was not because she was growing weaker, but because older chickens were now coming home to roost. The fact was that Britain never had been capable of controlling an empire as widespread as hers had now become. Before 1914 she had got away with not controlling it, except in parts, but instead had maintained it by persuading it – and her European rivals – to go along with her. This had been getting progressively more difficult for some time now. The problems she encountered dramatically just after the war, and chronically from then on, resulted from some of her subjects' reluctance to acquiesce any more. When that happened Britain found herself clearly overstretched, as she had been potentially for years. It was one of the inherent weaknesses of her situation, which broke to the surface more and more frequently after 1918.

Commercially, too, Britain was as fully committed overseas as she had ever been. In 1921, for example (to take a date well clear of the war and the artificial boom that came in its wake), she imported £1,085 million and exported £703 million worth of goods, which was 38 per cent more in money terms than in 1913, and comprised about the same proportion of her economic capacity as then.[3] The spread of her trade was also as wide as it had been before the war, and with a great deal less of it being done with Europe: a mere 30 per cent at this time, as against 38 per cent in 1913.[4] Her capital stake in the outside world was massive too. In 1938 she had £4·5 billion invested abroad, which was double the American figure, and was, again, spread all over the world: 23·8 per cent in North America, 21·4 per cent in Latin America, 22·9 per cent in Asia, 14·6 per cent in Australasia, 9·4 per cent in Africa, and only 7·5 per cent in Europe.[5] All this comprised an enormous and vital national interest, flung across every ocean and every continent of the world. It made Britain by far the least self-sufficient, or self-providing, of any nation anywhere, and the country therefore which depended on the rest of the world most.

All these interests involved her in defence commitments which would have been onerous at the best of times. Some of the onus she could, and did, devolve on her colonies, but much of it her own taxpayers had to bear, to the tune for example of £604 million in 1919.[6] Theoretically Britain might have defended all her overseas interests adequately, but only at enormous cost, which would probably have dried up those interests by starving the metropolitan side of her trade. Her financial problems were aggravated too by other, and new, demands on her exchequer. The most burdensome of these was the immense public debt the Great War had created, most of it owed to the United States, to whom Britain was still making massive annual repayments throughout the 1920s and 1930s, amounting in some years to as much as 40 per cent of her total budget.[7] Another new burden was social expenditure – unemployment pay, education, national insurance and the like – which was double or treble what it had used to be before the war.[8] All these factors meant that Britain in any case was having to spend far more between the wars than she ever had before: £781 million in 1930, for example, as against £184 million in 1913. This public expenditure had to be financed largely from income tax, the standard rate of which had been 1s 2d (6p) in the pound in 1913, but rose to 6s (30p) in 1919–22, and never thereafter fell below 4s (20p).[9] The burden of defence, therefore, now had to be added to other burdens, all of which together appeared crippling by contrast with happier days. During the great world depression which began in 1929 they seemed even more crippling, as Britain's exports, for example, fell to only half their level in 1924, and her balance of payments, for the first time in more than a century, moved permanently into the red.[10] There was another problem too. As well as needing more money, adequate defence would involve more soldiers, which ran against some deep-seated, and still surviving, liberal prejudices. Just after the war it was tried, when Britain's huge wartime army was not immediately demobilised but was kept on: and parts of it mutinied in protest. It was doubtful anyway whether the fabric of a liberal society could stand being militarised much more without crumbling, any more than a liberal economy could. What had happened to it in the war had not been encouraging. All these were very substantial obstacles in the way of Britain's stretching her cloth to make an adequate military coat out of.

So the coat was cut: from 1,332,854 men under arms in 1919 to 630,024 in 1920, and then to 422,897 by 1930, which latter figure was 200,000 fewer than at the beginning of 1914 (though they still cost a little more).[11] The potential task facing these 400,000 men was daunting. As well as defending Britain from attack by Germany (probably from the air, which made the Channel a less reassuring frontier than it had used to be), they might be called upon to defend her empire against Japan, and her Mediterranean trade routes from the Italians. Every strategist of the time agreed that they could not hope to provide simultaneously against all three of them, with the resources at their command. Most politicians of the time agreed that those resources could not be increased, without enormous damage to Britain's domestic base. Therein lay Britain's dilemma. 'If we were now to follow Winston's advice,' wrote Neville Chamberlain in 1936, 'and sacrifice our commerce to the manufacture of arms, we should inflict a certain injury on our trade from which it would take generations to recover.'[12] As well as this it might not really strengthen Britain militarily, for it was arguable (and argued by Sir Thomas Inskip in 1937) that 'economic and financial stability', which a massive rearmament might imperil, 'were as vital a component of British war potential as the strength of the defences'.[13] It was the same old problem as before. Defeat for Britain in a war would be disastrous; but so too would be preparing adequately to resist.

Another consideration was that Britain was not only being threatened from the outside at this time, but also — it was thought — from within. The size of her 'social budget' was an indication of this relatively new problem British capitalism was having to grapple with in the 1920s and 1930s: the cost of insuring and cushioning men and women against the inadequacies and failures of it, which were becoming increasingly evident by then. Strikes and hunger marches and 'extremist' politics were at any rate a sign that more people were coming to regard it as inadequate, which had implications for the stability of the country. At the other side of the fence (and on it) they raised doubts in many minds as to the capacity of Britain's capitalist society to withstand the tensions they gave rise to. This sense of political and social insecurity was quite new. There were other things behind it besides the depression. The war may have had much to do with it, by exacerbating proletarian resentments that had already been widespread on its eve, and stimulating expectations among certain groups of workers who had done comparatively well out of it. The main factor, however, was the events of 1917 in Russia, which were widely believed to put an entirely new complexion on everyone's affairs.

The Russian Revolution was a surprise, even to some Marxists, who found it something of a puzzle too. By rights Russia, because she had been 'behind' Britain and America before the war had begun, should have been the last to pass through capitalism entirely and into the next 'stage'; instead of which she had chosen to overleap the more advanced capitalist societies completely and achieve socialism first – a tadpole (to resume our amphibian metaphor) turned into a prince before his time. Whether the spot she had landed on was the same spot she would have evolved to if she had been less impatient no one would ever know; but her transformation clearly added a new dimension both to international and to individual nations' domestic affairs. Domestically it was feared – much like the French Revolution 128 years before had been feared – both as a warning of infection, and as a source of it. All governments, including Britain's, took it greatly to heart as an indication of what, if they were not very careful, might happen to them (and indeed did happen briefly to Germany and Austria in 1918). For other governments this was nothing very new, haunted as they had been by the *spectre rouge* for decades. Britain however, for seventy years at least, had never been susceptible to this kind of fear: and so it made a difference for her. The difference it made could be seen in the coalition government's response to the George Square riots in Glasgow in January 1919: with troops and tanks, as if a British revolution were imminent; and a few years later in the fuss over the 'Zinoviev letter' during the 1924 election campaign, which (irrespective of its authenticity) was significant in revealing a degree of anti-communist feeling in the country that was new.

This clearly had implications for Britain's foreign policy, which could no longer be conducted from a position of economic and social stability, as before. Russia obviously posed more of a problem now than she had done when she was exclusively an external threat (no one before 1917 had been afraid of any tsarist viruses catching among the working classes); as did any other potential enemy, with these rumblings of discontent at home. These domestic difficulties and fears added to the problems Britain was bound to face anyway arising from the defence of her vital interests abroad. The depression made it worse, giving a new edge to the old call for 'retrenchment', to the frustration of service chiefs, who were always – and rightly, from their viewpoint – calling for defence spending to be increased. At the same time as the dangers to her proliferated, therefore, Britain grew less and less able to cope. The greater her difficulties became, the more she needed her worldwide interests, and the greater the pressures were on her to defend those interests, if she could, on the cheap.

It was a vicious circle, and one that was tightening more and more as the years went by. Something eventually would have to break: either Britain would have to shed some of her overseas interests, or she would need to fit herself better, at the expense of some fundamental domestic changes, to defend them all. Some of those changes showed signs of taking place between the wars, as Britain's political base was affected by the loss of confidence in capitalism in ways that could have had a very great impact on her foreign policy if they had gone far enough. The decline of Victorian liberalism was one such change, which we saw had set in several years before, but accelerated now. Politically the plainest reflection of this was the demise of the Liberal *Party*, which had been the main repository of liberal capitalist values in the past but hardly knew its own mind on them now; and the domination of British politics thereafter by a Conservative Party which carried on the Liberals' capitalism without their regard for its liberal aspect, and a Labour Party which affected to reject the capitalism too. That left no one to guard British capitalism's old liberal soul. Economically too Britain changed in this period: she became more 'corporatist', her economy more deliberately planned, and subject – after that first flush of maidenly virtue following the war – to greater degrees of government interference and control.[14] The state increased its powers in other areas too. One important though not widely noticed one was internal security, where all kinds of developments took place under the terms of measures like the Emergency Powers Act of 1920, and also without any statutory authority at all. Police powers were extended far beyond what had been considered proper in the old days, and also the role of the security services, away from counter-espionage into counter-insurgency as well. A new pattern of secret domestic surveillance was established: spies, letter-opening, phone-tapping and the rest.[15] At the same time a considerable effort, and fortune, were poured by government into propaganda against the Left, and especially into manipulating a press which was anyway not nearly so independent or informative as it had once been.[16] In these ways, and in others, Britain was losing a lot of her old liberal shine. It may all have been justified, and necessary; but it marked a radical departure from the past. No longer, it seemed, could capitalism be trusted, as the Victorians had thought it could, to flourish on its own. It now had to be policed and doctored in order to survive, and thereby prised away from the liberalism, as they understood it, which had given it its moral legitimacy before.

For those who were anxious to abolish the contradictions in Britain's international situation then by toughening her to enable her to continue as a great power, these changes augured well. The decline of liberalism took away some of the ideological bastions that had supported the old foreign policy, and to that extent nudged the door open for alternatives to take hold. Earlier, as we saw, Britain had been constrained in what she had been able to do abroad by her adherence to free trade and free enterprise and a certain kind of liberalism at home; which is what in the end had wrecked the schemes of men like Joseph Chamberlain, and possibly Disraeli before him, who had had a more canny instinct than most for the deep-laid inconsistencies of Britain's position in the world. What those schemes had required to stand any chance of success was a new kind of domestic social and economic base; which base had been created briefly during the war, for example, and now looked as if it might be slowly emerging again. The object of those schemes had been to restore Britain's world leadership, which was – in theory at any rate – not impossible, despite her economic decline. Foreign policy may be largely determined by economics; but that is not the same as saying that it is determined exclusively by the state of a country's economic well-being. There is no exact correlation between power and prosperity, any more than there is a correlation between prosperity and who wins the World Cup. In the nineteenth century, for example, one common explanation for Britain's prosperity had been that she did *not* squander it on 'power' and its trappings; which made the correlation in this case an inverse one, if there was one at all. It did not necessarily follow, therefore, that because Britain was relatively poorer in the world between the wars she needed to be relatively weaker; not if her relative poverty helped to undermine the values that had discouraged her from exerting 'power' before. This was what kept alive still the ambitions of those imperialists – called 'new imperialists' before the war, and sometimes retrospectively called 'imperial visionaries' today – who in these years offered the most likely alternative to the old foreign policy of free enterprise.

The imperialists' idea, formulated before the war and carried on through it, was to preserve Britain as a great power by uniting and exploiting the colonies: consolidating the empire into a single economic unit, big enough to hold its own against Russia and the United States. During the war they had been greatly encouraged by the additions to the empire that had resulted from it, by the share the dominions had taken in the war effort, and by the scope they had been allowed to pursue all kinds of grandiose plans of 'colonial development', quite in the Chamberlain manner, in tropical Africa and elsewhere. All this was made possible by the special domestic circumstances of the war, which required liberal capitalism and the values and principles that were supposed to nurture it to be subordinated to

91

the requirements of security and defence, conceived – as of course they were bound to be in that situation – very narrowly. The new imperialists believed that these circumstances were not peculiar to wartime: that incipient war was the normal condition of international relations in peacetime too; and they hoped that if the people – or a strong government – got a taste for these wartime expedients now, some of them might be made to survive into more 'normal' times, to furnish the framework for a lasting new order. In this they were disappointed. When the war ended most of the new imperialists' hopes died with it. The empire shrank, the dominions retreated into particularism and the plans to 'develop' the tropics withered up. The economic base too, as we saw, returned to its prewar norm. In 1923 protectionism – a prerequisite for the new imperialism – was put to the electorate, and turned down. The experiment was abandoned: but the imperialists did not lose heart.

In the 1920s they regrouped and started propagandising again. At the most popular level of debate their efforts surpassed even Joseph Chamberlain's. One of Chamberlain's main difficulties had been getting ordinary people to expand their vision far enough to appreciate the empire; to which problem the imperialists of the 1920s responded by trying to make it homely. The Wembley Empire Exhibition of 1924–5 was directed to this end, as also were the Imperial Games that accompanied it, in a new and suitably monumental sporting arena which, after the occasion was over, continued to reiterate the imperial message year after year to the 100,000 working men who converged on it every Cup Final day, as they passed into the stadium along the 'Empire Way'. One year a great show was made of an 'Empire Christmas Pudding' made for the King out of ingredients from all the colonies; and there was an Empire Day, and books of Empire Songs, and a host of other ploys. People appreciated it all hugely, but perhaps did not always appreciate the serious message behind it; Leopold Amery – Chamberlain's heir in the 1920s – recounted how he had met ladies coming back from the Wembley exhibition under the impression that Japan was a British colony, and how the Empire Marketing Board, which was an official organisation set up in 1926 to push empire wares, was continually coming across shopkeepers who thought Californian tinned fruit was one.[17] But this effort was only one prong of a more widespread campaign, some of whose other prongs made a bolder impression. The imperialists' chief immediate aims were imperial tariff preference and colonial development, both of which made some progress in the 1930s. It was not before time. The first occasion they had been strongly mooted in British politics had been around 1900 by Joseph Chamberlain. They had not found favour then, or after the war. Now they seemed to be winning through at last. Chamberlain's eggs were beginning to hatch.

Some imperialists may have attributed this to their powers of persuasion: but eggs do not hatch because they are persuaded to. These particular eggs needed a special kind of environment to warm them, which had not, as we saw, existed before. They were not as innocent as they looked. Tariff preference required tariffs to be set up first, which went right across the economic grain. 'Colonial development' involved a degree of state interference ('the development of the State by the State for the State', as Milner put it once[18]) which had always been unthinkable before. Both required a revolution to make them possible. Imperialists believed the revolution was needed. *Laissez-faire* capitalism, they thought, was doomed; shortly Britain would be faced with a choice between socialism, and a new kind of capitalism protected and guided and imperially buttressed by the state. They argued that as this choice would need to be made eventually it had better be made early; but they expected too much if they thought that politicians could act with foresight like this. Until 1930 the situation was just not critical enough yet. Britain and her economy seemed to be surviving well enough along the old lines, and so there was none of that urgency about it which alone could bring about the change.

Then the world depression hit. It was this that eased the way a little for change. The situation that the imperialists (in common with Marxists) had been waiting on for years had finally come about. *Laissez-faire* had failed. If capitalism and the British way of life were to be saved from socialism, then they would have to be helped. One way of helping them, among a host of others suggested at the time, was import duties; which once they were introduced could then be manipulated to favour imperial trade. General import tariffs came in finally in February 1932; and the opportunity was immediately seized, at an imperial conference held in Ottawa later the same year, to negotiate preferential treaties with the colonies. The other imperialist panacea, colonial development, was given a modest start with an Act passed in 1929 which provided for small grants and loans to colonies, with a view to stimulating colonial demand for products made in Britain and so generating jobs there. It was hardly a complete revolution, but it showed – together with one or two other little schemes the government had been induced to fund before this, like the 1922 Empire Settlement Act and the Empire Marketing Board – that the imperialist cause was not lost yet. Domestic crisis was turning the country's face towards the light.

Quite apart from this, Britain's material interests in the world had for some years now been converging more and more on her empire.

Before the First World War we saw that Britain's imperial trade, though substantial, still comprised only about a third of her total trade; which made it doubtful whether it ought to be favoured at the expense – if this was the effect of imperial preference – of the rest. Britain's trade was not *concentrated* anywhere: not in Europe, nor the empire, nor elsewhere, which is why her national interest had consisted always in encouraging as wide and as open a commercial system as possible. In the 1930s this began to change. Empire trade increased enormously, while trade with Europe and trade with the rest of the world both lagged. In 1910–13, so far as exports were concerned, the three categories of trade had been roughly equal: just over 35 per cent to the empire, just under 35 per cent to Europe, and about 30 per cent elsewhere. In 1935–9, by contrast, the empire accounted for very nearly half of Britain's exports, while Europe took only 30 per cent and the rest of the world only 20 per cent. Imports showed a similar pattern, with the empire in third place in 1910–13 (25 per cent, compared with 40 per cent from Europe and 35 per cent from elsewhere), but top in the later 1930s (40 per cent from the empire, 30 per cent each from Europe and elsewhere).[19] Whatever the reasons for this may have been – the greater growth potential of the less 'developed' colonies, perhaps, or their relative immunity to the depression, or foreign tariffs, or the terms of trade, or Britain's declining competitiveness outside – it was a very major shift. The empire was coming to be, or to appear to be, Britain's major overseas economic interest; which was likely to affect the priorities of her foreign policy too.

But it was too late for it to make any substantial difference to the broad direction of that policy: too late for example for the empire to be turned into any sort of political force – a 'superpower' – that could make an impression on the new Balance of Power that was emerging in the world. It never had been an institution that could be easily rationalised, or disciplined, or harmonised, or fitted into a scheme, as most of its guardians had always known. The reason it had endured as long as it had was that Britain had allowed it a very loose rein, adapted her colonial policies to local circumstances, and not tried to make anything *of* the empire at all. As time went by the natural tendency of things was for colonies to grow away from Britain, to become more self-reliant and assertive, and to gravitate towards suns nearer by. To try to draw them in again, against nature, would take an unprecedented effort, and more so in the 1930s than before. The military capacity was not there any longer, and neither was the political will. Despite their little victories the imperial visionaries were still a very tiny, élite band of men, with no widespread backing in the country, or even among imperialists, many of whom had totally different ideas of how the future of the empire should go. For the fact was that however friendly the climate then seemed to be for Leopold Amery and his ilk, for others and for other ideas it was more friendly still. Which spelt defeat eventually for Amery's vision, and also, probably, for any last hope of preserving Britain's independent status in the world as a major power.

Theoretically there may still have been other ways to do it. If, for example, Britain had been prepared to embattle herself at the expense of nearly all her traditional values and interests – the fascist way – she might have done it on her own. Alternatively she could have sunk her own great power status in a wider European one, which was the choice offered to her by the 'Briand Plan' for European integration first mooted in 1929. That however was out of the question for her, for the same reason that it should have been out of the question in 1973: because her industrial and commercial interests did not point that way. This of course did not mean that she had to disapprove of any union the continentals might like to arrange among themselves, which on the whole she encouraged, but any chance of that foundered on the inveterate hostility that always simmered between Germany and France. Another alternative was an alliance, or at least an understanding, between Britain and Germany alone which would divide the world between them: the *Wehrmacht* taking Europe and the Royal Navy ruling the waves (if it still could). This had been one of the Kaiser's favourite dreams before the war, and it sometimes occurred to Hitler too. It never however appears to have been seriously considered in British official circles, partly because of the objections that still remained to open-ended alliances with anyone.

None of these alternatives, in fact, was a remotely realistic one. Nor was the possibility that Britain could ever have considered abandoning her world role, and been content with something less. Her existing interests were too deeply vested, the implications of any more far-sighted action than she in fact took too serious, and her people too sluggish or conservative to be moved to drastic action until the urgent necessity of it was staring them full in the face. Instead they opted for the more comfortable 'middle' course, as they usually have done in times of difficulty and crisis, then and since. In the 1930s the middle course became institutionalised in the form of the National Government, which most sections of opinion in Britain seemed contented with, except those who were stigmatised as 'extremists' to the Left and Right. The National Government represented the 'national interest' as it was broadly understood then; that same national interest which this book maintains has lain at the root of Britain's foreign policy from the middle of the nineteenth century until fairly recent times. It was not necessarily Britain's *best* interest, viewed in the longer term; but then it never had been. It is arguable that right from the beginning Britain had consistently pursued foreign policies that secured short-term profits at the expense of future ruin, but that was the only kind of 'national interest' the nature of her society would permit to be recognised. This it was, at bottom, that limited the options open to British foreign policy-makers between the wars, and prevented their pursuing courses which in the long run, and by wiser ways of looking at things, might possibly have conduced to her benefit more. The line that had to be taken was the line that her material situation resisted least. In the 1920s and 1930s this meant, very broadly, keeping to the path they knew, and hoping — against hope — for the best.

Britain's best hope — not in the sense of the most likely solution to her problems, but the ideal one if it could have been achieved — was to create a situation where peace was guaranteed in the world, but without the need for too much effort or commitment to secure it on Britain's part. That would have reconciled the contradiction that existed between her needs and her capabilities; for her needs, so far as diplomacy was concerned, did not go much further than peace, which she was, as we have seen, incapable of ensuring on her own. In the end, of course, this hope turned out to be an illusion; but it may have been a necessary illusion for Britain to cherish, and it did appear to have some chance of succeeding in the first few years. The hopes for it were encouraged considerably just after the war by everyone's war-weariness, and by the promise offered by the League of Nations which grew out of that war-weariness. The League of Nations was essentially an attempt to return to what Britain had always regarded as rational ways of conducting international relations: ways that were based, that is, on the premiss that war was bad for all. To a great extent its working principle harked back to the much earlier British 'Balance' idea: that if every nation agreed to resist aggression then no nation would be able to aggress, because if it did then it would have all the others on its neck; and at a minimal — because shared — cost to all. This was the attraction of it to a country in Britain's situation.

It did not work, because not every country had quite the interest in it that Britain did. In an abstract kind of way they all seemed to share the same interest in world peace, at least until the late 1920s; but even that shared interest marked differences of emphasis between them which were crucial. Germany, Italy and Japan, for example, clearly placed world peace lower in their scales of priorities than certain other desiderata, such as getting more territory; but even leaving the warmongers aside, and before they came to figure large on the international scene, there were enough differences between the non-aggressive countries to make it unlikely that they could ever agree together on the practical details of any war-prevention plan. France, for example, was bound to put a greater emphasis on European defence than Britain, whose main priority was the prevention of any – even a defensive – kind of war. The United States appeared to be closer to Britain in her diplomatic aims; but even her priorities differed slightly from Britain's, because it was more likely that she could *avoid* a war if one broke out. One of the first blows dealt to 'collective security' after the war was when the American Senate in 1919 rejected Woodrow Wilson's Tripartite Guarantee with Britain and France to defend the latter's borders against German aggression, and then withdrew America from the League; which meant that whatever system of general security did manage to emerge thereafter would have to do without the support of the world's richest power. It could not stand many such defections. The point of collective security was that it was all-inclusive; any lesser combination of powers smacked too much of *alliances*, which prewar experience suggested were no substitutes at all for a system to maintain peace. This was one of the complaints, for example, levelled against the 1923 Draft Treaty of Mutual Assistance, which proposed regional pacts which looked very much like alliances, and which was rejected by the British government in 1924 partly for that reason.[20] More general proposals, however, met with other objections, some of them very similar to the objections that had prevented a more effective peacemaking before the war. Efforts at disarmament were dogged by different countries' differing perceptions of their own military and naval needs. Grand proclamations renouncing aggression – such as the 1928 Kellogg Pact, which more than thirty nations signed – foundered when attempts were made to put them to some practical use by defining what 'aggression' actually meant. The most meticulous and detailed schemes for counter-aggression and arbitration, like Ramsay MacDonald's Geneva Protocol of 1924, were objected to on the grounds that they were so detailed that they undermined national sovereignty, as they did. Even the less ambitious schemes that did get through were not always unqualified successes. In 1922, for example, five interested powers signed a series of treaties in Washington which, among other things, limited naval strengths in the Pacific and guaranteed the integrity of China. For Britain the great advantage of this was that it prevented a crippling naval race with the United States; but it had its disadvantages too. One was that it made Britain much more dependent than she had been on America, who as it turned out – when she did nothing to stop the

Japanese invasion of Chinese Manchuria in 1931 – could not be trusted to do the right thing. 'It is always best and safest', commented Neville Chamberlain later, 'to count on nothing from the Americans but words';[21] which was perhaps not altogether fair on the Americans, who were not the only offenders in this regard. The problem was a general one: that while every nation could conceive of some act of aggression somewhere which would affect it, very few nations could accept that every act of aggression everywhere would. The effect of this was to make them – and Britain especially – reluctant to be the first to commit themselves to general guarantees. 'Collective security' was all very well if it was truly collective, but not if it rested on the shoulders of just one or two nations to enforce. Consequently it failed.

Its failure was clearly a blow to Britain's ultimate interests and objectives: but it did not alter them one whit. Nor did it alter the outlook on world affairs which stemmed from those interests and objectives, and which to a great extent guided her European policy between the wars. This was quite irrespective of the 'realities' of the situation outside – especially the growing menace of Germany – which in any case were never so clear at the time as some people afterwards claimed they had been, or as the 'realities' of Britain's situation at home. The charge of 'unrealism' is one that has stuck to British interwar diplomacy, but it may not altogether be deserved. External 'realities' in diplomatic affairs, after all, are very rarely absolute and unmistakable, but are open to interpretation; and they can just as well be interpreted to fit a nation's internal convenience as to conflict with it. This is what had happened before the war, and it tended to happen after it too. Britain's perception of the situation in Europe was very largely coloured by her domestic circumstances. Another way of putting that is to say that her view was distorted by those circumstances: but if that was true it was no less true of other countries, like France, who took a different line over the German threat. Both powers were equally 'realistic' about Germany, at least initially, when it is arguable that the 'reality' of her threat was not as set and inexorable as it later became. That France saw it then as inexorable, and Britain did not, arose from subjective factors, rather than from any greater percipience on France's part.

For example: Britain was still far more commercial a nation than France was – three times more commercial judging by their respective foreign trade figures in 1938[22] – which naturally gave her a commercial nation's view of what was best for the world. Because she depended so much on world trade, the prosperity and stability of other countries was to her advantage, because it meant larger markets and consequently prosperity for her. Therefore she was likely to favour anything that would encourage the prosperity of other countries, including Germany, whose fortune, as J. M. Keynes put it in a famous book published in December 1919, was 'deeply and inextricably intertwined' with those of her neighbours 'by hidden psychic and economic bonds'.[23] So if the victors in the last war persisted in trying to keep Germany prostrate it would be to the detriment of themselves, and especially to Britain's; whose motive therefore in urging German regeneration is clear.

But it was justified on other grounds too. Trade, it was said, was conducive to peace, and prosperity to pacifism. This of course was a familiar liberal line. Applied to this situation it meant that if Germany were rehabilitated she would be less likely to aggress, and less likely to go communist – which was another thing that naturally concerned a vulnerable capitalist society deeply. Rehabilitation involved a restoration not only of Germany's old economic position but also, within limits, of her national integrity and dignity. This was Lloyd George's line, for example, right from the start. 'You may strip Germany of her colonies,' he wrote in 1919, 'reduce her armaments to a mere police force and her navy to that of a fifth rate power; all the same in the end if she feels that she has been unjustly treated in the peace of 1919 she will find means of exacting retribution from her conquerors.'[24] The best hope of a lasting peace was to give Germany the means again to break it: but without the motive. So her recovery was fully compatible with – indeed essential to – European security.

This was the argument from principle; and the fact that it also fitted in with Britain's material interest did not necessarily make it cynical or selfish or wrong. There was a good case for saying that German recovery was in everyone's interests, if only they could see it; a case which came to be very widely accepted, for example, after the Second World War. The fact that it suited Britain materially in the 1920s however does help to explain why Britain perceived this 'truth' then, and not other nations, whose different material interests inclined them other ways. In this sense Britain's policy towards Germany in these years can be said to have been rooted in her particular needs: just as France's less generous policy was rooted in hers. Because the French were not a commercial nation to the same extent as Britain they could not share her commercial outlook; they were also concerned, as they were bound to be, with security above everything and feared that a revived Germany would imperil it again. Consequently they wanted her kept down. From their viewpoint Britain's attitude seemed unrealistic, foolhardy, maybe even treacherous. This was one reason for the mistrust that existed between them in the 1920s and 1930s, and soured the European diplomacy of these years.

In other ways too Britain's attitudes towards the problem of European security – her assessment of the external 'realities' – were quite clearly influenced by her domestic needs. These may account for example for the fact that the notion of German war guilt – that Germany had been solely responsible for the first war – came to be so widely called in question in Britain afterwards. If Germany had caused the war, it would follow that she was likely to cause wars again; against which the only safeguards were to suppress her, or to prepare militarily against her. If she was not to blame, however, the options were different. Perhaps it had been military preparedness itself – the naval race – that had brought the first war on; or maybe it was the fault of all the powers, or of the diplomatic conventions of the time: all of which suggested alternative solutions to the problem which were likely to be better suited to Britain's situation, especially her military situation, then. In much the same way the notion of 'collective security' had the effect – and possibly the purpose – of reassuring Britons that the inconvenience and expense of unilateral security were unnecessary. Any excuse was welcome, to avoid the hideous prospect of another arms race, or another European commitment, like the ones before.

Though it may have been a wishful view of the international situation, however, it was a plausible one. Even the notorious events that followed do not necessarily prove that it was wrong. Until Germany started arming illicitly in the early 1930s, and even perhaps later, it was reasonable to maintain that her transformation from an 'unsatisfied' power to a 'satisfied' one would pull her sting. If it had been done, it might have worked. It is possible, and even likely, that Nazism would have withered away in a healthier German soil. Nor is it surprising – though it may be more blameworthy – that the rise of Nazism should have made as little difference as it did to this attitude. Until 1938 it was quite possible to hold, on the available evidence, that Germany was not really bent on conquest but only wished to expand into lands which, if there had been any justice at all at Versailles, should have been hers by a kind of right. Some of them – such as the Eger district of the Sudetenland – Britain had urged should be ceded to her in 1919. The word Hitler used to justify these ambitions – self-determination – was one that struck a chord. Lord Halifax pointed out to Neville Chamberlain in November 1937 that for the *Sudetendeutsche* Germany wanted 'much the same things . . . as we did for the Uitlanders in the Transvaal'.[25] Now there was a thought. This was probably a mistaken view, but it was a rational one, and it sufficed therefore to justify the line of policy Britain was anyway constrained, by the whole bearing of her economic situation, to take.

And then there was also Soviet Russia: whom it was natural, and also right – 'realistic' – as it turned out, to regard as far more ominous a factor than Nazi Germany in the longer term. Even before the October Revolution it had been possible to predict, on the basis of past experience, that within a year of the war's ending British politicians would be 'calling out for a strong Germany to balance a threatening Russia',[26] which was indeed what occurred. The need was made the more urgent by the revolution, which Lloyd George believed was likely to make Russia more formidable than ever eventually, by imbuing her army with so potent a cause to inspire it when other armies had none. In 1918 he sent a force to Archangel to try to stop the revolution, but failed. Thereafter the danger, as he wrote in the memorandum he presented at the beginning of the Paris peace conference, was that Russia's cause might seduce to her side a demoralised Germany too, whose resources and 'vast organising power' then would be 'at the disposal of the revolutionary fanatics whose dream it is to conquer the world for Bolshevism by force of arms'.[27] In his eyes this was another powerful argument for regenerating Germany economically, to deprive Bolshevism of the conditions it flourished in best. It may also have been a prime motive for the Locarno treaties of 1925, which by excluding Russia erected what was in fact a Western alliance against her.[28] Hitler's rise to power in Germany eight years later was seen in much the same light by many influential Englishmen, including one of the foreign secretaries of the 1930s, Lord Halifax, who told him in 1937 how appreciative ministers in Britain were that 'by destroying Communism in his country, he has barred its road to Western Europe and that Germany therefore could rightly be regarded as a bulwark of the West against Bolshevism'.[29] Hitler of course fostered this idea sedulously. It was only when the bulwark began to seem to threaten Britain herself that many British Tories, and others, changed their tune, and allowed what was in most cases a genuine abhorrence of Nazism precedence over their deeper and older anti-Russian and anti-communist fears.

All these things considered it is not surprising that in Britain the German issue should have been a little clouded. For France, who was constantly thwarted by Britain's lack of co-operation with her own plans for stopping Germany, the issue was a comparatively simple one; but for Britain it was not. It was not merely that she did not have – or feel she had – the means to stop Germany: though until the middle of 1939 this was clearly germane. It was also that Germany was not the only threat to her, because of the particular state of her economy at that time. Because of the legacy of that economy in the past she had widespread interests in the world which were especially vulnerable in the condition it was in now; which condition also caused her to fear more than she had in the past the communist menace from Russia. Stopping Germany might mean endangering those interests, and letting the communists in. This may or may not have been a good or a wise argument for what came to be called 'appeasement'. But it was enough to make an imperial and late capitalist Britain, whose people were not certain anyway that Germany had been fairly treated since Versailles, pause a little in her progress towards a war that it was unlikely she could ever, in any real sense, win.

This last may have been the crucial factor, the joker lurking in the pack. If Britain went to war and lost it she would of course suffer, as she would too by expending too much treasure, and sacrificing too much of her liberalism, in building up her defences against that contingency. But even if she were victorious in a war it might do her nearly as much harm. 'The fact is', said the Foreign Office in 1926, 'that . . . so manifold and ubiquitous are British trade and British finance that, whatever else may be the outcome of a disturbance of the peace, we shall be the losers.'[30] One other reason for this, apart from the destruction of British assets, was the situation then of the United States, economically and politically poised to supersede Britain in the world. A German diplomat taunted Lord Gladwyn with this in May 1939: if there were a war, he said, and Britain were the victor, then 'one thing was certain, the Empire would disappear', and Britain would be 'reduced to the status of an American dominion.' (Gladwyn's retort was that he would sooner be an American dominion than a German *Gau*.[31]) That was one strong possibility; another was that Russia might take advantage of Germany's defeat to spread the tide of Bolshevism westwards. In either event it would go badly for Britain. Because of her economic state (and 'stage') relative to these two nascent superpowers, Britain was in no position to fight even to win. If she fought she would probably, in this sense, be destroyed. This was bound to affect her propensity to fight: like a bee whose only sanction is its sting.

So Britain went on after 1918 roughly as she had gone before: holding herself back from any broad military commitment in Europe, and seeking to preserve, as far as possible, what Chamberlain called a 'free hand to consider the circumstances and merits' of any case for intervention that might arise.[32] Her isolation was not absolute. Shortly after the war, for example, she joined with the United States in promising military help to France if she were attacked again; an arrangement which as we saw turned out to be stillborn when it was abrogated by the American Senate, but which was revived again without America in 1925 at Locarno. On paper Locarno was easily the most binding military commitment Britain had made in Western Europe for half a century, and was just the kind of commitment it had always previously been assumed her interests, and 'public opinion', would never allow. That Britain consented to it might suggest that at last she had been prised away from her blinkered self-interest by a tardy realisation of what the situation really was in the world outside. But in fact the shift was very slight. If Germany did ever violate France's eastern frontier Britain was bound to intervene, whether she was pledged to or not. To promise intervention beforehand therefore, as she did at Locarno, involved no new real commitment at all. Apart from this pledge to France she made no other serious commitments in Europe before 1939. She always baulked against any general guarantee against aggression, for example, on the ground that some aggressions might not affect British interests as much as others. Usually when she said this she had Poland in mind, which was where any future German aggression was most likely to be. 'British interests' were assumed to be distinct from European security, which consequently she did nothing in a diplomatic or military way to promote. It was much like before the war again, with Europe shored up with treaties of mutual assistance, and Britain lending a hand – or a finger – at the nearest point. Apart from this she stayed aloof.

To countries with other concerns and priorities than Britain all this seemed merely negative and obstructive, but it was not really so. It was in fact an alternative constructive approach to the problem of international security, based primarily on disarmament and economic reconstruction, which was the only approach, as we have seen, Britain's interests could ultimately stand. Both these aims, sadly, turned out to be unattainable, and eventually had to be scrapped. Reconstruction, which required some easing of Germany's reparations burden for it to stand a chance, never overcame the barriers set against this by the temerity of French stategists and the avarice of American creditors, and in the end it was left to Hitler to effect his own reconstruction of his country – and counter the Bolshevik menace – in quite another way. Disarmament made a little progress – some grand-sounding declarations and one or two limited bilateral agreements; but any really effective multilateral disarmament proved impossible while so many nations, including Britain in the naval field, remained suspicious, and some of them ambitious too. By 1935 German, Italian and Japanese ambitions clearly rendered Britain's alternative strategy irrelevant. If it had succeeded then, it would have been too late.

But by 1935 Britain had already staked her all upon it; and so when

Italy invaded Abyssinia in October, for example, there was no convincing countervailing action she could take. The feebleness of Britain's reaction to that invasion is notorious; it was reminiscent in some ways of Russell's reaction to the Prussian invasion of Schleswig seventy years before, and derived from much the same causes: low armaments, and an abhorrence of war. Germany's remilitarisation of the Rhineland in March 1936 was greeted in a similar way; but by then Britain had at least begun to rearm. In 1936 her defence budget was increased by 35 per cent over the previous year's, and in 1937 by 50 per cent more.[33] This was the context of Britain's policy of appeasement in the later 1930s, which had two aims: firstly, and optimistically, to ward off a war; but secondly, and realistically, to give Britain time to prepare for one, if it could not be warded off.

The first aim of course turned out to be wildly over-optimistic; and it is his apparent disregard of this that has made Neville Chamberlain in retrospect appear something of a fool.[34] On the other side there were the clear-sighted ones, history's winners, men like his protégé Eden, who resigned over the issue, and Churchill, who had been pressing for rearmament for years; both of whom almost certainly had a better appreciation of what Hitler was up to, but neither of whom arguably was as realistic as Chamberlain in his assessment of the long-term implications of it all. What Chamberlain may have sensed, and they did not, was the ruinous effect on Britain – 'with our wide trading and financial ramifications'[35] – a European war would have. Certainly his horror of war was more intense than theirs, and in this he reflected both the national mood of the time and also – which is more important – Britain's national interest in this very broad sense. It was this that made him cling for so long to the hope that a 'general appeasement' might 'save the world from chaos':[36] for so far as Britain was concerned if that hope was extinguished, then everything was lost. While there was hope there was life; without it, none.

Chamberlain therefore, with all his illusions and his lack of dignity, mirrored perfectly the necessities of Britain's economic and political situation then. The indignity he was big enough not to care about, if it was the price of the chance to save millions of lives;[37] the illusions he perhaps only half believed in, and at the best of times. (It was probably at one of those times that he 'got the impression' of Hitler 'that here was a man who could be relied upon when he had given his word',[38] which with hindsight appears more than a little naïve.) At other times he was quite firm in his assessment of Hitler as a 'madman', who could not be depended on to stop short of the line he – Chamberlain – always felt was the limit of Britain's forbearance; so that however much he may have hoped from his talks with him he never *relied* on them, to the extent of leaving Britain unprepared for the war that would result if they failed. Those talks, and the concessions (of other countries' territories) that were made during the course of them, may not have been intended primarily to buy Britain time. But this was the effect of them; and it was an effect, and an advantage, of which Chamberlain was well aware.

And there can be no doubt that Britain was not yet ready for war before 1939. 'Canning lays it down', wrote Chamberlain just before Munich, 'that you should never menace unless you are in a position to carry out your threats'; and as yet (in September 1938) Britain was 'certainly not in a position in which our military advisers would feel happy in undertaking to begin hostilities if we were not forced to do so'.[39] If she did fight it would probably be alone, because France in Chamberlain's view was too divided and demoralised and ill-prepared herself to be of any practical help at all; and so it seemed clear to him, in January 1938, that 'in the absence of any powerful ally, and until our armaments are completed, we must adjust our foreign policy to our circumstances'.[40] This is precisely what appeasement did.

Beyond this however there was another and more important factor making for delay. This was the sheer desperation of Britain's position in the world if it came to war: which made it essential that before Britain took this step everything else must be right. If she went to war it had to be a war that was worth the unique sacrifice it involved for her. This was why every avenue for avoiding it had to be explored, for example, so that no one could call it unnecessary; and why no lingering doubts could be left as to the justice of it, which might still have remained in many people's minds if the pretext had been Czechoslovakia, where Germany was felt to have a kind of case. This was what Austen Chamberlain meant when he talked of places being far away and unknown and not worth the bones of a British grenadier: not that they or the issues that arose there were intrinsically un-important, but that they were not 'irresistible' as *casūs belli*. 'If we have to fight,' believed Neville, 'it must be on larger issues than that',[41] like a clear proof that Britain's own security was being threatened, which alone could counteract the massive weight of her vital national interests which pulled the other way. Public opinion, which on this occasion mirrored those interests, had to be persuaded that there was no other way; and the dominions too, who as late as 1938 let it be known to Britain that in the event of a war over a European issue their support could not be counted on.[42] This took a lot of doing, but by the spring of 1939 it had been done. The alternatives had been tried, and failed, and almost every little corner of doubt and resistance swept clean. And so in September Chamberlain was able to lead a prepared and united nation into a war from which it could not emerge except as a pale and played-out shadow of the power it had been before.

Maybe if Britain had threatened force earlier Hitler might have been stopped before then. This was the line Chamberlain's critics took against him, which it was impossible of course to disprove. It was, and remains, an interesting debating point; but it had little practical relevance at any time. For Britain could not have stood firm any earlier than she did, for reasons that went back a long way. Appeasement, after all, was not a new policy in the 1920s and 1930s, except in name. In essence it had been a main plank of British foreign and colonial policy for fifty years or more: giving way to others — territory, or markets, or influence, or principles — in the interests of a quiet and peaceful life. Every surrender of authority to obstreperous white colonists was a kind of appeasement, for example, as was every 'sphere of interest' abandoned, and every retreat before Bismarck in the 1860s, and all of Grey's offers to seduce the Kaiser away from war.[43] Or if they were not, then they were all part of the same tradition with this policy of Chamberlain's in the 1930s; which derived fundamentally from the imperative needs of Britain's economy right through these years for an extensive overseas market with only the minimum of force. Those needs, as we saw, had first been those of a flourishing capitalist economy; but they were no less applicable to a capitalist economy in decline. Britain in decline needed her overseas markets at least as much as ever, but could afford to defend them even less; so that the contradiction which had bedevilled her situation for decades was intensified, and the knot pulled tighter still. The other newer factors in the situation merely added to her discomfort: Japan's rise, America's ambivalence, Russia's ideology, and the decline of reason and moderation and 'civilisation' everywhere. It was, quite simply, no world for Britain to live in: for an open and still relatively liberal commercial society, whose well-being at this time more than any other depended on worldwide prosperity and unarmed peace. Which is why between the wars her best and most committed diplomatic efforts were directed — perhaps misdirected — towards *changing* the world; and why, failing that, she was forced to appease.

Clearly the renewal of the Anglo-German conflict in September 1939 marked the failure of this policy; a much greater failure, even, than Grey's in August 1914. Appeasement had not appeased: had neither satisfied the dictators nor prevented Britain's involvement in a damaging war against them; and so whatever incidental benefits Britain may have gained from it, like a space to rearm, the outcome of it in the end was a diplomatic defeat. In other ways, however, British diplomacy had succeeded remarkably well over the previous fifteen years or so, especially in preserving most of Britain's interests in the wider world; so that when she did go into the second great European war she did it with her empire, for example, very nearly intact. Some of its new 1919 accretions had gone, and other older parts of it (as well as Ireland) had loosened the control Britain had once exercised over them; but the empire was still strong in the 1930s, in the sense of being strongly attached in other ways to Britain, with very few signs indeed that it would soon – if ever – break up. The economic and geopolitical facts of life may have been against its survival, but those facts of life had been pretty smartly outwitted so far.

Many people in Britain, probably most of them, saw no reason why they should not be outwitted for many more years to come. One person who very much hoped so was Churchill, who throughout the war saw himself as leading the fight for the preservation of the British empire, as if this was still on the cards. But it would have been difficult, for a number of reasons that became more and more apparent to some others as the war went on. In the first place there was the economic damage the war did to Britain, which more than justified Neville Chamberlain's prewar fears. By 1940 she had lost 40 per cent of her overseas markets, been forced to sell a billion pounds worth of her foreign stocks, accumulated a national debt three times as large (£21 billion) as in 1938, raised her standard rate of income tax to 10s (50p) in the pound, and been obliged to borrow heavily from the United States on terms ('lend-lease') that seemed deliberately designed to profit the American business community – again – at her own long-term expense.[44] Secondly there was the unrest the war provoked or encouraged in many of her colonies, and especially in India in 1942 and in the Middle East. Some of her Eastern colonies she lost during the course of the war to Japan. All these blows weakened her, and consequently eroded the base upon which her world power might have been rebuilt.

And then there was the intervention in the war of the United States in December 1941, which created the same kinds of problems for Britain it had created in 1917, only worse, because now she depended on America to help her get her lost colonies back. Once again Britain was compelled to modify her broader objectives to fit in with America's very different views. What those views were was a matter for dispute; Americans themselves presented them as straightforward liberal anti-colonialism, but many Britons suspected that behind that façade lurked some less reputable ambitions for an 'informal' empire of America's own. Years of wrangling between them over the future of Japan's and Italy's colonies, the British and French colonies retaken from the Japanese, and the old mandated territories of the defunct League of Nations, in the end left the British Empire (except for her mandates) formally unaffected, but internally unsettled somewhat. The colonies became 'problems' in ways they might not have been if America had not been involved:[45] discussed and dissected as never before, and justified by Britain, more and more as the war went on, in ways that were supposed to recommend them to American opinion but had the further effect of committing Britain to courses of action she might otherwise have been able to avoid. By the end of the war Britain had come to persuade herself, and enough Americans, that really her empire was a philanthropic venture, a great international 'trust'; which was likely to make it more difficult for her after the war to treat it, if she wanted to, in any other way.

On the other hand 'trusteeship' had been a major motivation behind her colonial rule for many years now, quite apart from any pressure the Americans brought to bear; which meant that that pressure was less effective in initiating new lines of policy than in teasing out trends that were already there. Generations of Indian and colonial civil servants had long been accustomed to justifying their actions to themselves by the belief that they were ruling their native 'wards' for their own good, and had expended much energy in resisting the more rapacious demands of certain capitalists, for example, for years. It was this tradition among the administrators of Britain's dependent empire which must modify, as we have seen already, the common picture of Britain's imperialism as simply an aspect of her capitalism. Whatever it may have been in origin, once the India and Colonial Offices took it over it became something more: a capitalist exploitative empire still in part, no doubt, but with many of its roughest capitalist corners rubbed down. This was another manifestation of the phenomenon we noticed at home too: the failure of capitalist or bourgeois values to triumph completely over the paternalist past, partly because in nineteenth-century Britain, and afterwards, 'freedom' had been one of the leading bourgeois values, and freedom was taken to mean the freedom of anyone to choose to reject the other bourgeois values if he wished. This was one of the main contradictions in Britain's society, whose effects were seen particularly vividly in the colonies because it was to the colonies that so many old-fashioned paternalists fled for refuge, and the reactionary public schools looked for jobs for their boys. It was one of the reasons why the 'trustee' element in British colonial policy was so pervasive, and why therefore the empire lacked the ruthlessness which may have been one requirement for its survival after the war; this, and the American lever too.

Another obstacle to the empire's survival was that the British people did not particularly want it to survive – or at least did not want to make the sacrifices that its survival might require. Whatever Churchill and others in the wartime government were fighting for between 1939 and 1945, most Britons saw themselves as fighting first for their own national self-defence and secondly for the cause of 'freedom' against Nazi tyranny; in so far as they wanted anything beyond that it was something for themselves, in the shape of improved social welfare, rather than the continuance of an empire it is doubtful whether a majority of them had ever felt strongly about at any time.[46] This was only to be expected. The war subjected millions of people to hardships and dangers many of them had not known before. People do not suffer extreme hardships unquestioningly; at the very least it is likely to make them think and doubt. This was the effect the war had on public opinion: to politicise and radicalise it as seldom before. People's main memory of before the war was of the depression and unemployment; if they were to sacrifice themselves now, many determined that it would not be for a return to that. The empire was widely regarded as something alien to ordinary people, an upper-class distraction from welfare (despite years of propaganda by imperialists to try to associate them together), and not worth subordinating welfare to. So it was that in July 1945 the postwar electorate – and the serviceman's vote in particular – turfed the imperialist Churchill out, despite his acknowledged services in the war, and returned to power in his place, with a large majority, a government pledged to turn over an entirely new social and economic leaf.

All this was symptomatic of an underlying condition which was likely to sap Britain's capacity to hold on to her empire anyway. The fact was that she was functionally unfitted to hold on to it: to run an empire against, rather than with, the odds. Because of the way her empire had originally been acquired, as an incidental and in some ways unwanted by-product of her liberal commercial structure, and because of the way it was run, mainly paternalistically, Britain had developed neither the machinery nor the right imperial ethos nationally to defend it in hard times. Before 1939 she had been able to get away with it nevertheless: managed to keep hold of her empire with most of her home population apathetic towards it, and with military and administrative forces totally inadequate for it if it were seriously threatened. Many of the more committed imperialists had worried about the long-term implications of this for years. Now those long-term implications had arrived. Ravaged by two costly world wars, challenged by colonial nationalist movements all over, and over-shadowed militarily and economically in the world by two 'super-powers' she could not hope to emulate, Britain now, if she wanted to keep her empire, would need to put far more effort into it than she had done up to now. But where was that effort to come from? Circumstances were no more favourable now than they had ever been for a real national dedication to the cause of empire to begin to flower. In many ways they were less favourable. If dedication meant sacrifice, most Britons considered they had done as much sacrificing recently as could reasonably be expected of them. If it meant compromising their liberalism, was that not what they had just been fighting to prevent? Britain had never been an imperial *people* in this sense, and it was too late for her suddenly to be forged into one now. Her society would not tolerate the necessary injection of steel.

She could perhaps have managed it if she had had the constructive co-operation – no longer just the tacit connivance – of the Americans; if America had agreed, in other words, to share Britain's imperial burden with her after the war. This was a solution with quite a long pedigree in British imperial thought, among those who had predicted America's inevitable displacement of Britain as the world's leading power years before, and seized on it as the only way in this situation to preserve the empire intact.[47] There were clearly ways in which this might have been to America's advantage, helping her to police the world for the benefit of her commerce and capital just as it had done for so many years for Britain; but it was never a likelihood while the United States mistrusted the idea of formal empire as she did, and while Britain so mistrusted the United States. Which made the eventual outcome unavoidable: that in the conditions of the postwar world Britain would lose her colonies; in the event far more quickly than any but the most optimistic of anti-imperialists foresaw.

At bottom it all went back to the nature of her society, which explained not of course the blows that fell on her after 1939, but why she could not have put up a better fight against them than she did. Her power and influence in the world had never been based on solid social foundations, foundations that would carry them through less favourable conditions than the ones they had been laid down in. The foundations could not be strengthened, without revolutionising Britain's society in more ways than would have been acceptable at any time. This was her weak spot, revealed glaringly during the war; after which the whole building, as it was bound to, came tumbling down.

5

Revolution 1945–86

During the century before 1945 Britain's foreign policy was determined by the nature of her economic interests in the world. The word 'determined' is used here deliberately, to indicate that no alternative courses of foreign policy were ever realistically open to her. Some courses might have been wiser in the longer run than the ones she took, but she was incapable of acting to her long-term benefit while the short-term pressures on her were so overwhelming. A change of policy was inevitable eventually, if only because of the contradictions which were implicit in the policy to which those short-term pressures had given rise. But it could only come about once the contradictions had bitten so deep that there was no longer any possibility of ignoring them, despite the trauma and pain the acknowledgement of them was likely to cause.

That moment came shortly after the end of the Second World War, and explains Britain's diplomatic and some of her domestic problems in the decades since. The result of the war had three broad effects on Britain. The first was to save her from Nazi tyranny. That undoubted advantage, however, was only secured at a price. This was the second effect of the war on Britain: that it greatly impoverished her. During the course of it, and in order to secure her share in the victory, Britain had lost two-thirds of her export markets, and been reduced to selling at least a quarter of her foreign stocks to pay the bills.[1] That, for a country as dependent on foreign trade and investment as Britain, was economically crippling. It also, clearly, affected her military strength. In 1947 Hugh Dalton, Labour's Chancellor of the Exchequer, put it almost apocalyptically. The whole question of national defence, he minuted to Attlee, had to be considered 'no longer against the more distant possibility of armed aggression, but also against the far more immediate risk of economic and financial overstrain and collapse'.[2] The position was as serious as that. Fundamentally, however, it was not new. What Dalton was describing was just one more twist in the basic contradiction that had bedevilled Britain for decades. It was the war's third main effect on her to highlight this: the underlying weakness which had been there, in Britain's situation, all along.

It arose, as we have seen already, from her dependence on overseas commodity and capital markets, coupled with her need to secure those markets cheaply and liberally. It was this fundamental national interest which had lain at the root of all her activities in Europe and the wider world since Palmerston's time, when the conditions for pursuing it had been far more favourable. They were favourable then because no-one who was powerful enough to do anything about it took exception to Britain's economic objectives in the wider world. Most nineteenth-century Britons had believed that this acquiescence was the natural condition of international relations under capitalism, because capitalism was so self-evidently conducive to the wellbeing of all. The peaceful exchange of goods and services, in a world progressively enlightened by the benefits of that exchange, would not require to be expensively policed. This turned out to be a delusion; but by the time that had dawned on her, Britain was ineluctably committed to an economic and diplomatic strategy predicated on the assumption that it was true. This was the cause of most of her international difficulties from the 1880s onwards, and now, after 1945, of her ultimate decline and fall.

It was the policing that was the problem. Britain had inherited from palmier days a pattern of international interests which by now, in a different kind of world, far outstretched her capacity to defend it all. Even with the losses occasioned by the war that pattern remained extensive. In 1960, for example, she exported £3,280 million worth of goods abroad, most of it – 67 per cent – to countries outside Europe.[3] No other country except America and West Germany had a larger export trade than Britain; no other country exported so large a proportion of its total production; and no other European country did anything like as much trade in extra-European markets. Much the same applied to her private capital investment abroad, which came to about £10,000 million in 1960, with perhaps 90 per cent of it going outside Europe.[4] All this gave Britain a massive and vital interest in the world market, which was a factor of continuity with the past. As ever, it was an interest only in access, and not in exerting control. Consequently it could theoretically have been secured by agreement, or by the new United Nations, if that organisation had been created strong enough properly to police the world. But that was never a possibility; which left Britain's fundamental dilemma unresolved. Even after she had recovered economically from the effects of the war, as she had done by and large by 1960, there was no way in which she could safeguard her peculiar and vital national interests on her own.

The main threat to those interests now was no longer Germany, but the Soviet Union: as in some politicians' minds it had been for many years. The Soviet threat was a triple one. In the first place, as a military superpower she was felt to endanger Britain's security directly. Some people were reluctant to acknowledge this initially, after Russia's heroic contribution to the Allied effort during the war; but that was soon forgotten in the light of her postwar conduct in the 'liberated' Eastern European states. That was supposed to indicate her aggressive and expansionist designs, which may have been unfair. The Russians themselves presented their Warsaw pact of East European satellites as a defensive alliance against aggressive designs by the West which they had as much genuine reason to fear as the West had to fear *their* ambitions; but that in a way was beside the main point. It is arguable that more conquests in recent world history have been made, and more wars started, for 'defensive' reasons than for overtly acquisitive ones; which made Britain no less vulnerable to a paranoid than she would have been to a predatory power.

A direct military attack was the most catastrophic of the threats which were felt to be posed to Britain by the Soviet Union after 1945; but it was not – and was not widely regarded as – an immediate one. The other Soviet threats were. Both of them arose from Russia's subversive proclivities: first of all in Britain itself, amongst the political left, and secondly in her areas of economic interest in the wider world. The domestic threat was not taken so seriously in Britain as it was, for example, in America during the McCarthy years; except for the slightly different problem of treachery, which was largely confined to a group of public school and Cambridge educated *naïfs*. Communist subversion in the wider world, however, was both serious and immediate. It undermined Britain's situation fundamentally, because it attacked the ideological premise on which it was built. What seemed to her to be a mutually beneficial system of international commercial and financial exchange was presented by the communists as 'capitalist exploitation' of the poor by the rich; especially when, as was often the case, the poor were formal colonies of the capitalists. Russian and later Chinese and Cuban support for colonial nationalist movements exacerbated problems which were already becoming critical for Britain long before those powers came on to the scene. It was one reason for her rapid decolonisation after the war ended, in the face of indigenous colonial pressures made even less resistible than they would otherwise have been by Eastern bloc aid, and American indifference.

America's role in this was, in a negative kind of way, crucial. For very many years now she had been widely regarded as the friendliest of Britain's several rivals for world power. Even before the First World War some percipient critics of the international scene had predicted Britain's eclipse by her before the century was out, as an inevitable corollary of the natural advantages the United States enjoyed.[5] The two great wars hastened that process, and left the latter immensely strengthened relative to the British empire, of whose existence she disapproved on grounds of principle. That was the problem. American support was Britain's only hope of holding on to her empire, and that support was never forthcoming, or likely to be. In 1956 this was demonstrated unmistakably. Britain and France tried to reassert their old pretensions as guardians of the international trading community against one of the new generation of colonial nationalists in Egypt, and failed. It was the active obstruction of the United States, backed by the threat of economic sanctions, which forced them to retreat. America was as firm against European as she was against Soviet imperialism. If she would not help, then no-one else could. And if no-one else did, then the British empire was doomed.

Doomed, that is, in a formal sense; for the dissolution of the British empire did not bring about an end to imperialism in other guises. In a way what happened was a return to the 'informal' commercial and financial imperialism of the mid-nineteenth century, dominated this time by the United States in place of Britain, whose adjustment to this shift in the balance of world economic power was, as we shall see, one of her major postwar difficulties. America herself did not regard this kind of dominance as 'imperialistic', just as Britain had not in mid-Victorian times, because of her ideological commitment to the market definition of 'liberty'; but there is a case for saying that in some ways it was more tyrannical in its impact, because less responsible, than more overtly colonial relationships have sometimes been. It was certainly more in line with the best preferences of most of the capitalist classes than was the kind of British imperialism which was in the process of being dismantled then, and which had always, in the eyes of many capitalists, been far too fettered by old-fashioned notions of service and trusteeship ever to be able to maximise its profits – and hence its long-term benefits – efficiently. In this sense American imperialism, like American industry, was a whole stage ahead of its British predecessor: a fully-developed, perfected, super-frog.

The effect of all this on British foreign policy was to throw it into a spin from which it has still not (in 1986) quite steadied itself. The world had changed utterly. Britain had become a second-rank power. She had always, as this book has tried to show, been weak relative to other countries; now, and far more significantly, she was weak relative to her *needs*. Those needs – based on her far-flung economic interests – she had inherited from former days. They were her downfall. None of the past few years' power shifts in the world would have mattered half so much to her if her responsibilities had been more compact, better fitted to her circumstances then. There is little charity in the modern world for a *nouveau pauvre* with estates in the country to keep up. In this sense Britain was far worse off when she was a middling-sized power than she would have been if she had never been great: less free to manoeuvre, and to cut her coat in the style that suited her best. To a great extent she was the prisoner of her past, and of the economic interests she had carved out for herself then.

For a few years after the war she may also have been the prisoner of an illusion: which was that she was not really a prisoner at all. The result of the war encouraged this. Britain had come out of it, after all, on the winning side: which was not quite the same as saying she had won it, but was close. In May 1945 her troops were encamped on the Elbe, and three months later Churchill was lording it over Germany with Stalin and Truman at Potsdam, apparently on equal terms. At the time of the Berlin blockade in 1948 Britain contributed 40 per cent to the airlift to relieve the city, against the Americans' 60 per cent.[6] She also had troops engaged, and not ineffectively, over much of the rest of the world. America, for her part, did not behave as if she thought Britain's day was done. There could be no knowing for sure that it was, before 1968; which was the year when Britain finally, under the pressure of a financial crisis, and after a succession of foreign policy débâcles, came to abandon her 'East of Suez' defence role. That was when the illusion was finally pricked.

There were two other main reasons for its survival until then, one of them familiar, the other quite new. The familiar one was Britain's empire, which had survived the war against all the odds. The new one was the nuclear bomb. Both were supposed to compensate in some measure for the advantages Britain had clearly lost over the past few years. The empire made up for Britain's smallness on her own compared with the superpowers, and was a potential source of the things – materials, manpower – that could make her great again. 'The Bomb' was a bonus: a card that trumped even the best conventional hand, because for the first time it put utter destruction – which could be regarded as a kind of victory – into the hands of those who would not have been able to afford it in the ordinary way. Together they seemed to offer a means of prolonging Britain's great power role, beyond what otherwise would have been its natural span. And if that could be done it was worth doing; for Britain, as we have seen, had interests in the world that only a great power could defend.

To a post-imperial generation it may seem strange that one of these factors – the hopes people placed in their empire – persisted for so long. The dismantling of the empire after all began as early as 1947 with India, which in the past had always been regarded as its 'keystone', and whose emancipation was surely a sign of things to come. That it was not more widely seen as a sign of things to come may have been because it was not really such – not really the start of a process that could not have been halted, given a sufficient degree of political will (or American help); or it may have been for other reasons, which obscured the truth for many people at the time. One of those reasons, perhaps, was an imperial habit of mind which will have been difficult to break among those who had been nurtured in their youth on Kipling and Henty and the great red-bespattered world maps that had used to dominate geography classrooms, and who had been persuaded by the history books of the day that the empire was central to Britain's 'destiny', instead of extraneous to it, as we have seen it really was. The empire always had been a bit of a fraud in many ways – giving out an impression of purpose and strength and permanence that never really belonged to it; and if people had been fooled by this in the past there was no reason why they should not continue to be fooled by it now. Nations have been known to be subject to sillier illusions than this.

But there were other, better reasons for staying with the empire. One was that in material terms it was actually more valuable to Britain now than it had ever been. Before the war we saw that it had never taken quite as much of Britain's trade as imperialists would have liked, or as would have justified the more ambitious of their *Zollverein* schemes, which is one reason why those schemes never caught on. After the war, however, the imperial share of Britain's trade increased yearly, until by the 1950s it accounted for 49 per cent of her imports, 54 per cent of her exports, and 65 per cent of her capital investment abroad.[7] For the very first time, therefore, the empire had to come to comprise Britain's majority economic interest in the world; which may have boosted its political stock, and also the reluctance of people to accept the dominant, anti-imperial, trend.

It was in any case perfectly possible to regard India (and Ceylon and Burma, who left at about the same time) as being quite apart from any dominant trend, and not at all the forerunner of an overall imperial decline. Many imperialists had already cut their Indian losses some time before, and centred their imperial ambitions in Africa, where most of the dynamic imperialism of the 1940s and 1950s was taking place. So far as the tropical parts of Africa were concerned it was as if real imperialism – exploitative imperialism, Lenin's 'final stage' – was only just beginning, after years of quiescence; certainly to most white men working there there was no sure sign that it was about to end. With a bit of constitutional gerrymandering in places, like the setting up of the Federation of Rhodesia and Nyasaland in 1953, it looked as though Africa could still remain British for many years to come. Imperialist hopes therefore were by no means utterly dashed by India's departure, but merely redirected a little, and remained moderately convincing for some time afterwards.

They were encouraged too by the fact that after independence India did not completely cut her ties with the empire, but remained within what was now called the 'Commonwealth'; which gave credence to the view that all that had happened really was a kind of internal adjustment to the colonial hierarchy – India's promotion to the rank held by the 'white dominions' already – which need have no significant repercussions on the cohesion and strength of the whole. Which was correct in a way, but *in*correct if it was inferred from this that the emerging self-governing Commonwealth could ever be the force in the world that the old empire was commonly supposed to have been; but again people's appreciation of this was obscured by myths about the old empire, and the uncertainties of the world situation then. 'Commonwealths' of this kind had not been tried before; there was no way of telling for sure how much unity of purpose Britain's Commonwealth would be able to generate, or how far its constituent members would be drawn apart by stronger gravities nearer by. There seemed therefore to be room for alternative scenarios, one of which had a place in it for Britain still as a kind of third force in the world. It was fostered by the way Britain decolonised in the later 1950s and 1960s – usually with enough good sense and grace to feed the idea that it was not forced on her, but granted as a kind of favour; and by the adhesion of most of the rest of her ex-colonies to the Commonwealth too. This again preserved the illusion of continuity with the past.

It was, however, undoubtedly an illusion, and in hindsight rather a gross one; for which reason postwar imperialists have come to cut sorry figures, especially in 'progressive' circles, in recent years. After the 1960s they began to assume another important hisorical role: which was of scapegoats for most of Britain's worst diplomatic blunders before then. They were responsible for the over-extension of her defence commitments, for her nuclear pretensions, and for her tardiness in joining the EEC. They were also probably to blame (together with trade unions) for Britain's failure to roll up her sleeves and get down to the sort of solid industrial work which would restore her competitiveness in the markets of the world. All this is a heavy weight of responsibility to bear.

To load it all on to the shoulders of the imperialists, however, may be unfair. It is also misleading. In the first place it does many imperialists an injustice, if it sees them all as men concerned chiefly with national power. Many of them were not. By the 1950s Britain's colonial hierarchy had become deeply imbued at every level with the 'trusteeship' idea. It was not always implemented consistently, to put it kindly; but it was a more compelling ideal for most imperialists than that of national aggrandisement. It was the feature which distinguished self-styled imperialists from unconscious ones, like the Americans: the acknowledgment of the responsibilities that attached to the colonial relationship. Sometimes, and paradoxically, those responsibilities involved them (as we have seen) in actively resisting capitalist exploitation of colonies: in a kind of anti-imperialism, therefore. To people like this the metamorphosis of empire into Commonwealth was natural, welcome, and had very little to do with the preservation of Britain as a great (in the conventional sense) power. It was far more tied up with notions of co-operation, multiracialism, and world peace. These ideas may have been no less illusory than the other; but they were different, in many essential ways. And until the later 1970s, when they all went out of fashion together in the wake of the Great Reaction, no-one could be certain that they did not offer at least a straw of realistic hope.

Blaming imperialists for Britain's postwar mistakes not only misrepresents them; it also obscures the real problems which underlay most of their concerns. The formal empire may have been an anachronism, but it never had been of central importance *per se*. Britain's fundamental interests in the world had always been commercial and financial, with the empire as a kind of accretion on them. This remained true after the Second World War. However hopeless and pointless the cause of the empire was by then, this did not apply to the economic interests it had originally been called into being to guard. They were not merely sentimental, atavistic, illusory, but very rational and real. They may have been much more at the root of Britain's policies than her empire was. The two were often confused, partly because 'empire' conjured up a more tangible and to some people attractive image than mere trade, or imperialism of the 'informal' kind. Men and women recognised and related more easily to it; it meant more to them, warmed – or repelled – them more than Britain's ordinary business in the world ever could. This had been going on since Kipling's time, distracting people's attention away from fundamentals, to what was really just a show. The show was large and impressive, and significant in some ways (especially to the performers); but it was never, so far as Britain was concerned, intrinsically vital, for itself and on its own. Many things which were done in its *name*, therefore, were not really done for its *sake*. And when its name failed to inspire people, and the formal empire collapsed, some of the structure that had supported it remained intact below. That was the position in the 1950s and 1960s. The empire was doomed and lost; but the interests that were miscalled 'imperial interests' were not. In this sense Britain's empire was not illusory at all; but it was if it was regarded as a source or sign of 'power'.

Britain's nuclear bomb, too, was widely regarded as a source of national power in the early stages, though later on it became clear that it was not. Her capacity to develop the bomb arose out of the close co-operation which had taken place during the war between American and British scientists on the project ('Manhattan') that gave rise to the Hiroshima and

Nagasaki bombs, and which, when it was abruptly ended by the Americans in 1946, still left its British participants with most of the data they needed to continue on their own. The decision to do so was taken secretly, with Parliament and even most of Attlee's cabinet kept wholly in the dark,[8] and was publicised more widely only when the bomb was already made. Britain's first atomic 'device' was tested in 1952, which marked her entry into what was at that time a very exclusive nuclear club.

Its exclusiveness was one of the attractions of it; for could it not be said that sharing this particular distinction with the two superpowers gave Britain just a touch of superpower status too? Then again, the very force of the new weapon seemed to augment her strength enormously, if strength was measured – as it often had been in the past – by a nation's capacity to destroy. Even Napoleon and Hitler had not been able to raze Moscow with a single blow. A clutch of atom bombs could do this; and a thermonuclear (or hydrogen) bomb could do it on its own. So, said Julian Amery in the House of Commons in 1956, 'It would seem that the hydrogen bomb, when we have it, will make us a world power again'. It was 'a great leveller', cancelling out disparities of size and population between large powers and small. (The atomic bomb in Amery's view did not quite do this, because America and Russia unlike Britain could 'stand up to atom-bombing and hope to survive'.[9]) That was the view of others, too, and was the basis for the accusation that was sometimes made, that the nuclear bomb for Britain was a national virility symbol, and no more.

More important than this, however, was the 'independence' Britain's nuclear weaponry was supposed to confer on her, in two senses at least. In the first place it was supposed to safeguard her national independence from any threat that might come from the Soviet Union, who would – according to the prevalent defence doctrine of the day – be 'deterred' from any designs she might have on Britain by the certainty of her own destruction if she tried. In the second place, it was supposed to make her independent of the Americans, who could not be guaranteed not to retreat into isolationism again at any time. That was always a possibility in the days before NATO, and even after NATO, when America had developed the capacity to strike from afar. While she needed Europe to launch her deterrent from, said the British defence secretary in 1957, America could be relied upon to defend Europe too. But 'when they have developed the 5,000 mile intercontinental ballistic rocket, can we really be sure that every American administration will go on looking at things in quite the same way?'[10] The 'independent deterrent', therefore, was a means of prising Britain away from dependence on anyone, which was a mark of a 'great power' again. It was also supposed to give Britain some sort of leverage over America, though it was never convincingly demonstrated how.

Lastily, it freed Britain from the necessity of providing vast conventional forces for defence, which was no less desirable than it had ever been from an economic and also perhaps from a political point of view. Just as significant, therefore, as the decision to build nuclear weapons in 1946 was the decision to rely on them to the exclusion of almost everything else, which was announced in a famous Defence White Paper of 1957. Three years afterwards military conscription came to an end, to the dismay of many who thought that the experience of it did young men good. Britain could get by again with a small army of regulars, despite the rising threats to her in the world. This the new weapon had achieved for her: or so it was generally believed.

The trouble was, however, that her bomb did not really give her either the power or the independence she expected from it, for reasons which she should perhaps have been smart enough to see. In the first place, it was totally unsuited to the kind of position she had traditionally taken in the world, which was one that depended on her exerting active – not just 'deterrent' – influence outside. The disadvantage of the nuclear bomb was that it was so destructive, and so invulnerable, that it could never be used 'tactically'. This at any rate was the orthodox view of it for most of the post-war period, though at the beginning President Truman may have considered using it in Korea, and at the end American strategists began thinking in terms of 'limited' nuclear warfare again. So far as Britain was concerned, however, there was never any possibility that she would unleash her nuclear arsenal except in the very last resort; which meant that that nuclear arsenal did nothing to augment her military strength in situations that fell short of that. She could not police her colonies and trade routes with nuclear bombs; and so they did nothing to restore the particular kind of world 'power' she had used to have. Later on when she fought (and lost) the 'Cod War' with Iceland, they did nothing for her except make her humiliation the more intense; and in 1982 when Argentina seized the Falkland Islands from her no one seriously suggested that Britain could ever drop a nuclear bomb on Buenos Aires. Then again, the notion that Britain's bombs put her on a footing with the great powers rested on the idea that a country needed only enough nuclear weapons to destroy a country once. Any bombs over and above that did not count; if you could fill your quota it put you into the top league. This idea, however, was soon overtaken by new developments in nuclear strategic theory,[11] and by the consequent nuclear arms race which was bound to leave a more impecunious Britain far behind.

The third reason why her bombs did not give her the kind of independent strength they were supposed to was that very early on it became obvious that in order to 'deliver' them Britain depended on American technology, and American technology was only to be had at a price. At the beginning Britain's nuclear bombs were carried by bomber aircraft, which Britain could make very well herself. When America and Russia started putting their bombs into unmanned missiles, however, Britain lacked the knowledge and also the money to develop her own. 'Blue Streak' was her attempt to do so, which in 1960 expensively failed. Thereafter she relied on the United States for all her delivery systems: 'Skybolt' first of all, until it was cancelled, then 'Polaris', and finally 'Trident'. In return for this help America was allowed facilities for her own nuclear missiles in Britain,[12] which thus became a kind of forward post for America's own system of defence. If after this she was still 'independent', then it was in a completely different sense from before. In exchange for an independent capacity to strike, Britain could be said to have compromised her independent capacity to go to war. This was an exact reversal of her traditional policy, whose priority had always been to maintain this latter kind of independence above all.

The origin of that change of policy, however, predated the Skybolt decision by a decade. It went back to the Dunkirk treaty of March 1947, and the Brussels treaty of March 1948, subsumed a year later in the North Atlantic treaty, which gave birth to one of the two major alliances – NATO – that dominated Britain's foreign relations in the postwar years.

The decision to form NATO was the most momentous act of British foreign policy for more than a century. It entirely changed the whole nature of her external relations in peacetime. This was because it went against what had long been one of the main purposes of her diplomacy, which was to avoid open-ended commitments that might drag her into war. In the past, as we have seen, she had always tried to maintain her freedom of choice in the matter of alliances, the overriding principle being that if she went to war it had to be for reasons arising out of her own interests, and not because she was simply obligated to. The argument that by promising to support allies she might deter enemies had never carried much weight with her, by comparison with the weight of the risks on the other side. Those risks were still considerable in 1949. Yet this time they were not allowed to stand in NATO's way. By the terms of the treaty Britain committed herself to go to war in defence of eleven (later fourteen) other countries if they were attacked, whatever the circumstances of the attack and whether or not she was directly threatened herself. Later the commitment deepened. By allowing America, the senior partner in the alliance, to station nuclear weapons and bases in Britain, any chance Britain had of wriggling out of her obligations in the event of war melted away. Even if she did nothing positively to help America in any war that might flare up, she would be certain to be blasted anyway to kingdom come.

The risks attaching to the alliance, therefore, were horrendous. Britain could be dragged into a war she had no hand in herself, with results far more devastating than any she had ever risked before. There was even the possibility that she could be used as a kind of battlefield for a proxy war between the superpowers, taking almost the whole brunt of it herself. There was also the danger that the alliance might itself provoke a war, by being seen as a threat to the other side. That sort of thing had happened before. And there was no absolute guarantee that America might not renege on her part of the bargain, if it meant her own destruction otherwise.[13] It was an awesome commitment, and one that could hardly – surely – have been contemplated by Britain before.

The main reason it could be contemplated now was that Britain felt more vulnerable, both because of her relative military decline and because of Russia's increasing threat. When she had been 'isolationist' in the past she had had the Channel to protect her, and no rival who threatened to overwhelm her as Russia now seemed to. Since the advent of bomber aircraft and missiles the Channel had become irrelevant; they were no longer, wrote Attlee in 1944, 'a semi-detached country ... but a continental Power with a vulnerable land frontier'.[14] Russia's military expansion in the war years had been enormous, and clearly made her unstoppable, if she took it into her head to attack. That she might attack Britain was thought to be likely, and at the time of the Berlin blockade seemed to have some basis in fact. Churchill believed it would have happened already, if it were not for America's atomic bomb.[15] At that time the main British worry was that America might not use the deterrent capability of her bomb to safeguard Europe as well as herself; 'isolationism', after all, was a sturdy tradition in American politics too. Possibly this – the difficulty of winning it – made the prize appear more desirable than it was. In any event, to have enticed America into the alliance was widely seen as an achievement; and thereafter on both sides of the Atlantic the assumption remained, that America was doing her European partners more of a favour than they were doing her.

For this reason it was by no means an alliance of equals, but one in which Britain played a very subordinate role. This sometimes produced friction. It did not help either that America regarded herself as Britain's shining knight in two world wars, and entitled to some gratitude in return, which is probably the worst basis for friendship that any two nations can have. Occasionally the tensions between them erupted into open disagreement. In 1951, for example, there was a row over appointments to NATO commands; in 1956 another one over Suez; and in 1962 over the cancellation of the Skybolt missile programme.[16] As well as this, British support for America was severely strained at one stage over the Korean War, when she was supposed to be contemplating ending it quickly and cleanly with an atomic bomb; at several points during the Vietnam War;

and by various more covert activities of the American government abroad in the 1970s, like in Chile and the Shah's Iran. The Americans in their turn greatly disapproved of what they suspected were Britain's continuing imperial proclivities; her 'socialism'; and her irresolution, which was perhaps connected with it, over what to them were the clear moral issues raised by the communist menace at home and abroad.

Personal factors may have been involved too, especially with the smoother British diplomatic operators like Eden, whose aristocratic guile Dulles was supposed to distrust greatly,[17] and Lord Carrington, whom Secretary of State Alexander Haig was reported to have privately described as a 'duplicitous bastard' in October 1981.[18] (On the other hand Kennedy by all accounts got on famously with Macmillan, who had more than a touch of class himself; but then so also did Kennedy, uniquely among American presidents since 1945.) America had never had this caste of pure-bred diplomatic specialists to feather her cruder bourgeois blows for her, which may account both for these frictions, and for some of her more alarming blunders in the world; but it was not merely a difference of style. America's 'Manichaean' view of the world, as Enoch Powell put it in March 1981 – her division of it into 'two monoliths, the goodies and the baddies' – was a 'nightmarish distortion of reality' which most Britons simply could not share.[19] Consequently from 1945 to 1979 Britain was consistently more anxious to come to terms with the communist world than the United States generally was, which made the latter's attitude appear foolhardy to Britain, and Britain's faint-hearted to the United States.

The United States, however, was the dominant partner of the two; and this is reflected in the fact that in nearly all these controversies between them Britain was the one to give in. A more visible sign of it was the plethora of American military bases and installations which had appeared all over the country, but especially in the south-east, and which in 1980 were estimated to number at least a hundred.[20] Of course it could be said – and was – that these bases were protecting Britain's security as much as America's; they were also supposed to be under ultimate British command. Serious doubts existed, however, over whether in a crisis that command would be worth the paper it was (presumably) written on. In the 1970s and 1980s, especially, the feeling grew in some British circles that the country was, in a way, 'occupied' in much the same way that Russia's east European satellites were, though this comparison ignored some essential differences between them. It made NATO, under whose auspices all this was done, a very one-sided alliance indeed; and a much more demeaning kind of alliance, so far as Britain was concerned, than any alliance she had ever contemplated in the past.

It was often claimed that Britain had a 'special relationship' with

America, closer than her other NATO partners', but this term was misleading if it was taken to imply a more equal standing than theirs. In a way it was closer because she submitted more. Of course that submission was voluntary, in the sense that Britain could always withdraw her favours (could she not?) if she wished. The trouble however was supposed to be that if she did, then her protector might abandon her, to a fate that would be far worse. The choice was still there, but it was a choice between submission and rape. If it was accepted that the other side were rapists, then submission was probably the wisest course. It had its dangers, but then so too did chastity. If the Russians were not rapists, however, or no more 'imperialistic' than the Americans were, or if they were but the nuclear deterrent for some reason failed to deter, then the calculation could go horribly wrong. Britain might come to wish that she had heeded the old wisdom yet.

Britain's international situation after the war was objectively uncomfortable, even impossible. There was no ideal response to it that she could make. The imperial response was shown to be impractical early on; the Atlanticist response also had its drawbacks. A third response, for Britain to join with her European neighbours in a regional bloc large and powerful enough to maintain its corporate independence against the superpowers, posed other problems for Britain. Nevertheless in the 1960s this was the path she determined to follow. By that time there already existed a continental union, the European Economic Community, with its own constitution and rules. Britain's decision to seek membership of that body was as remarkable a reversal of traditional policy in its way as NATO was, and acknowledged as such, though not always for the right reasons.

It was revolutionary in two ways. The first was that it meant abandoning – in a sense – the Commonwealth. This was the angle that was highlighted at the time. Britain had been an imperial and dominating and rather aloof power for centuries; now she was content with a very much humbler and more co-operative role. Not that there was any longer any chance that she could return to the other one; but still it was supposed to be significant that she should finally have accepted this. The other reason why Britain's new European policy was revolutionary was that it required her to turn her back on internationalism as well. This was less widely understood in the 1960s, because internationalism had by then come to be confused with 'Europeanism'; but this only went to show how narrow Britain's international vision had become. In the nineteenth century internationalism had meant freedom of trade and of association throughout the world. It had not meant organising into protective, self-sufficient blocs. This 'regional nationalism'[21] offended as much against Britain's old ideals as national nationalism did, and was just the kind of thing she had resisted – for practical reasons too – for years. Now she stopped resisting, and at length, in 1973, joined the EEC.

At first the move seemed to do her very little good. It was always likely to be a much more painful one for Britain than for her partners, because of the disparity between their economic interests. In the first place her trade was still more widely scattered than theirs, even as late as 1960, as we have seen. This had always been the chief material difference between Britain and her continental neighbours, and may have been at the bottom of her reluctance to join a European union right from the start. When the idea had first been mooted after the war she had not been at all obstructive, but had in fact taken a leading part. She started obstructing when continental integrationists hit on the idea of a customs union as the means to achieve their aim – a 'functional' way, as it is called, to promote unity from below. The difficulty here was that a customs union was not as 'functional' for Britain as it was for them, because whereas most of them did most of their trade within Europe, Britain did most of hers outside. This made it much more rational for the countries of the continent to unite economically than it was for Britain to join them: the fact that they were forming their 'common market' out of the area that was their majority market anyway, whereas Britain's majority market lay elsewhere.

Much of that market consisted of her Commonwealth, with which she still did more trade than with the whole of Western Europe right through to 1962.[22] Advocates of Britain's entry into the EEC later tended to forget this, and to assume – or pretend – that her attachment to the Commonwealth was a matter of 'tradition and emotion and affection' alone.[23] For those who prided themselves on having outgrown these sentimental ties the empire was an easy target; so easy as to draw attention away from the solider national interest, Britain's pattern of trade, which lay beneath. That pattern of trade was a more rational obstacle to entry than the Commonwealth, and a real cause of difficulty when Britain entered all the same. In order to adjust to the EEC she had to uproot and replant, while her neighbours cultivated the fields they already had.

There were other problems. Britain was, and had been for a century, more dependent on food imports than other Common Market countries, which meant that the Market's common agricultural policy involved her in disproportionate expense. Then again, it could be said that the very weakness of her industry by comparison with most continental countries' made her less able to cope with the new continental competition her accession brought, than those countries were able to cope with hers. In the first two or three years of her membership her trading balance with her EEC partners plummeted quite dramatically into the red: from a mere 3 per cent deficit (excess of imports over exports) in 1970, for example, to a 39 per cent deficit in 1974. Pro-marketeers talked of this competition as

a 'bracing wind'; but for an economy in the fragile state Britain's was in
during the 1970s it was arguable that the last thing that was wanted was
a wind. Winds might brace healthy economies, but not an economy in
decline. For all these reasons the hopes that were held out for Britain's
membership in the 1960s were very quickly disappointed. Economically it
seemed to have damaged Britain's interests; or at the very least to have
prevented her repairing them in her own best way.

Some pro-marketeers were turned into anti-marketeers by this; others
got over the difficulty by maintaining that the economic arguments for
joining had not been the important ones anyway.[24] But there was no
reason to disown them. The pro-marketeers had undoubtedly been too
sanguine about, for example, what they called the 'dynamic effects' of
membership;[25] but despite the problems there were still good reasons for
Britain to be in. Her Commonwealth trade, for instance, which was
supposed to be a rival attraction, was a declining commodity; in 1972, the
year before she joined, the value of her exports to the Commonwealth was
already a mere 65 per cent of the value of her exports to the countries of
the enlarged (1973) EEC.[26] After 1973 the proportion of Britain's trade
that was done with her Community partners gradually increased, from
32.7 per cent in 1973 to 39.2 per cent in 1978; which showed that Britain
was adjusting to her new commercial allegiance, whether or not it was
wise for her so to do. As well as this the sizeable trade deficit with her
partners which had followed her accession was gradually whittled down
after 1975, until by 1980, helped by North Sea oil and the recession, it had
virtually disappeared.[27] There was still much to be done before Britain's
membership could show a profit in book-keeping terms – before any
visible benefits would accrue to make the cost, her contribution to the
Community budget, worthwhile; but by 1980 her position in the EEC was
no longer looking as incongruous as before. The most painful part of the
transition was over; now was the time perhaps – or when the recession
had lifted – for those 'dynamic effects' to begin working at last. European
competition might prove to be bracing yet. Besides, if British industry did
not learn to live with it, it was unlikely anyway to be able to survive very
long. So the Community may not have been the economic disaster for
Britain it seemed at first sight to be. All could still come right in the end.

In any case, the costs of joining had to be weighed against the costs of
staying outside, or later against the costs of coming outside again, after she
had once gone in. At the time Britain joined it was possible to argue that
she could manage with EFTA – the European Free Trade Association –
and the Commonwealth; but how long could that be expected to last?
EFTA, though it was structurally better suited to her needs, did not really
have any convincing existence except as a kind of *salon des refusés* by the
'Six', which would be bound to disintegrate, and did, as the *refusés* became

acceptés one by one. It never anyway took as much of Britain's trade as the Six did. The Commonwealth too seemed to be on the way out. If size was the thing – and pro-marketeers maintained it was – then in the long term there was no alternative to the EEC.

This was probably the key argument. In the sophisticated technological world of the 1970s and 1980s small economic units just could not compete any more. To be efficient, industry had to be organised 'on a truly continental scale'.[28] There was also the matter of sheer muscle. Trade required diplomacy, and successful diplomatising depended on size. Otherwise how could Britain, in the state she was in now, hope to compete against America and OPEC and the rest? The same argument applied, even more beguilingly, to defence. There was of course an alternative to a European defence system – NATO – but we have seen that there were drawbacks to it. Those drawbacks became more apparent in the early 1980s under the populist President Reagan, whose views did not mirror those of many people in Western Europe. If Europe could be fashioned into a real 'third force' in the world, independent both of America's moral crusaders and of the frankly *realpolitischer* USSR, then she might be worth sticking with: with the French conception of Europe, that is, rather than the more pro-American German and (up to then) British one. The problems were that not many Europeans outside France, or even British anti-Americans, saw Europe as an alternative to NATO yet; and that a truly neutral Europe would need to include the Eastern bloc satellites, over which Russia gave no sign of wishing to relax her grip. But as a long-term aim, or a position to fall back on if America withdrew from Europe, it was an attractive proposition to some. For those who believed that the future lay with the superpowers it was clearly more sensible to join up with a potential like-minded superpower, than to remain stuck between two alien superpowers and treated as little more than a buffer or a base.

This kind of reasoning made sense; but it was not the kind of sense that had usually won Britons over in the past. In the past, as we have seen, the sort of considerations that generally determined Britain's foreign policy had been shorter-term, and not nearly so far-sighted as these. Nothing could be done that threatened her established economic interests in the short term, unless those interests seemed doomed in any case. This attitude had been the object of constant complaints by certain politicians for years; and especially by those 'new imperialists', for example, who had long foreseen the rise of America and Russia to superpower status, and warned that if Britain was to hold her own against them she would need to expand and fortify. They had not been heeded in the past. Now they were. By this time, of course, it was too late for their favourite nostrum to be applied. An imperial *Zollverein* was no longer practical politics. But a European *Zollverein* was. So far as Britain was concerned her entry into that *Zollverein* was the culmination of the 'new imperialism': not because the 'new imperialists' had ever wanted it, or anything like it, but because it was what their basic outlook implied.

In essence a European customs union was very little different from an imperial customs union, except that it was less well adapted to Britain's particular interests when she joined. The rationale behind it was similar, and especially the emphasis on size. This was why so many old imperialists came to accept it so easily, once it became clear to them that their first preference – the imperial one – had failed. Imperialism is usually regarded as having been an obstacle to Britain's entry into the European Community, which in the early stages it probably (though not exclusively) was. But in another way this sort of imperialism prepared the ground for entry because it *conceded the principle*, which the older free trade internationalist tradition of British policy never had. By the time the opportunity to join Europe came along, people were used to the idea of trading blocs and tariff unions and the like. Imperial preference had been established for decades, and very few objected to the principle of it now. The transition was a natural one, therefore: from imperialism to 'Europeanism' in one jump. The 'new imperialism' was the vehicle that carried Britain over from her isolationist past into the alliance politics of modern times. Paradoxically, it and 'Europeanism' were two sides of the same coin; just as 'isolationism' and 'internationalism' had been two sides of another coin in the old days.

It is scarcely surprising, in view of all these difficulties and adjustments, that foreign policy was so controversial a subject in the years after the war. Some of the controversies were conducted along party lines, but most of them were not entirely: which may be a measure of their depth. Rows over various stages of decolonisation and over southern Africa divided the Conservative party; disputes over American bases and the Falklands war split Labour; and the Common Market debate cut right across conventional political allegiances on both sides. One whole new major party, the Social Democrats, with a mission to 'break the mould' of politics in Britain entirely, owed its origins chiefly to the latter issue.[29] At very few other times in Britain's recent history have foreign affairs had more disruptive an impact on her domestic politics; which is an indication both of their crucial importance to her after the war, and of their intractability.

To a great extent attitudes and policies towards them depended on ideology. This was new, and uncharacteristic of the British, who traditionally have spurned – possibly because they were too lazy to try to understand them – overtly ideological points of view. Such pragmatism is possible in situations in which there is a broad consensus about fundamentals, as there was by and large in the hundred years before 1945;

but it becomes less tenable when a nation loses all sense of where it is and where it is going, as happened with Britain after then. In conditions like this there is more room for argument, and more need, perhaps, for the certainty which an abstract ideology can give you: for a star to fix your eye on, while the boat drifts out of control.

In the nineteenth century it was plain where the boat was, and where it was making for. Societies were seen as developing in 'stages'. Most countries in the middle of the century were still in the aristocratic or feudal stage, except Britain, who had passed on to the higher stage of liberal capitalism. She was, to revert to our running metaphor, the first tadpole in Europe to become a frog. Later in the century some of the other tadpoles became frogs too, which was good for Britain, because they all helped each other to prosper in the pool. The frogs themselves regarded their stage of development as the highest possible, and sustainable in perpetuity, so long as the laws of their nature were obeyed. 'Progress' consisted in the metamorphosis of more and more of the tadpoles in the pool to the same stage, until that happy time in the future when the whole world would be liberal, capitalist, and consequently 'free'.

Doubts about this scenario existed from the very beginning of Britain's capitalist revolution (whenever that was), and grew larger as that revolution got properly under way. One of the doubts, first sown by Marx, was over whether the frog stage really was the apex of the creature's historical development. Marx saw it, on the contrary, as containing within itself fatal contradictions, which in the end would lead inevitably to a further mutation, into (if this is not straining our metaphor too far) a handsome socialist prince. In October 1917 some frogs who had been reading Marx tried to effect that metamorphosis, possibly before the time for it was ripe. They then set about trying to incite all the other frogs to do the same. This created problems, and compounded the fears of those non-Marxists who before then had begun to suspect that there might be some aspects of froggy nature which should not be given free rein. A once clear picture had become a little muddied; what before had been assumed to be the natural process of amphibian evolution could no longer be taken on trust.

This affected Britain's position in the world fundamentally. Where she was, and where she stood in relation to other countries, depended very largely on one's viewpoint in this broader debate. The dominant country in the 'free' or 'Western' world was America, of whose essential frogginess there could be very little doubt. But where did that put Britain? She was less froggy than America – less wedded to the free market system, more highly taxed, more bureaucratic and 'socialist' – and also less dynamic and prosperous. Were the two connected? Did Britain's peculiarities, by comparison with America, indicate that she was 'ahead' of her, or 'behind'?

Was her welfare state, for example, a mark of the progress she had made over her own free enterprise past, or a regression, in part, to the tadpole stage? These questions were important. On the answers that were found for them rested not only the solutions (hopefully) to Britain's domestic problems, but also her response – insofar as she had any control over it – to the international situation she found herself in.

Immediately after the war there was a large measure of agreement that Britain's new welfareist path of development was the progressive one. The only people to dissent from this were unregenerate free marketeers on the right of the Conservative party, for obvious reasons; and those socialists who preferred to dismiss welfareism as a degenerate capitalism's last prop. Both were minority, and regarded as 'extremist', groups. Neither had any influence on the conduct of Britain's external policy. Those people who did ranged widely in their opinions, but well within these two extremes. Some were paternalists, like most Colonial Office personnel. Others could be described as interventionists, or collectivists, or corporatists of various kinds. They believed in co-operation, conciliation, consensus, compromise, community. Some of them were imperialists of the protective and benevolent sort that has been described already, infusing notions of 'welfare' into their colonial policies, for example (in the Development and Welfare Acts of 1940 and 1945), and later becoming ardent champions of the new, free, multi-racial Commonwealth. The Fabian Society, which was supposed to be a scion of the socialist movement, had a significant hand in this.[30] Others became Europeanists, again largely as a result of their corporatist frames of mind, and their belief in the importance of active international combination as a protection against what they saw as the jungle anarchy of an unregulated world. It was within these kinds of parameters that the debate over foreign policy was conducted, until the later 1970s, when quite suddenly the ideological climate changed.

One reason for the change was undoubtedly the failure of the consensual policies of the past to deliver what had been promised and expected of them, both at home and abroad. At home they came to be associated (however unfairly) with stifling bureaucracy, high rates and taxes, over-mighty trade unions, disrespectful students, 'scrounging', and general economic decline. Abroad, the Common Market was portrayed as another bureaucracy which drained Britain of money in order to subsidise inefficient foreign farmers to produce food that could not be sold, and the Commonwealth as a glasshouse for black hypocrites to throw stones at their white betters from. There were also pockets of concern in Britain about 'new Commonwealth' immigration, which was one way in which foreign policy had a direct bearing on the domestic scene. The reaction built up, fuelled by the inevitable frustrations of a declining power. In

America, and also in one or two odd little right-wing seminaries in England, preparations were made for certain ideologues to take advantage of it. Ancient Victorian woodwork started creaking with the excited activities of all the old notions (death-watch frogs?) making ready to crawl out from under it. Some of them crawled into the Conservative party, which they took control of in 1975. Not everyone at the time credited this. There was a general feeling that experience, especially of power, must moderate them. But it did not happen to any great extent. For most of the 1980s Britain was run by a government whose main boast was that it did *not* trim and turn in response to outside pressures, but remained true to the 'convictions' its leader, in particular, espoused.

Those convictions turned out to be pretty well all-embracing. Mostly they had to do with domestic politics; but they also took in the world. This was because they were absolute, derived from first principles, and consequently applicable to any human condition anywhere. The last thing Margaret Thatcher was was a relativist, someone who believed that different societies had different requirements and needs. The needs of every society were, in broad terms, the same. They were: free enterprise, low taxation, incentives, a work ethic, labour mobility, and strongly-enforced property laws. Political democracy was also desirable. These were fundamental human rights, the main planks of 'liberty', and the secrets of prosperity, opportunity and happiness in any part of the known universe.

This package of ideals and values was marketed as 'Victorian', partly because of the association with past greatness which was suggested thereby. There was, to be sure, a familiar nineteenth-century ring about much of it, though not many genuine Victorians would, without prompting, have immediately recognised Thatcher as one of themselves. One difficulty was the values that she *omitted* from her litany: including charity, service, and what today are called 'civil liberties'. The main difference was the divorce between economic and political liberalism which had been taking place slowly over the past hundred years, and was now almost complete. In the nineteenth century the two things had been intimately associated together, so that capitalism was justified for many of its aficionados, for example, by the political freedoms it was supposed to bring in its train. In the 1980s the same identification was sometimes made between capitalism and 'liberty', but by then it could only be sustained in a tautological sense. The champions of the free market now were also, by and large, the defenders of strong laws, a powerful police, centralised government, the 'right' to manage, leadership, and – in foreign affairs – military might and *Realpolitik:* which in Victorian times they generally were not. Perhaps it had something to do with the fact that twentieth-century British capitalism was more under threat than its predecessor had been. All of which suggests that it may have been their confidence in their capitalism which made the mid-Victorians' liberalism possible, rather than the nature of the system itself.

Of course this created tensions and difficulties for the free marketeers themselves. It was not an easy marriage of policies, because law and order and military strength cost public money, which it went against the economic liberal grain to spend. One manifestation of these tensions came during the Falklands crisis of April 1982, when the economic liberals' hearts and heads clearly came into conflict over whether to save money on the navy (which may have encouraged the Argentines to invade the islands in the first place), or to engage in an expensive naval war. Materially speaking Britain could gain little from war, over a distant and isolated population of Britishers who were an anachronistic and unwanted legacy from the past. Yet she went into it with resolution, and even enthusiasm; which is another indication of the sudden change that had come over British foreign policy. Some politicians and commentators drew parallels with the past, either in support of the exercise or in order to ridicule it; but in one way the past provided no precedent for it at all. No British government before had ever made so great a material sacrifice over a principle – whatever that principle may have been: 'aggression shall not pay', or injured national pride – as Thatcher's government did in 1982; not Palmerston or Disraeli, for example, though they may have come close to it on a couple of occasions, and not Gladstone, though he sometimes would have liked to.[31] Every other war Britain had fought over the past century and a half had either been for her advantage, or for her defence, or both; principles may have come into it too, and very often did, but not if principles were the only matters at stake, in which case, whatever the humiliation, Britain had always put convenience first. Of course there may have been other, less elevated motives behind this Falklands policy as well. Two that were suggested at the time were electoral profit, and distraction from economic ills at home; both of which were certainly a convenient bonus for the government while the crisis was on and for a little time afterwards. But it still marked a major revolution in attitudes. In the nineteenth century free marketism and warmongering had been at opposite poles. Now, in a remarkable (though explicable) geological shift, the two poles had come together as one.

The Falklands war also marked the eclipse, for a while, of the British Foreign Office, and of its whole way of going about its work. The Foreign Office was badly caught out by the Falklands crisis. It was aware, as the Prime Minister seems not to have been, both of the irrationality of Britain's continued possession of the Falklands, and of the questionable legality of her case. For years before the crisis it had been engaged in tentative negotiations over some kind of conditional cession of sovereignty over the islands to Argentina. It does not appear to have foreseen that Argentina's ruling junta might take it into their heads to invade. That invasion, of course, did not invalidate the theoretical merits of the Foreign Office's case, but it made it appear weak and irresolute in the heat of actual war. The result was to confirm the distrust which many ministers felt for it already. Lord Carrington, who was a typical creature of the Foreign Office in many ways, was forced to resign early on. Effective control of foreign relations during the crisis was taken out of the next Foreign Secretary's hands. One effect of this was undoubtedly to place a lower premium on conciliation, and possibly to scupper one faint chance of conciliation – a Peruvian peace plan mooted in May 1982 – deliberately.

All this happened after Lord Carrington had engineered a typical Foreign Office transfer of power from a white minority to the black majority in Zimbabwe; and too late to make any difference to the negotiations going on for the cession of Hong Kong from Britain to the People's Republic of China in 1997. The latter was upsetting for those who regarded Hong Kong as a paradigm of all the capitalist virtues, and even a model for the more laggardly British; but it could scarcely be avoided in view of China's firm legal title – which a capitalist had to respect – to the mainland part of the territory. These were two considerable successes for the traditional Foreign Office approach. But they were uncharacteristic of the policy of the Thatcher government generally.

That policy, once it had slipped its Foreign Office leash, soon showed itself to have a very different set of teeth. Margaret Thatcher, and some of those about her, as 'conviction politicians' abhorred compromise with what they regarded as 'wrong'. This in itself is likely to have made them impatient with diplomats, who were trained to sup with devils and to keep their own convictions (if they had any) quiet. The bedrock of Thatcher's conviction was her belief in both the efficacy and the moral rectitude of free commercial and financial exchange. That this was more than just pious rhetoric was demonstrated very early on when her first government lifted exchange controls. That put Britain's economy almost completely at the mercy of the world market, in which the new ministry, like their Victorian forefathers, reposed absolute trust. In Victorian times, when Britain had dominated the world market anyway, this had been easy; but it took a great deal of faith and courage when the economy was so relatively weak. The argument from theory, of course, was that exposure to market forces would toughen it. The market was the surest path to all-round prosperity, and also to 'freedom', defined in other than economic ways. This very Cobdenite view may be what set Thatcher so much against South African sanctions in 1986, which she regarded as not only ineffectual, as they may have been, but 'immoral' too.[32] The way to liberalise countries was to trade with them, so long as they were integral parts of the international capitalist community, and so susceptible to trade's liberalising effects.

The perfect international society, by this way of looking at it, was one in which capitalism had almost entirely free play. Nothing more than this was needed, except in the area of defence. Existing international organisations were pointless or downright harmful, according to how much they helped the process of economic liberalisation on. The United Nations and the Commonwealth seem to have been matters of complete indifference to Thatcher, who did not see why different races and cultures needed to come together except as vendors and vendees. When they started trying to push Britain into sanctions against other capitalist economies they turned – in her eyes – into something worse. Her 'contempt' for the Commonwealth was the cause of much anguish among some of the older-fashioned of her followers in July 1986, during the South African crisis, but it was entirely consistent with her particular tunnel ideology.[33] For similar reasons she was the least *communitaire* of all British prime ministers since Britain's entry into the Common Market, whose bureaucratic and protectionist aspects deeply offended her.

Defence had to be an exception, because of the existence in the world of a strongly-armed anti-capitalist bloc. Thatcher's position on communism was firm and clear. Socialism in every guise was an aberration, a monster: not a handsome prince at all. Even if it had never given any signs of malevolent intentions towards the West, which of course it had, those intentions would have to be presumed because they were inherent in the nature of the beast. Against a threat such as this to the whole basis of 'freedom' in the world, the ordinary liberal rules did not apply. For a less-than-superpower like Britain defensive alliances were clearly necessary, and the best defensive alliance was one with the power which on this question of communism was most ideologically sound. Thatcher consequently was never at all worried by United States domination of NATO, but on the contrary found it more reassuring than, for example, a European alternative dominated by a wetter power might be. It was this ideological affinity which lay at the root of her relationship with President Reagan, which was, for the whole period they were both in office, the centrepin of her diplomacy.

Its most dramatic manifestation came in April 1986, when American aircraft bombed Libyan cities in order to stop Colonel Gaddafi giving support to Arab terrorists. The reaction of most Europeans to this was hostile; the British government, however, after a personal appeal by Reagan to Thatcher, allowed him to use British bases for the exercise. This was at some political risk to Thatcher herself, and at what was perceived to be a risk to Britain of Arab reprisals, not least by large numbers of

Americans who, notwithstanding earnest appeals to them by the prime minister, cancelled holidays in Britain out of fright. Libya was not the only token of British fidelity to the American alliance. In 1980 Thatcher followed Reagan in imposing sanctions on Russia over her invasion of Afghanistan, possibly against her better judgment, though in Russia's case, of course, the South African arguments against sanctions did not hold. She welcomed cruise missiles into England positively. She also backed Reagan's pet 'Star Wars' scheme, for a vast protective shield against intercontinental nuclear missiles, despite the misgivings of most experts and of her own, normally dutiful, Foreign Secretary. Her banning of trade unions at GCHQ Cheltenham, which intercepted signals for the benefit of US as well as British intelligence, may have been at the insistence of the Americans. She did what she could to ease American takeovers of the Westland helicopter manufacturing company and the profitable parts of British Leyland, in the former case successfully, but again at the cost of considerable political damage to herself. By the middle of her second term she was widely regarded in Britain and elsewhere as Reagan's 'lapdog' though kinder names were also found for it.

She deserved something kinder, because in fact her loyalty to Reagan was not at all the deferential sort. It is not even the case that she invariably supported him: they fell out, for example, over the question of a gas pipeline in 1982, and over the American invasion of Grenada in October 1983. When she did support him, then it was because of a genuine marriage of their minds. On terrorism, trade unions and communist tyranny her instincts, which she came to trust the longer she was in power, were very close indeed to his. On American takeovers it is unlikely that fears of foreign industrial 'dominance', or anything of that kind, meant anything at all to her. In this sort of field, if in no others, she was a true and total internationalist.

The internationalism of the free market had been a noble conception in Victorian times. Some of its champions then had seen it as the path to universal brotherhood and peace. It is not clear whether its advocates in the 1980s had quite such large expectations of it: most of them still had enough of the old Tory in them not to expect too much of anything in this world; but they certainly believed that its general effect was to benefit everyone. That being so, it was clearly wrong for purely nationalistic factors, like the fear of 'domination', to be allowed to obstruct it. 'Domination' in any case was a totally inapposite word for a relationship in which both sides – employer and employee, buyer and seller, creditor and debtor – were essentially 'free'. It was not at all like the political tyranny of one country over another: Russia's over Poland, for example, or

Britain's over India in the bad old days. Free marketeers denied absolutely, if they were even aware of it, the whole notion of 'free trade imperialism'. It was a contradiction in terms, an impossibility, and consequently nothing which Britain, now that she was a much smaller fish in the international capitalist ocean than in former times, ought to fear.

Not everyone, however, agreed. Many Britons in the 1980s came to resent what *they* saw as American domination over them, whether or not this was fair. The government's attempt to sell British Leyland to an American corporation in 1986 was widely resisted, because it would have meant Britain's last indigenous motor manufacturing firm passing out of Britain's 'control'. The political row over Westland was fuelled by the fact that in this case defence considerations were involved. All this came at a time when anti-American feeling was running high in Britain for other reasons too. One of those reasons was undoubtedly the person of Ronald Reagan, who was widely lampooned in Britain as amiable but simple-minded, which was the public image he seemed to want to convey. Amiable simpletons are harmless in most situations, but not when they have nuclear missiles stationed on your soil. The arrival of those missiles in 1984 saw a movement of popular protest in Britain unrivalled – in sheer numbers – for more than a hundred years. Much of that protest was inevitably anti-American; and although it died down once the deed was done, and the missiles were installed, it never went entirely away. Demonstrations outside American bases in England and Scotland became part of the normal pattern of national life. In April 1986 even Tories living near the bases were found joining in, when the American raid on Libya seemed to endanger their homes. Anti-Americanism was at a greater pitch than it had been (probably) since the war of 1812; which was ironic in view of the closeness of the two countries' leaders at this time, and the popularity of Thatcher, by all accounts, in the United States.

The reason for this was that, on many quite fundamental questions, her views were closer to the Americans' than they were to her own people's. For a time this fact may have been obscured by the size of her parliamentary majority, which the ingenuity of the British electoral system had managed to contrive from an actual minority of the votes cast. 'Thatcherism' probably always had more power than popularity in Britain, whose basic political culture it may have shifted a little way, but failed to overturn. This was her problem. She did not represent Britain in any real sense, as Reagan at this time undoubtedly represented America. Most Britons did not share her clear, bright vision of a Western world dominated by an inherently benevolent American capitalism, and defended against the anti-capitalists by inherently benevolent American bombs. They did not share it because their underlying ideologies, such as they were, were not of a kind to predispose them towards such a vision, as their prime minister's underlying ideology seems to have done.

Free marketeers were well aware of this problem: that many Britons' cultural values were antipathetic to the new faith. Some of them traced the roots of it back a long way: to the survival, for example, of pre-bourgeois attitudes in post-bourgeois times.[34] Other roots were more recent, though in essence they were just as 'backward': movements like democratic socialism and trade unionism, for example, and the welfare state. All these things, and the anti-individualist attitudes that sustained them, were more firmly established there than they were in America, and consequently were a clear obstacle to the dissemination of American values in Britain. The question for the free marketeers was whether they could be eroded, or else bypassed. If they could not be, then capitalist internationalism might have a tough fight on its hands, against the alternative foreign policies to which Britain's other ideologies could give rise.

What those foreign policies might be was not certain. None of them was likely to be quite as clear cut as Thatcher's. A more neutral stance between the two superpowers was one obvious line. This would involve a slight distancing of Britain from the United States, especially over matters of defence. One practical possibility mooted was the removal of American bases and cruise missiles from Britain. This carried the risk of America's retreat into isolationism, but that might be a lesser risk than Britain already ran. Europe offered a more positive option. Membership of the EEC was no longer the bone of contention it had been during the previous decade, now that the inevitable problems of British adjustment had, for better or worse, been overcome. Europe had so far proved a disappointment to those who had hoped that it might some day pass beyond the 'common market' stage, into a proper regional political federation and a force in foreign affairs; but the potential was still there. A little more community feeling from Britain herself might help. 'If we are not to become *de facto* the 51st state,' claimed one newspaper, 'then Europe is the way we must go, at the double.'[35] The Commonwealth, if it survived the Thatcher years, could be a force for good in other ways. Perhaps even the much-derided United Nations could be looked at again.

What was needed above all was a little more flexibility; a return, in other words, to 'diplomacy' in the old Foreign Office sense. One particular and very tangible problem which a more flexible foreign policy might solve was Britain's relations with South America, which were still bedevilled by the issue of the Falklands. The problem here was the price, in blood, that had already been paid by Britain to retain the islands, which made any concession now seem a betrayal of young men's lives; but it should not have been beyond the powers of those clever men in Whitehall, if they were given their heads again, to reach a compromise that would end the absurd state of affairs that the war had brought about. That would be a great relief to America, whose support for Britain over the war had not been without its cost to her. But other alternative British foreign policies, clearly, would not.

Whether, in view of this, any of those policies were really practicable, was not something that had been properly tested yet. America's domination sometimes seemed overwhelming. She could blow up half the world, bankrupt it, or subvert it, at the stroke of a president's pen. Her financial tentacles were everywhere; her military forces and advisers were nearly everywhere; and her secret agents were everywhere else. Her popular culture was pervasive, especially where there was no language barrier to hold it up. She was puffed up with patriotism, and with a sense of her own essential rightness, to a degree which either amused, irritated or frightened those of a more sceptical cast of mind. Under Reagan she had decided to make a stand against communism, and to roll back its frontiers if she could. Looked at in another way, this spelled expansion. Thatcher's devotion to America was genuine, and her compliance with most of her demands consequently a matter of real choice. The question remained, however: if a prime minister chose otherwise – came to the actual point, for example, of sending back cruise missiles – would it be possible for him or her to get away with it, without bringing down an awful vengeance in the form of economic sanctions, or even a CIA-engineered plot?

That this question could be seriously put in Britain was another indication both of the mistrust of the United States that existed there, and of people's awareness of Britain's weakness in the world. That weakness was probably greater now than it had ever been. Economically her long-established relative decline continued, despite the Thatcherite revolution, possibly because the benefits of that revolution had not yet had time to filter through. In 1985 she passed a significant milestone when for the first time for two centuries she imported more manufactured goods than she exported; and generally she was only kept solvent during these years by the diminishing asset of North Sea oil. About her only other growth sector was the 'service' industries, including tourism. Years before, in 1908, Lord Curzon had painted a picture of a future Britain, without her empire, full of unemployed workers, 'with no aspiration but a narrow and selfish materialism', and living mainly off foreign tourists, who would 'come to see us just as they climb the Acropolis at Athens'.[36] By the 1980s that prediction had come to seem quite remarkably prescient. In 1986 an ex-head of the English Tourist Board described Britain, enthusiastically, as 'one gigantic genuine historic theme park', dotted about with stately homes, and with 'some lovely decrepit dukes to wheel out for the tourists'.[37] Some less-than-decrepit Royals were also wheeled out, for weddings, jubilees and the like, in order to exhibit to paying visitors what Britain 'did best': which by then was to put on Disneyland displays of a pomp and circumstance whose reality, the power beneath the shell, had long since evaporated. She had sunk to living off her history, or a kind of invented history; the deposit left by ancient aristocratic forests, whose advantage over coal and oil was that – with plenty of marketing enterprise, and perhaps a little more invention now and again – it need never, like them, run out.

When this kind of thing had first originated, it had been at a time (the 1880s) when Britain could still reasonably regard herself as powerful. Later, in 1952 for example, it may have given her the illusion of strength. By 1986 she did not even have that. Everyone knew that the carriages would be turned back into pumpkins on the stroke of midnight, when the watching crowds would have to go back to scratching a living from the North Sea, or their service industries, or the local office of the DHSS. Because they were poorer, Britons believed they must be weaker: which does not of course necessarily follow (it depends very much on the cost of your national *needs*), but in this case has the ring of truth. Weakness generally means dependence, and restrictions on the options that are open to you. A narrowing of options may have been an effect of Britain's weakness in the 1980s. She was no longer as much her own mistress as she had used to be, able to pursue the policies either abroad or at home that best suited her condition then.

One of the arguments of this book has been that she never had been her own mistress, in the sense that she was always entrapped by the imperatives of her economy; but this situation was different, because what was now entrapping her was not her own imperatives, but someone else's. That, at any rate, was a possibility. Her government denied it on the grounds that *their* reason for going along with those imperatives was that they agreed with them, and regarded them as identical to Britain's own: in other words, that the way of the market was no less conducive to her real interests than it was to America's. That may have been so. If it was not, however (and the proof of the pudding was an awfully long time coming out in the eating), then it remained to be seen whether drastically different options were open to her in practical terms. That could only be put to the proof by a government which believed those options were preferable. A good test would be to see what happened if Britain asked for the cruise missiles on her soil to be withdrawn.

Britain's relations with the world after 1945 were as much governed by her material situation after 1945 as they had been before, except that by now that material situation no longer unambiguously indicated where her national interest lay. This uncertainty was reflected in her foreign policy. Reduced to a husk of her former international self, with neither the power to pursue her own inherited interests nor enough shared interests with other powers to make it clear which of them, if any, she should join, and uncertain about where she should be going domestically, she seemed to lurch from an outmoded imperialism in the 1950s, to a reluctant Europeanism in the 1960s and 1970s, and then on to a passionate Atlanticism in the 1980s, with no thought at all for consistency, or for the damage her sudden changes of route might inflict. By 1986 she had reached a position where the direction and style of her policy were clearer and more coherent than they had been for decades; but there was still no certainty that the lurching was about to stop. That would depend, firstly, on whether her national interest came to be more generally seen to lie in this direction; and secondly, on whether Britain had sufficient freedom of action to assert any other national interest, if it was not.

Conclusion

That political power and international influence rest to a great extent on economic strength almost goes without saying today, though it might not have done so in the mid-nineteenth century, or at least not if it were put as crudely as that. This in the end was Britain's undoing: the relative failure of her diplomacy's industrial, commercial and financial base, which determined – or may have determined: it is too early as yet to be sure – that whatever her future in international affairs might be it would not be a future of her own choosing. This, or something like it, has been the main theme of nearly every book on British foreign policy that has been produced over the past ten or fifteen years, whose authors all agree nowadays in recognising the influence of economics on diplomacy to this extent. The argument of this book, however, goes a little beyond that. The connection between economics and foreign policy has never been one merely between prosperity and power, but is far more complicated: partly because economics is not just a question of prosperity, and foreign policy not just a matter of power. In the nineteenth century the nature of Britain's economic and social *structure* was every bit as important as her gross national product in determining what her relations with other countries would be; and if it has been less important after 1945, because stronger outside forces have made it so, still the connections are there, on many levels, helping first of all to explain some of the tensions in Britain's international situation today, and secondly to indicate – though it may be merely academic – where Britain's best international interests might lie.

That is a moot point, and in any case beyond the competence of a historian to judge. The future is treacherous territory for anybody, but especially for a profession which relies for its judgements so heavily on hindsight, and whose function for that reason should be restricted to trying to explain, merely, how things have come to be how they are. The main explanation offered here for Britain's present predicament is that it arose out of the nature and the basis of the 'power' she used to wield long ago, which was what engendered her peculiar vulnerability to the blows that she was subjected to after 1939. Chiefly it arose out of a contradiction implicit in her national economy in the nineteenth century, between the stake it gave her in the wider world, and the means it allowed her to safeguard that stake.

Initially – to recapitulate – the contradiction was not widely perceived, because it was assumed that the particular nature of the stake Britain had in the world was not such as to require any special measures to safeguard it. She was not looking to subdue anyone, or to steal anything, but only to exchange things with other peoples, to the benefit of them all. Because everyone must realise that it was to their benefit, it should not require to be forced on them; and indeed in a way Britain's commercial and financial penetration of the world was supposed to represent the very antithesis of force. The health of Britain's economy depended on this being so: for the deployment of too much force would have financial and also social implications that were fundamentally inimical to it. It was her release from the many burdens of militarism and imperialism that had enabled her economy to expand so phenomenally; to have to defend that expansion militarily and imperially now would mean a slow but inevitable death for the goose that was laying the golden eggs. This was, to say the least, a simplistic analysis of Britain's industrial and commercial rise in the eighteenth and early nineteenth centuries; but it contained enough truth to indicate where the weakness of her position thereafter lay. Her 'greatness', which was a commerce-based greatness, depended on the preservation of a kind of political and economic liberalism which major wars and conquests could only undermine, and consequently required that situations did not arise where major wars and conquests would need to be undertaken. The difficulty was that to a great extent this was beyond her control. Her only real hope of avoiding wars lay in the progressive realisation by other countries that wars were not in their interests either, but when that realisation failed to dawn, Britain was doomed. With customers and competitors both disputing Britain's sincere claim that her domination of the world's markets was good for them, situations were bound to arise where the only way to defend that domination was to annex a market or to fight a rival off. Every time she did this it eroded the conditions that were necessary to support her economic vitality at its centre; which vitality anyway by the end of the nineteenth century was being drained by internal weaknesses – maybe other 'contradictions' – too. The new empire she accumulated then was necessary to the maintenance of her leading position in the world, but also ultimately fatal to it; for it was bound in the end to destroy the foundation on which that leading position had been built. So the very thing that had made Britain 'great' was to engender, indirectly, her decline.

That she was able to live with this contradiction for so long was due to luck, and skill, especially in minimising the domestic repercussions of the defensive measures she was forced to take, and some compromise; but it could not possibly last for ever, or for very long in the 'century of total war'. Throughout that century her wealth and power declined steadily, relative to other countries' wealth and power and to her own needs; though for some people that decline may have been masked by the fact that she won, or seemed to win, the century's two most total wars. But this of course was misleading. By 1980 she was clearly reduced to penury and impotence, and to a position where she no longer seemed to have an effective foreign policy, beyond bowing and scraping and posturing, at all.

It was of course a great decline. But it is arguable whether it was quite as great as it looked. In the first place, by any way of looking at it, it was only a relative decline, and not absolute, at least until the end; which meant that in terms of real national wealth, for example, Britain was no worse off than before. Secondly, we have seen that there was a way in which it could be regarded as not a decline at all, but rather a transformation: depending on the criteria used and the angle chosen to measure how societies develop and progress. In the third place it is possible to argue that Britain in the second half of the nineteenth century had not really been as powerful as she had seemed to be, in one sense at least: taking 'power' to mean freedom of action and the freedom a nation has to impose her own national will. Britain's freedom was always limited in this respect: limited latterly by her resources, but earlier by the checks which the peculiar nature of her economic and political system placed on the extent to which those resources could be diverted into imposing her national will. Thus she had command of the seas, but was supposed to use it only to maintain access for everyone, even when she used it to accumulate her 'new' empire at the end of the nineteenth century, which itself was far less a source of strength to her, or even controlled by her, than many people at the time believed. In Europe she had scarcely any authority at all, except what Palmerston was able to conjure up before he was rumbled, because of her aversion to fighting there, which was a necessity rather than a choice, and the difficulty she had finding allies with the same basic objectives as herself. All of which is not to deny that in most senses she was far better placed in the nineteenth century than she later became, but only to emphasise that the contrast was not between simple 'power', and abject decline.

In the mean time her foreign *policy* remained broadly the same for a very long while, and then changed with a rush after the Second World War. The continuity of her foreign policy until then derived from the fact that her fundamental interests and responsibilities in the world continued too, and it contributed towards her decline, by prolonging the contradiction that was the cause of it. That this would be the effect of it was perceived very early on by the 'new imperialists', who sought to break the vicious circle by adapting Britain's policy – which meant sacrificing some of her liberalism – to her new needs. They failed in this, mainly because British policy in a matter like this could not be shifted except by the sheerest necessity, and for a long time that necessity was obscured. There was no chance, therefore, that drastic enough changes could be made early enough to halt the decline. On the other hand some changes were forced by circumstances: chief among which was the gradual hardening of Britain's 'informal' interest in the world into a formal imperial one, so that a relationship that the Victorians had preferred not to regard as a power-relationship now indisputably became just that. One of the effects of this was that their older way of looking at the world was slowly forgotten, at the same time as many of the liberal values and assumptions that had underpinned it were being eroded from other directions as well. At the very heart of the mid-Victorians' liberalism had lain the notion that men's interests did not conflict but naturally – in conditions of 'freedom' – complemented each other, which notion could be extended to international relations also. From this had derived, in broadest outline, the fundamental principles of Britain's foreign policy in the nineteenth century: especially her free trade internationalism, and her 'isolation' from Europe because Europe followed an entirely different creed. From about 1880 onwards, however, this type of liberalism slowly decayed, until the middle of the twentieth century when economically, politically and diplomatically it hardly survived – was hardly even understood – at all. The liberal soul of Britain's foreign policy, therefore, had gone out of it; which made the collapse of that policy, when it came, all the more sudden and complete. Britain's society had become transformed over the course of the century in more ways, perhaps, than she realised. This was one of the reasons – though not the only one – why her relations with the rest of the world also became transformed.

Initially the course of the transformation was highly confused. This was because the situation Britain found herself in after 1945 gave no firm indication of how she should proceed thereafter: the best path to follow away from the wreckage of the past. There was no clear, happy or even likely solution to her new predicament; merely a number of different options, all of which seemed to have flaws which greatly outweighed their advantages. One theoretical option was for Britain to try to go it alone in the world. That was never properly on, because of her dependence on other countries. The remaining options involved collaboration with other countries, but in different combinations and different ways. Between 1945 and 1986 Britain tried out three of those combinations, but none of them with the same degree of national consensus and commitment that had marked her foreign policy in the past.

Which option she preferred at any one time depended largely on the ideological preconceptions of those in power. Her foreign policy went through three broad stages, corresponding roughly to the stages of development of her domestic policies at the time. The first was an imperial, or post-imperial, stage, which in retrospect has been somewhat

144

misunderstood. Imperialism is generally associated with crude power; from which it is inferred that the leading intention of the most unregenerate postwar British imperialists was simply to maintain Britain's power in the world. There is a great deal of truth in this. The post-1945 era furnished a congenial climate for such illusions, which however evaporated (except for the stupidest of the unregenerates) around 1956. But British imperialism had always had another side. Not all imperialists were seekers after national power. Some were driven by different motives, like 'service' to those they governed; these were the imperialists who set such store by colonial 'welfare' in the 1940s, for example, and were so enthusiastic about the new 'Commonwealth' which developed out of the empire after 1945. The multi-racial Commonwealth of free nations was the culmination of this particular strain in the British imperial tradition: the paternalistic strain, altruistic to an extent, racially and culturally tolerant, undogmatic, and drawing inspiration from the friendly image of the 'family'. It was related in some very obvious ways to the consensual welfareism of Britain's domestic policy at this time, and flourished when that policy flourished, in the ten or fifteen years immediately after the war.

The trouble was that it could not actually *effect* very much. On its own terms the Commonwealth had its uses, which some Britons valued more than others; but it was clearly inadequate as a substitute for the old empire as a source of power. Those who had hoped that it might prove such a substitute were consequently bound to become disillusioned eventually, and to turn to other groupings of nations to provide what they felt Britain now lacked. The most likely grouping for imperialists of this persuasion, as well as for some people of other persuasions, was the newly formed European Economic Community, which Britain joined – at some short-term cost, because of the distinctive lie of her trade – in 1973. This was the second stage in the development of her postwar foreign policy. It was widely billed as a movement away from isolationism to a more 'internationalist' outlook on Britain's part, but it could also be regarded as no more than a shift from one kind of internationalism to another. Commonwealth internationalism had rested on the idea of informal co-operation between widely scattered and differing cultural traditions whose association together was, in a way, no more than a historical accident. European internationalism was based on the notion that close neighbours with a common culture should band together as formally as possible against the rest. It was corporatist in conception, and bureaucratic in form: again reflecting a contemporary domestic frame of mind. This was the climate in which Britain harnessed herself to the 'European idea'. Unfortunately for the further development of that idea it did not last very long. Towards the end of the 1970s it was superseded, in its turn, by a totally different climate, and hence a different policy.

The climate was 'free marketism'; and the foreign policy it gave rise to was a *competitive* internationalism, in succession to the co-operative and corporatist sorts. Free marketeers claimed to be trying to return Britain to the ideals and values of Victorian times, which was justified to a point, but did not take full account of the distorting impact of the events of the intervening years. The new gospel differed from its Victorian model in being far less optimistic about its own chances of prevailing in the world without help, and consequently less relaxed, or liberal, politically. The target it set itself was a free enterprise economy within a strong framework of managerial power and law and order; in the diplomatic field this was translated into a policy of free international exchange within a framework of firm 'leadership', and a defensive alliance with the United States. The cash nexus was now bonded with steel. Anything outside it was devalued; including, in the 1980s, the ideals represented both by the European Economic Community, and by the British Commonwealth.

The links between this and the earlier tradition are plain to see; but so also are the breaks. The wheel had not quite turned full circle. A mid-Victorian liberal spirited back to life in Britain in the 1980s would no doubt have braced himself for certain changes, but it is likely that he would still have been surprised and distressed by modern free enterprise capitalism's less liberal political side. Examples of this, if he could have found out about them, were Britain's political police, and her laws against aliens, neither of which had had any British equivalents – only *foreign* ones – in mid-Victorian times. In the realm of diplomacy the contrast was even starker. The old confidence in the peaceful spread of liberal enlightenment in the world was altogether gone. So was the prejudice against military alliances. In 1848 Palmerston had declared that Britain had 'no eternal allies, and no perpetual enemies'. In the 1980s she had a perpetual enemy in the shape of Russia, and an open-ended alliance with the United States of exactly the type that it had been a main priority of the Victorian Foreign Office to avoid. She spent more on her military than any other European country, whereas in the later nineteenth century she had spent a good deal less than three or four of them. She had foreign troops on her soil, and foreign weapons of unprecedented destructive power, probably outside her effective national control. The nearest she had come to that in peacetime in the later nineteenth century was the alliance that was periodically mooted then with Germany; but even if that had come to anything, which it never did, it is difficult to imagine Britain's ever allowing Prussian garrisons to be stationed in England with Prussian heavy artillery, under German command. These changes were dramatic, and constituted a revolution in British foreign policy which makes comparisons with earlier times meaningless.

It may have been justified and necessary, or even inevitable. The Victorians may have been – probably were – wrong. The world they believed they inhabited may have been an illusion, which was saved from being shattered sooner than it was only by the fact that, whatever their theory said, they had the *power* to disregard the truth. Their chief mistake was to think that their liberal vision was self-sustaining, which blinded them to the fact that it needed artificial conditions to sustain it: conditions that were ultimately bound to fail. Whatever their other virtues may have been, free trade and liberal enlightenment had not spread and filled the world with sisterly feelings, or even arguably benefited Britain herself much in the longer term. Instead of peace, the result of her efforts to diffuse the blessings of her commerce abroad had provoked colonial wars, which in turn heaped burdens upon her that eventually tore the heart out of the vision itself. Instead of contentment the free pursuit of profit at home had led to growing resentments, which had forced compromises and adjustments that soon consumed the remnants that were left. The vision stood revealed as a flawed one, free marketism on its own not really the universal panacea for all ills: either because of the inability of people to see what was good for them, or else, possibly, because it was not good for them at all. So, by the last quarter of the twentieth century Britain's situation had entirely altered. She was weak; she was threatened; and – more importantly – she was without a broadly accepted faith to sustain her any more. What was left was just the economic shell of the old vision: capitalism without its liberal soul; and that needed new measures to keep it alive.

Whether this kind of policy represented the end of her long postwar search for a new, consistent role in the world to replace her old one is impossible as yet (the summer of 1986) to say. It is still highly controversial. There are two main points at issue. The first is whether such a policy is in Britain's real national interest. The second is whether she has any choice in the matter anyway. The two questions are connected. If being a cork on America's free enterprise ocean is good for Britain, then it does not really matter whether or not it is a matter of choice. If it is not a matter of choice for her, then the question of whether it is beneficial is of no consequence. Both questions are vexed, and probably intractable. For that reason it may be prudent to duck them, in a work of this kind.

Whatever the future held for Britain in 1986, however, there could be few doubts about what had brought her to that pass. Her collapse as a world power had been determined by the particular nature of her historical development up to that point, which in its turn was governed by the structure of her economy from the time of the industrial revolution on.

There was no escaping it, just as there is no escape from death for our man with his head in a noose, without the intervention of an outsider to un-pinion him or cut him down. Some such intervention was always theoretically possible in Britain's case, but it was never within her control. So she declined and fell, inevitably; and afterwards scrabbled about from one line of policy to another, in a way which was less 'determined' by her previous history, except in the negative sense that that history dictated that her choice of policies would be peculiarly difficult. In the end – if it is the end – she settled on a kind of reversion to her mid-Victorian line of trusting (broadly) to the market, but with crucial differences; the most crucial being that she was now one of the lighter corks in the water, instead of the heaviest one. The implications of that are a matter for conjecture. One possibility is that it effectively took the control of her own affairs out of her hands. If that is so, then it follows that one of the themes of this book, which is that Britain's foreign policy arose out of her economic infrastructure, has to be cut short in or around 1945. From then onwards her progress became subordinated to the progress – if that is not too whiggish a word for it – of another power. Her superstructure had come to rest on someone else's base. Or not: if on the one hand the free marketeers are right, and their infrastructures are identical; or, on the other hand, she ever manages to break loose.

Notes

(All books are published in London unless otherwise stated.)

Preface

1 On Victorian foreign policy there is R. W. Seton-Watson, *Britain in Europe 1789–1914* (1937), and Kenneth Bourne, *The Foreign Policy of Victorian England 1830–1902* (1970); and for the later period F. S. Northedge, *The Troubled Giant, Britain among the Great Powers 1916–1939* (1966), and *Descent from Power: British Foreign Policy 1945–1973* (1974). On the imperial and colonial aspect there is my own *The Lion's Share: A Short History of British Imperialism 1850–1970* (1976); P. N. S. Mansergh, *The Commonwealth Experience* (1969); Ronald Hyam, *Britain's Imperial Century 1815–1914* (1976); Colin Eldridge, *Victorian Imperialism* (1978); and James Morris's more flavoursome trilogy, *Heaven's Command* (1973), *Pax Britannica* (1968) and *Farewell the Trumpets* (1978). On defence policy there is Corelli Barnett, *Britain and her Army 1509–1970* (1970), and Paul Kennedy, *The Rise and Fall of British Naval Mastery* (1976). Very recently Paul Kennedy's *The Realities Behind Diplomacy* (1981) has appeared, which explores much of the same ground covered in the present book.

Chapter 1

1 Samuel Laing, *Observations on the Social and Political State of the European People in 1848 and 1849* (1850), pp. 15–16.
2 But not, for example, Professor Norman Gash, whose *Aristocracy and People: Britain 1815–1865* (1979) comes to a different conclusion (e.g. p. 8).
3 *Annual Register 1848*, p. 124.
4 Viscountess Enfield (ed.), *Leaves from the Diary of Henry Greville,* 1st series (1883), p. 388.
5 Charles de Bussy, *Les Conspirateurs en Angleterre 1848–1858: étude historique* (Paris, 1858), pp. 75, 180.
6 [Lady Charlotte Campbell], *Conduct is Fate* (Edinburgh, 1822), Vol. I, p. 76.
7 This general impression is gleaned from the recorded testimony of many of those mid-Victorians – travel writers, journalists, a few novelists – who were *interested* in the continent, and whose opinions by virtue of that may be atypical, but who are almost the only witnesses we have.
8 J. P. C. Roach, *Public Examinations in England, 1850–1900* (1971), p. 203.
9 The defeat of Palmerston's first ministry in February 1858 is a possible exception, though there was a domestic issue involved here too. Another is the resignation of Rosebery's government over the 'cordite affair' in June 1895.
10 See Valerie Cromwell, 'The Private Member of the House of Commons and Foreign Policy in the Nineteenth Century', in H. M. Cam *et al.*, *Liber Memorialis Sir Maurice Powicke* (Louvain and Paris, 1965).
11 See Sheila Lambert, 'A Century of Diplomatic Blue Books', in *Historical Journal*, vol. 10, no. 1 (1967). It is only fair to add that if British practice in these regards left something to be desired, continental governments behaved much worse.
12 Charles Lever, *The Fortunes of Glencore* (1857; new edn, Routledge, n.d.), p. 78.

13 Roach, *Public Examinations in England*, p. 211; M. Wright, *Treasury Control of the Civil Service 1854–1874* (1969), pp. 82–3.

14 See D. C. M. Platt, *The Cinderella Service: British Consuls since 1825* (1971).

15 Bulwer to Russell, 28 March 1855: Russell Papers, Public Record Office, PRO 30/22/12D f. 56.

16 Richard Millman, *Britain and the Eastern Question 1875–1878* (Oxford, 1979), p. 168.

17 The rare examples include the ditching of the Conspiracy Bill in 1858, and Gladstone's despatch of Gordon and then Wolseley to the Sudan in 1884–5.

18 See John H. Gleason, *The Genesis of Russophobia in Great Britain* (Cambridge, Mass., 1950).

19 See Richard Millman, *Britain and the Eastern Question;* Robert Blake, *Disraeli* (1966) chs 26 and 27; and Bernard Porter, 'British Foreign Policy in the Nineteenth Century', *Historical Journal*, vol. 23, no. 1 (1980). pp. 199–200.

20 Britain's greatest foreign secretary, Lord Salisbury, recognised this later in the century, and used a similar metaphor to describe it: 'Governments can do so little and prevent so little nowadays. Power has passed from the hands of statesmen, but I should be very much puzzled to say into whose hands it has passed. It is all pure drifting. As we go down stream, we can occasionally fend off a collision; but where are we going?' – Letter to Cranbook, 1 January 1895, quoted in Robert Taylor, *Lord Salisbury* (1975), p. 145.

21 Of course this cannot be proved, and it could be put another way: that the aristocracy still retained their old power, but used it more in Manchester's interest than before. This is how it will have seemed to them; but then it would need to, if they were to agree to do the job demanded of them.

22 The best-known attempt to discover economic motives behind Britain's European diplomacy is V. J. Puryear's *England, Russia, and the Straits Question, 1844–56* (1936). Even the most overtly economic actions of the Foreign Office often turn out on further study to have deeper political causes, like for example the 'Cobden treaty' (see Barrie M. Ratcliffe, 'The origins of the Anglo-French Commercial treaty of 1860: a reassessment', in Ratcliffe (ed.), *Great Britain and her World 1750–1914: Essays in honour of W. O. Henderson*, Manchester, 1975), and the Ottoman loans (see D. C. M. Platt, *Finance, Trade and Politics*, 1968, pt III, ch. 2).

23 William Woodruff, *Impact of Western Man* (1966), p. 313.

24 Phyllis Deane and W. A. Cole, *British Economic Growth 1688–1959* (2nd edn, 1967), pp. 187, 196, 225.

25 Woodruff, *Impact of Western Man*, pp. 318–30.

26 ibid., pp. 314–16.

27 Kissinger's *A World Restored* (1964), about Anglo-Austrian relations 1812–22, contains statements (for example, on p. 33, 'Because command of the seas had enabled Britain to survive ten years of isolation, maritime rights acquired a significance out of proportion to their real importance') that could only be made in ignorance of the continuing significance of Britain's extra-European interests. Hence too Kissinger's approval of (the relatively 'European') Castlereagh in preference to Canning, and of Metternich in preference to both.

28 Below, p. 44.

29 B. R. Mitchell and Phyllis Deane, *Abstract of British Historical Statistics* (1962), p. 397.

30 Except Inkerman, and perhaps the Alma.

31 See Queen Victoria to the Earl of Clarendon, 15 January 1856, in A. C. Benson and Viscount Esher (eds), *The Letters of Queen Victoria . . . 1837–1861* (1907), Vol. III, p. 207: 'The Queen cannot conceal from Lord Clarendon what *her own* feelings and wishes at this moment are. They *cannot* be for peace *now*, for she is *convinced* that this country would *not* stand in the eyes of Europe as she *ought*, and as the Queen is convinced she *would* after *this* year's campaign. The honour and glory of her dear Army, is as *near* her heart as almost anything, and she cannot *bear* the thought that "the failure on the Redan" should be our last *fait d'Armes*, and it would cost her more than words would express to conclude a peace with *this* as the end.' Later she became reconciled to the peace on the grounds that 'France

would either not have continued the war, or continued it in such a manner that *no* glory could have been hoped for by us' (to Clarendon 31 March 1856: ibid., p. 235).

32 W. S. Hamer, *The British Army: Civil–Military Relations 1885–1905* (Oxford, 1970), p. 1.

33 W. E. Mosse, *The European Powers and the German Question, 1848–71* (1958; repr. 1969), p. 183.

34 None of this should be taken to imply that all or any of these principles originated with nineteenth-century capitalism or the middle classes; many of them had roots – Whiggish roots – that went much further back. But they were associated with the liberal and capitalist middle classes now.

35 Clive Emsley, *British Society and the French Wars 1793–1815* (1979), p. 31.

36 ibid., p. 21.

37 C. K. Webster, *The Foreign Policy of Palmerston 1830–1841* (1951), Vol. I, p. 414.

38 Russell to Queen Victoria, 29 December 1851, in Benson and Esher (eds), *Letters of Queen Victoria . . . 1837–1861,* Vol. II; p. 427.

39 The main occasions were in the 1850s, 1872 and 1881: see Bernard Porter, *The Refugee Question in mid-Victorian Politics* (1979), p. 64 and *passim*; and 'The *Freiheit* prosecutions, 1881–1882', *Historical Journal*, vol. 23, no. 4 (1980).

40 Christopher Bartlett, 'Britain and the European Balance, 1815–48', in Alan Sked (ed.), *Europe's Balance of Power 1815–1848* (1979), p. 145.

41 Hamer, *The British Army*, p. 31.

42 A. J. P. Taylor, *Europe: Grandeur and Decline* (Harmondsworth, 1967), p. 236.

43 In the common nineteenth-century sense: that 'nationality' (however defined) should form the basis for statehood. The word has taken on other meanings since.

44 The same solution, of course, that Britain at that time was beginning to apply to Canada.

45 See Palmerston to King Leopold, 15 June 1848, printed in Bourne, *Foreign Policy of Victorian England,* pp. 294–5; and, for his arguments in favour of Austria's retention of Hungary, H. C. F. Bell, *Lord Palmerston,* Vol. II (1936), p. 14.

46 See G. B. Henderson, *Crimean War Diplomacy and other Historical Essays* (Glasgow, 1947), pp. 238–41.

47 For example, M. S. Anderson, *The Eastern Question 1774–1923* (1966), p. 132: 'The Crimean war was thus the outcome of a series of misjudgements, misunderstandings and blunders, of stupidity, pride and obstinacy rather than of ill will. More than any great war of modern times, it took place by accident.' And J. B. Conacher, *The Aberdeen Coalition 1852–1855* (1968), p. 268, regards it as an 'unnecessary war', which could have been avoided at several stages in the diplomacy leading up to it had not on each occasion 'some mischance' stepped in to spoil things.

48 Karl Marx and Frederick Engels, *Articles on Britain* (Moscow, 1975), p. 203; and cf. the *Spectator*, quoted in *The Times*, 29 December 1851, p. 3: 'Lord Palmerston had always been one of those men who engaged in politics as sportsmen follow the fox, more for the excitement of the chase than from an earnest desire to attain the object in pursuit.'

49 Bourne, *Foreign Policy of Victorian England,* p. 374.

50 See Richard Millman, *British Foreign Policy and the Coming of the Franco-Prussian War* (1965), pp. 89–92 and 205–7.

51 Some of Palmerston's statements appear at first glance to advocate a direct commercial role for the Foreign Office, but can be seen not to if they are examined carefully. For example, to Lord Auckland in January 1841 he wrote: 'We must unremittingly endeavour to find in other parts of the world new vents for the produce of our industry'; but by 'we' in this context he did not mean the Foreign Office but the nation in a more general and unofficial sense. He went on to say that it was 'the business of the *Government* to open and secure the *roads* for the market' (my italics); which defines quite clearly his view of the state's more limited role. (The quotation appears in J. Ridley, *Lord Palmerston,* 1970; new edn, 1972, pp. 354–5.)

52 See G. S. Graham, *The China Station* (1978), *passim*.

53 ibid., pp. 207–8, 382, 389.

54 See J. A. Gallagher and R. E. Robinson, 'The Imperialism of Free Trade', *Economic History Review*, vol. VI, no. 1 (1953).

55 W. N. Medlicott, *Bismarck, Gladstone, and the Concert of Europe* (1956), p. 10.

Chapter 2

1 David S. Landes, *The Unbound Prometheus* (1969), p. 194.

2 Calculated from the tables in Mitchell and Deane, *Abstract of British Historical Statistics*, ch. XI.

3 The latest treatment of this theme is M. Weiner's *English Culture and the Decline of the Industrial Spirit 1850–1980* (1981).

4 D. C. M. Platt, 'British portfolio investment overseas before 1870: some doubts', *Economic History Review*, 2nd series, vol. 33, no. 1 (1980); contrast Woodruff's figure of £1,225 million in *Impact of Western Man*, p. 150.

5 And thereafter, her competitors' ability to compete with Britain in supplying overseas capital markets too.

6 Deriving not only from Marx but also, for example, from J. S. Mill's *Principles of Political Economy* (1848; new edn, 1909). p. 731, and from Sismondi, Malthus and Edward Gibbon Wakefield before that.

7 Lord Stanley (the future 15th Earl of Derby, and foreign secretary 1866–8 and 1874–8) is supposed to have taken this attitude to its extreme limit: according to Lord Clarendon in 1866 he had 'strange theories about our only being a manufacturing nation and that we have no business to meddle with Foreign Affairs' (quoted in Millman, *British Foreign Policy and the Coming of the Franco-Prussian War*, p. 30).

8 See Deryck Schreuder, 'Gladstone as "Troublemaker": Liberal Foreign Policy and the German Annexation of Alsace-Lorraine, 1870–1871', *Journal of British Studies*, vol. 17, no. 2 (1978), p. 113.

9 R. W. Seton-Watson, *Disraeli, Gladstone and the Eastern Question* (1935), p. 33.

10 Quoted by W. N. Medlicott, 'Bismarck and Beaconsfield', in A. O. Sarkissian (ed.), *Studies in Diplomatic History and Historiography in honour of G. P. Gooch* (1961), p. 250.

11 Gwendolen Cecil, *Life of Robert Marquis of Salisbury*, Vol. II (1921), p. 171.

12 C. J. Lowe, *Salisbury and the Mediterranean 1886–1896* (1965), pp. 87–9.

13 See Bernard Porter, 'Imperialism and the Scramble', *Journal of Imperial and Commonwealth History*, vol. IX, no. 1 (1980), p. 80.

14 For a recent interpretation of the socio-economic basis of Disraeli's early imperialism, particularly the Abyssinian expedition, see Freda Harcourt, 'Disraeli's imperialism, 1866–1868: a question of timing', *Historical Journal*, vol. 23, no. 1 (1980).

15 Of course it depends on what is meant by 'convincing'. There were colonial challenges earlier, especially from France, but not nearly so serious as the later ones, or so feared.

16 See J. P. C. Roach, 'Liberalism and the Victorian Intelligentsia', *Cambridge Historical Journal*, vol. 13, no. 1 (1957).

17 W. G. Hynes, *The Economics of Empire. Britain, Africa and the New Imperialism 1870–95* (1979), *passim*; and Barrie M. Ratcliffe, 'Commerce and Empire: Manchester merchants and West Africa, 1873–1895', *Journal of Imperial and Commonwealth History*, vol. VII, no. 3 (1979).

18 Woodruff, *Impact of Western Man*, pp. 316–30.

19 R. W. Seton-Watson, *Britain in Europe 1789–1914* (1937), p. 415.

20 Quoted in R. J. Sontag, *Germany and England: Background to Conflict 1848–1894* (New York, 1938; repr. 1964), p. 120.

21 W. L. Langer, *European Alliances and Alignments 1871–1890* (New York, 1931; repr. 1950), p. 18.

22 For example, neither 'extradition' nor 'foreign enlistment' appears in the indexes to the two fullest surveys of British foreign policy in this period, Seton-Watson's *Britain in Europe*, and A. W. Ward and G. P. Gooch (eds), *The Cambridge History of British Foreign Policy 1783–1919* (3 vols, 1922–3); though the *Alabama* and one or two other specific incidents relating to the Foreign Enlistment Act do.

23 See PP (1867–8) VII, p. 136. Britain's three extradition acts were with France, USA and Denmark.

24 ibid., p. 158.

25 On the *Ward Jackson* affair, see E. H. Carr, *The Romantic Exiles* (1933; new edn, Harmondsworth, 1968), pp. 208–10.

26 33 & 34 Vict. c. 90.

27 33 & 34 Vict. c. 52.

28 Extradition treaties were concluded with Germany in 1872, Italy in 1873, Austria in 1874, France in 1878 and Russia in 1887.

29 See *Halsbury's Laws,* Vol. 9 (2nd edn, 1949), pp. 875–7.

30 Bernard Porter, *The Refugee Question*, p. 220.

31 Above, p. 46.

32 Bernard Porter, 'The *Freiheit* prosecutions', p. 850.

33 Lisa Keller, 'Public Order in Victorian London' (Cambridge Ph.D. dissertation, 1977), pp. 279–91.

34 Quoted in P. J. Durrans, 'The Liberal attack on Disraelian imperialism', *Journal of Imperial and Commonwealth History,* vol. X, no. 3 (1982); and cf. below, p. 69.

35 Except in, or connected with, Ireland, where there were 'terrorist' campaigns in the 1840s and 1860s, which were not yet, however, directed at the civilian population on the mainland.

Chapter 3

1 For example, William le Queux, *The Great War in England in 1897* (1894), and Erskine Childers, *The Riddle of the Sands* (1903). Novels of this kind are a recurrent literary form; cf. G. T. Chesney *The Battle of Dorking* (1871); Sir John Hackett, *The Third World War* (1978); and Ray Flint, *The People's Scenario* (Hull, 1982).

2 C. H. D. Howard, 'The policy of Isolation', *Historical Journal,* vol. 10, no. 1 (1967), p. 80.

3 Michael Kennedy, *Portrait of Elgar* (1968), p. 140.

4 See W. L. Langer, *The Diplomacy of Imperialism* (New York, 1935), vol. I, ch. 3.

5 Turkey was the latest and most notable of these 'losses'; by 1900 Britain had more or less given up her old influence at the Porte to Germany. As well as this the boundaries of her commercial 'empire' were being delimited by more thrusting trade rivals, and annexations by countries with less open commercial principles than hers.

6 One of the reasons why Salisbury was initially so chary of going to war against the Transvaal was that the organisation of the home army was not up to it, and the Indian army 'so riddled with venereal disease and other complaints that they are comparatively unfit for service' (Andrew Porter, *The Origins of the South African War,* Manchester, 1980, pp. 234 and 237); and in the event the meal the army made of the Boer War did little for its reputation.

7 See Paul Kennedy, *The Rise and Fall of British Naval Mastery* (1976), ch. 8.

8 See Richard Price, *An Imperial War and the British Working Class* (1972).

9 See Andrew Porter, *Origins of the South African War, passim.*

10 Rosebery's expression, quoted in the Marquess of Crewe, *Lord Rosebery* (1931), vol. II, p. 570.

11 See R. Kubicek, *The Administration of Imperialism* (1969); and Andrew Porter, 'In Memoriam Joseph Chamberlain', *Journal of Imperial and Commonwealth History*, vol. III, no. 2 (1975).

12 Andrew Porter, *Origins of the South African War*, ch. II.

13 Mitchell and Deane, *Abstract of British Historical Statistics*, pp. 283–4.

14 Woodruff, *Impact of Western Man*, pp. 315, 317.

15 ibid., pp. 150, 154.

16 ibid., pp. 322–3, 154. None of these investment figures, however, has been exposed to the same kind of scrutiny D. C. M. Platt has given to the pre-1870 ones (see above, p. 35); if they were it is likely, in his view, that they would need to be reduced 'by as much as a third' ('British portfolio investment overseas', p. 16).

17 Michael Barratt Brown, *After Imperialism* (1963; new edn, 1970), p. 111.

18 Mitchell and Deane, *Abstract of British Historical Statistics*, p. 334.

19 See Woodruff, *Impact of Western Man*, pp. 317, 321, 323, 325.

20 See Memorandum by Salisbury, 29 May 1901, printed in G. P. Gooch and H. Temperley (eds), *British Documents on the Origins of the War 1898–1914*, Vol. II (1927), p. 68.

21 Classical liberalism assumed that in a contract between employer and employee, for example, both contracting parties were equally free: the employer free to employ someone else, the employee free to take his labour elsewhere. The 'New Liberals', as they called themselves, disputed this, on the grounds that in real life it was nearly always easier for an employer to find an alternative worker than it was for a worker to find an alternative job. From this it followed that under capitalism things were not so 'free' as they had been supposed to be, which made some measure of 'socialism' necessary to balance them up. See L. T. Hobhouse, *Liberalism* (1911; new edn, 1964), esp. p. 47.

22 Bentley B. Gilbert, *The Evolution of National Insurance in Great Britain* (1966), ch. 2.

23 For example the Old Age Pensions Act of 1908 and the Health Insurance and National Insurance Acts of 1911.

24 A. V. Dicey, *Lectures on the Relation between Law and Public Opinion in England during the Nineteenth century* (2nd edn, 1914), Introduction.

25 J. A. Hobson, *Imperialism: a Study* (1902), pt II, ch. I; and cf. above, pp. 53–4.

26 Howard, 'The policy of Isolation', p. 79.

27 Gwendolen Cecil, *Robert Marquis of Salisbury*, Vol. IV (1932), p. 298.

28 Though not, perhaps, in the full sense of the word, as Keith Middlemas defines it: 'the policy of meeting . . . demands and grievances without asking for firm reciprocal advantages; asking only for future "mutual understanding" ' (*Diplomacy of Illusion*, 1972, p. 8). Britain was not yet reduced to this.

29 Preamble to the Anglo-German Convention, 1898, in Michael Hurst (ed.), *Key Treaties for the Great Powers 1814–1914* (1972), Vol. II, p. 689.

30 G. P. Gooch, *Before the War* (1936), Vol. I, p. 201. Of course there are alliances and alliances, and from Germany's point of view when she looked at it realistically, a pact of neutrality in any future war was the most she could – and did – expect. For example, Richthofen quoted in B. von Bülow, *Memoirs 1897–1903* (1931), p. 504.

31 See for example Richthofen in 1901, quoted in von Bülow, *Memoirs*, p. 506; and Bülow himself, quoted in Gooch, *Before the War*, Vol. I, p. 231: 'English embarrassments will grow in the coming months, and therewith our price will rise'.

32 Paul Kennedy argues that Bülow was not really interested in a British alliance after 1897: 'German World Policy and the Alliance Negotiations with England, 1897–1900', *Journal of Modern History*, vol. 45 (1973).

33 See Gooch and Temperley, *British Documents*, Vol. II, p. 373, last sentence of Lansdowne's despatch; and *Parliamentary Debates*, 4th series, *Vol.* CXXXV (1904), cc. 516 (Percy) and 572 (Balfour).

34 See *The Times*, 12 April 1904, p. 7: 'The days have gone by when the Germans could assume with some shadow of plausibility that in the larger questions of international

politics Great Britain must follow in the wake of the Triple Alliance, and that the attitude
of France might be ignored.'

35   Langer, *European Alliances and Alignments*, p. 197.
36   Zara Steiner in F. H. Hinsley (ed.), *British Foreign Policy under Sir Edward Grey*
     (Cambridge, 1977), p. 69; and cf. Keith Robbins, *Sir Edward Grey* (1971), p. 371.
37   ibid., p. 237; and Robbins, 'Sir Edward Grey and the British Empire', *Journal of Imperial
     and Commonwealth History*, vol. I, no. 2 (1973).
38   Robbins, *Grey,* p. 35.
39   ibid., pp. 108, 140.
40   Seton-Watson, *Britain in Europe,* p. 606.
41   Robbins, *Grey,* p. 234.
42   Hinsley, *British Foreign Policy,* ch. 5.
43   Seton-Watson, *Britain in Europe,* p. 609.
44   Robbins, *Grey,* p. 262.
45   ibid., p. 297.
46   See ibid., p. 372.

Chapter 4

1   David Butler and Jennie Freeman, *British Political Facts 1900–1960* (1963), p. 161;
    Mitchell and Deane, *Abstract of British Historical Statistics,* pp. 394, 284.
2   Unless one counts as a coalition the Conservative–Liberal Unionist alliance of 1886–92.
3   W. Schlote, *British Overseas Trade from 1700 to the 1930s* (Oxford, 1952), pp. 123, 126,
    45–51.
4   Calculated from tables in Mitchell and Deane, *Abstract of British Historical Statistics,* p.
    317; the figures include Russia and North Africa.
5   Woodruff, *Impact of Western Man,* pp. 156–7.
6   Butler and Freeman, *British Political Facts,* p. 159.
7   Mitchell and Deane, *Abstract of British Historical Statistics,* pp. 398–9. The figure of 40 per
    cent is for Britain's public debt as a whole.
8   cf. ibid., p. 400.
9   ibid., pp. 398–9, 429. If we allow for price inflation the difference in public expenditure
    narrows a little; in 1930 prices were declining, but were still between 10 and 50 per cent
    up (according to the index one takes) on 1913; ibid., pp. 344–5 and ch. XVI.
10 ibid., pp. 284, 335.
11 From *Statistical Abstracts for the United Kingdom . . . 1913 to 1927* (1929), pp. 106–8, and
    ibid., *1925 to 1938* (1940), pp. 166–8. These figures include the Territorial Army, but
    not Reservists or the RAF; the latter was 27,664 strong in 1920 and 32,989 strong in
    1930. See also Robin Higham, *Armed Forces in Peacetime* (1962), Appendix II.
12 Keith Feiling, *The Life of Neville Chamberlain* (1946), p. 314.
13 Simon Newman, *March 1939: The British Guarantee to Poland* (1976), p. 16.
14 Keith Middlemas, *Politics in Industrial Society* (1979), chs 6–9.
15 ibid., p. 154; and Tony Bunyan, *The History and Practice of the Political Police in Britain*
    (1977).
16 Middlemas, *Politics in Industrial Society,* pp. 131, 153–4; and on the decline of the press
    before this time see Alan J. Lee, *The Origins of the Popular Press 1855–1915* (1976).
17 L. S. Amery, *My Political Life,* Vol. II (1953), p. 340.
18 Quoted in David Killingray, 'The Empire Resources Development Committee and West
    Africa, 1916–1920', *Journal of Imperial and Commonwealth History,* vol. X, no. 2 (1982), p.
    195.
19 Calculated from tables in Barratt Brown, *After Imperialism,* p. 111, and Mitchell and
    Deane, *Abstract of British Historical Statistics,* ch. XI.

20 F. S. Northedge, *The Troubled Giant*, p. 237.

21 Feiling, *Neville Chamberlain*, p. 325.

22 Woodruff, *Impact of Western Man*, pp. 315–21.

23 J. M. Keynes, *The Economic Consequences of the Peace* (1919), p. 3.

24 The 'Fontainbleau Memorandum', printed in Martin Gilbert, *The Roots of Appeasement* (1967), p. 189.

25 Feiling, *Neville Chamberlain*, p. 333 (from Chamberlain's diary).

26 H. N. Brailsford, quoted by A. J. P. Taylor in R. Pares and A. J. P. Taylor (eds), *Essays presented to Sir Lewis Namier* (1956), p. 479.

27 Martin Gilbert, *Roots of Appeasement*, pp. 191–2. Germany's vulnerability to communism had already been demonstrated in the last months of the war, when there were revolutions in Kiel, Munich and Berlin, and also in Austria.

28 Lionel Kochan, *The Struggle for Germany, 1914–45* (Edinburgh, 1963), ch. III.

29 ibid., p. 64.

30 Kennedy, *The Realities Behind Diplomacy*, p. 256.

31 Newman, *March 1939: The British Guarantee*, p. 24 n.; and see M. Cowling, *The Impact of Hitler* (1975), p. 398.

32 Feiling, *Neville Chamberlain*, p. 301.

33 Higham, *Armed Forces in Peacetime*, Appendix II. The figures were: 1935 £136.96 million; 1936 £185.08 million; 1937 £254.4 million.

34 Though it is fair to add that a reaction in his favour, very much along the lines of the present chapter, has been under way among historians for many years now. See D. C. Watt, 'Appeasement: The Rise of a Revisionist School?', *Political Quarterly*, vol. 36, no. 2 (1965).

35 Feiling, *Neville Chamberlain*, p. 252.

36 ibid., p. 375.

37 ibid., p. 368.

38 ibid., p. 367.

39 ibid., p. 360.

40 ibid., p. 324.

41 ibid., p. 362.

42 See D. C. Watt, *Personalities and Policies* (1965), ch. 8; and Ritchie Ovendale, *'Appeasement' and the English Speaking World* (Cardiff, 1975).

43 See Wolf D. Gruner, 'The British political, social and economic system and the decision for peace and war: reflections on Anglo-German relations 1800–1939', *British Journal of International Studies*, vol. VI, no. 3 (1980), and works cited therein.

44 *Annual Abstract of Statistics, 1935–1946* (1948), pp. 178 (comparing exports in 1939 and 1944) and 217; Butler and Freeman, *British Political Facts*, p. 227; A. Sked and C. Cook, *Post-War Britain: A Political History* (Harmondsworth, 1979), p. 27 n.

45 W. R. Louis, *Imperialism at Bay* (1977), p. 514.

46 Bernard Porter, *The Lion's Share*, pp. 311–12.

47 Louis *Imperialism at Bay*, p. 5 (quoting Milner in 1919); and see also H. G. Wells, *Anticipations* (1902), pp. 260–1; and 'Ogniben', 'The United States of Imperial Britain', *Contemporary Review*, vol. 81 (1902), pp. 312–13.

Chapter 5

1 Sidney Pollard, *The Development of the British Economy 1914–1967* (1962; 2nd edn, 1969), p. 357.

2 David Dilks (ed.) *Retreat from Power. Studies in Britain's Foreign Policy in the Twentieth Century* (1981), Vol. II, pp. 21–2.

3 Woodruff, *Impact of Western Man*, p. 317.

4   Pollard, *Development of the British Economy*, p. 452.
5   See, for example, 'Calchas', 'Will England Last the Century?' in *Fortnightly Review*, vol. 75 (1901), pp. 20–34.
6   F. S. Northedge, *Descent from Power. British Foreign Policy, 1945–1973* (1974), p. 89.
7   Barratt Brown, *After Imperialism*, p. 111.
8   Margaret Gowing, *Independence and Deterrence* (1974), Vol. II, p. 182.
9   Andrew J. Pierre, *Nuclear Politics: the British Experience with an Independent Strategic Force 1939–1970* (1972), p. 94.
10 ibid., pp. 100–1.
11 J. L. Moulton, *Defence in a Changing World* (1964), p. 63.
12 Lawrence Freedman, *Britain and Nuclear Weapons* (1980), pp. 8–9.
13 Moulton, *Defence in a Changing World*, p. 63
14 Dilks (ed.), *Retreat from Power*, Vol. II, p. 12.
15 Speech at the Massachusetts Institute of Technology, 31 March 1949, reported in *The Times*, 1 April 1949, p. 4.
16 See Richard E. Neustadt, *Alliance Politics* (New York, 1970).
17 Northedge, *Descent from Power*, p. 201, and see ch.6 *passim*.
18 *The Times*, 20 February 1982, p. 1.
19 Enoch Powell in the House of Commons, 3 March 1981: *Parliamentary Debates*, 5th series, Vol.1000, c. 157.
20 *New Statesman*, 31 October 1980, pp. 6–9.
21 Peter Jay's phrase, reported in the *Guardian*, 17 July 1979.
22 *Annual Abstract of Statistics 1968*, pp. 230–1.
23 Oliver Franks, recorded interview quoted in 'The Price of Victory', BBC Radio 3, 9 February 1981.
24 For example, David Marquand in the *Guardian*, 13 March 1980.
25 For example, *Britain and the European Communities: An Economic Assessment* (Cmnd. 4289, 1970), p. 42.
26 *Annual Abstract of Statistics 1980*, pp. 317–18. Strictly speaking the figures are for the ex-empire, not the Commonwealth.
27 ibid., *1984*, pp. 237–9.
28 Edward Heath, quoted in *Britain and the European Communities*, p. 3.
29 Just before their defection from the Labour Party to form the SDP, at a 'fringe' meeting at the 1980 Labour Party Annual Conference at Blackpool, Mrs Shirley Williams declared that if she left it would be over Europe, and Dr David Owen that the crucial issue for him was nuclear defence.
30 See Bernard Porter, 'Fabians, Imperialists and the International Order', in Ben Pimlott (ed.), *Fabian Essays in Socialist Thought* (1984), pp. 63–4.
31 There are one or two possible exceptions. One is the fairly costly naval measures that successive governments took against the slave trade around the middle of the nineteenth century; another may be the Crimean war.
32 Interview with Hugo Young in the *Guardian*, 9 July 1986.
33 Hugo Young in ibid., 15 July 1986; and see the letter from Elwyn Morris in ibid., same date.
34 See above, pp. 34–5.
35 *Guardian* leader, 7 February 1986.
36 Lord Curzon, 'The True Imperialism', in *Nineteenth Century*, vol. 63 (1908), pp. 157–8.
37 Quoted by Polly Toynbee in the *Guardian*, 14 April 1986.

Index

Index